JEW AND GENTILE:
THE PHILO-SEMITIC ASPECT

JEW AND GENTILE: THE PHILO-SEMITIC ASPECT

Solomon Rappaport

Philosophical Library
New York

Library of Congress Catalog Card No. 79-84854
SBN 8022-2354-0

Manufactured in the United States of America

CONJUGI CARISSIMAE
LILI
Prov. xxxi, 28

If you have called a bad thing bad, you have done no great matter; but if you call a good thing good, you have accomplished much.

Goethe

The good in the world is much more sparsely sown than one thinks; what we have, we must hold.

Goethe

It is sad not to see any good in goodness.

Gogol

CONTENTS

ACKNOWLEDGMENTS

The author has included brief quotations from the following, for which he expresses his grateful thanks:

Agus, I.A. *The Heroic Age of Franco-German Jewry.* (Yeshiva University Press, New York, 1969.)

Agus, J.B. *The Meaning of Jewish History.* (Abelard-Schuman, London, New York, Toronto, 1963.)

Baer, Y.F. *A History of the Jews in Christian Spain, Vol. 1.* (The Jewish Publication Society of America, Philadelphia, 1966.)

Baron, Joseph, ed. *Stars and Sand.* (The Jewish Publication Society of America, Philadelphia, 1944.) (The material is used through the courtesy of the copyright holder, The Jewish Publication Society of America.)

Baron, S.W. *A Social and Religious History of the Jews.* (Columbia University Press, New York, 1937.)

Bernard, M. *Zola.* (Evergreen Books, Ltd., London, 1960.)

Bonsirven, J. *Palestinian Judaism in the Time of Jesus Christ.* (Holt, Rinehart and Winston, New York, Chicago, San Francisco, 1964.)

Dimont, M.I. *Jews, God and History.* (W.H. Allen, London, 1964.)

Grunwald, M. *Vienna.* (The Jewish Publication Society of America, Philadelphia, 1936.)

Hoexter-Jung. *Source Book of Jewish History and Literature.* (Shapiro Valentine and Co., London, 1938.)

xi

Mahler, R. *Jewish Emancipation* (A selection of documents.) (The American Jewish Committee, New York, 1941.)

Marcus, J.R. *The Jew in the Medieval World*. (The Union of American Hebrew Congregations, Cincinnati, 1938.)

Modder, M.F. *The Jew in the Literature of England*. (Meridian Books and The Jewish Publication Society, New York, 1960.)

Parkes, J. *A History of the Jewish People*. (Weidenfeld and Nicolson, London, etc., 1962.)

Poliakov, L. *The History of Anti-Semitism*. (Reprinted from *The History of Anti-Semitism*, Volume I, by permission of the publisher, The Vanguard Press, Inc. Copyright © 1966 by Leon Poliakov and The Vanguard Press, Inc.) (Reprint permission also granted by Routledge & Kegan Paul Ltd., London.)

Rabinowicz, O. *Winston Churchill on Jewish Problems*. (Thomas Yoseloff, London, New York, 1960.)

Saron, G. & Hotz, L. *The Jews in South Africa*. (Oxford University Press, Cape Town, London, New York, 1960.)

Talmon, J.L. *The Unique and the Universal*. (Secker & Warburg, London, 1965.)

PERIODICALS

"A.J.R. Information," issued by the Association of Jewish Refugees in Great Britain, London.

"Contemporary Jewish Record," The American Jewish Committee, New York.

"Jewish Heritage, B'nai B'rith," Adult Jewish Education, Washington, D.C.

"Jewish Social Studies," The Conference on Jewish Relations, New York, October, 1947.

JEW AND GENTILE:
THE PHILO-SEMITIC ASPECT

TRENDS IN PHILO-SEMITISM

Philo-Semitism signifies a trend of thought which is motivated by sympathy for the "Semite" and indicates a positive evaluation of Judaism. This concept denotes a friendly attitude to the Jew, the chief representative of the so-called "Semitic Race", and an appreciation of Jewish life and culture. It constitutes a counter-trend to anti-Semitism, animosity towards the Jews, dislike of their spiritual qualities and contempt for their traditions.

While there is ample documentation concerning the nature and history of anti-Semitism, while innumerable publications exist about its origins, manifestations and consequences, the system of ideas and motives leading to philo-Semitism, a notable tendency existing throughout the history of Gentile-Jewish relations, has attracted scant attention. Though pro-Jewish attitudes appear to be rarer and less characteristic than antagonism towards the Jews, the motives of philo-Semitism are, nevertheless, as interesting and significant as those leading to anti-Semitic sentiment, thought and action.

Anti-Semitism or philo-Semitism have always played the role of the people's foreign relations, parallel to those affecting states in their relations with one another. While anti-Semitism is conspicuous in Jewish-Gentile relationships, philo-Semitism is a quiet, less obvious factor; it assumes normal relationships

1

between individuals and groups and rarely arouses special notice.

In every age, it was not only anti-Jewish sentiment and conduct but, in one form or another, it was also pro-Jewish thought and action which characterised the relationship of Jews with a section of their neighbours in the Diaspora. This, to a great extent, enabled them to go forward on their march through history and, fortified by their inner spiritual resources, to survive their tribulations, maintain their communal structure, practise their traditions and create their own culture, until they reached the present era of renewed sovereignty in the State of Israel and gained full emancipation in the Western Diaspora. The following chapters are not intended to serve the cause of either propaganda or apologetics. They aim at lending emphasis to a vital aspect of the complex phenomenon of Jewish-Gentile relationships throughout the ages — one which is generally overlooked and neglected — the recurring pattern of philo-Semitism. They propose to complement, not to replace or to minimize, the long and brutal record of anti-Semitism.

The following motives animate philo-Semitic thought, feeling and action in the Gentile world:

The Jew should be an object of Christian brotherly love and missionary activity, which would ultimately result in his conversion to Christianity, the only true faith. Judaism has frequently been cherished by people born outside the Jewish fold — even by theologians firmly rooted in the Christian faith.

The Messianic-Chiliastic motive aims at establishing friendly contact with the Jewish people, which, according to Romans 9-11, is chosen to play a special role in the ultimate act of World Redemption.

Admiration for the Jewish religion leads, not infrequently, to conversion to Judaism and complete integration with the Jewish community. Recently a feeling of guilt and a desire to atone for the horror of the Nazi era has prompted Gentiles to honour Jews and Judaism, and to make amends for past misdeeds.

Sympathy, even affection for the ancient people of Israel, the creator and bearer of great cultural values, induces the humanistic motive in philo-Semitism. Philo-Semites of this kind are imbued with love for the Hebrew Bible; prompted by regard for the Hebraic truth of the Old Testament (Hebraica Veritas), they are interested in Kabbalah, the mystic lore of Judaism.

Esteem for the remarkable qualities of the Jewish people — their endurance in the face of suffering, heroism through ages of persecution, unfaltering fidelity to tradition, family morality, and other characteristics — appears to endow the Jewish community with a special excellence.

The utilitarian aspect of philo-Semitism ascribes to the Jews commercial abilities which benefit the countries of their sojourn. The Jews should be welcomed and offered economic opportunities so that their financial activities may redound to the advantage of commerce and industry.

To the liberal type of philo-Semite the Jew is a fellowman and the Jewish situation a touchstone for the rule of tolerance and humanity in society. Liberal principles impose the duty of special concern for the under-privileged Jews. The humanitarian defender of the Jewish people affirms that he is not motivated by any shallow philo-Semitic sentiments, but by feelings of a common humanity, embracing all members of the human family. The feeling of all-human kinship directs particular attention to the fate of the generally persecuted Jewish people.

The romantic pro-Zionist type of philo-Semitism is motivated by respect for the Jews who, as a nation, are worthy to be replanted in their ancient homeland so that they may continue their ancient traditions in a modern State. Gentile pro-Zionists, such as Lloyd George, A.J. Balfour, Winston Churchill, Orde Wingate and Josiah Wedgewood, who were brought up on the Scriptures, believed that Britain was the country to liberate Palestine from the Turks and that, under British protection, the Jews, the people of the Bible, were the rightful nation to possess it. Thanks to their Bible-reading, they knew more about Palestine than about any country save their own,

3

and believed that it was Britain's destiny to settle the Jews in their historic homeland. Balfour believed that the ultimate justification of Zionism lies in the endemic anti-Semitism in the Gentile world; it is because the Jews of the Diaspora must remain in danger of homelessness, that a Jewish State is a necessity for Jewish survival.[1]

Philanthropic Zionism appealed powerfully to Christians as well as to Jews. Sharing in the language and sentiment of the Bible, Christians could not be emotionally indifferent to the drama of the Holy Land and the "Chosen People." Here, philo-Semites thought, was an opportunity to right an immemorial wrong. British statesmen, eager to justify Britain's role as bearer of the white man's burden, were particularly suscepti-ble to the fascination of the dream of Zion. In this sense, Churchill, an inveterate romantic, was entirely sincere, when he spoke of himself as a "veteran Zionist". Lord Balfour was similarly impelled and motivated by this romantic vision, even if the issuing of the Balfour Declaration was precipitated, not by romantic humanists, but by the hard-headed generals, eager to win the allegiance of the Jews of the Russian Pale against the Bolshevik regime that sought to withdraw from the war.[2] Weizmann was helped in his Zionist endeavours by England's religious tradition founded as much on the Old Testament as on the New.[3]

In the following pages an attempt will be made to present a few of the main representatives of these trends of thought and to delineate philo-Semitic attitudes, sentiments and actions in various cultural spheres from the beginning of the Diaspora till our day.

Anti-Semitism, like all manifestations of aggression and hatred, is conspicuous, prominent and notorious, while pro-Semitism, like all phenomena of sympathy and love, is taken for granted, considered as normal, difficult to discern and to classify. Reading an average history of the Jews it appears as if persecutions and expulsions were the main features of Jewish existence. It is forgotten that the Jewish people existed in many countries in the course of centuries, under various cultural systems, in comparative quiet and ease, enjoying a measure of tolerance and understanding. Frequently protected by pope and emperor, sultan and vizier, king and nobleman, cardinal and bishop; they were esteemed by Hebraic scholars as the people of the Bible and admired by humanists for their spiritual gifts. It is incorrect and depressing to assume that, generally speaking, the Jews were detested and Judaism scorned everywhere and by everybody, as the "lachrymose"* approach to Jewish history affirms. Numerous instances could be adduced for cases where Jews enjoyed protection and sympathetic treatment; frequently their faith and persistence were appreciated and libellous accusations denounced. The eminent humanist, the famous Dutch theologian and forerunner of the Reformation, Erasmus of Rotterdam (1466-1536) found great inspiration in the Jewish religion, ascribed great significance to the Hebrew Bible and considered the reading of it an obligation for every Christian. He defended the Jews against the accusation of usury by pointing to the Biblical prohibition. He was one of those who revived the study of the Bible in the original. One may recall the German protestant theologian, Andreas Osiander, the sixteenth-century Hebrew scholar and defender of the Jews, who, in his writings, took a firm stand against the ritual murder accusation. To the great humanists, the Jewish problem was incidental to the general problem with which they happened to be confronted — the conflict between Christian creed and deed. The tragic plight of the Jewish community served to bring into bold relief the anomaly of Christian conduct, which they sought to reform, and to emphasize the wickedness of bigotry and absolutism, which they sought to eradicate. Crotus Rubianus and Ulrich von Hutten, the great sixteenth-century German humanists and contributors to the famous *Epistolae Obscurorum Virorum,* a satire on benighted clericalism, saw in the cleric's contemptuous attitude towards

*NOTE: The term "lachrymose", describing the sorrowful character of Jewish history, has become an accepted term in Jewish historiography. It was coined by Prof. S. Baron.

5

Jews yet another manifestation of the stupidity and cruelty of the ecclesiastical order. There is biting sarcasm in the comment of Erasmus of Rotterdam, "If it be Christian to hate the Jews, then we are true Christians."[4]

The mediaeval Jews are often depicted as a completely helpless and defenceless group, wholly in the power of the lay or ecclesiastical princes and totally dependent on their goodwill and generosity. Yet the life of the Jews in the Dark Ages, their economic and political position, the security of their life and property, must be evaluated on the basis of the general condition at that time and place. Some contemporary Jewish historians even go so far as to declare that the Jews from the ninth to the twelfth centuries fared better than their Christian neighbours.[5] While the manifestations of anti-Semitism in the Christian world were engendered by the accusations of deicide and the anti-Jewish tendencies of Christian teachings, the protection the Jews enjoyed for hundreds of years in Christian surroundings was based on an attitude of mysterious reverence for the people of the "Old Testament", the hope of ultimate conversion of the remnant of Israel and the professed opposition of the Church to the shedding of blood. The popes offered guarantees for the safety of the Jews under their dominion and affirmed the indissoluble relationship between Israel and the Church.[6] This contradictory attitude which accounted for both the survival and the humiliation of the Jews in the Christian world is strikingly expressed in an address of Pope Innocent II (d. 1143) to a delegation of Jews. The pope praised the Holy Law (Pentateuch) "for it was handed to your ancestors by the omnipotent God through the hands of Moses. But we condemn your religious practice and your faulty interpretation. For the Messiah, whom you still expect in vain, has come long ago."[7] The theological motive thus ensured the bodily survival of the Jews in the Christian world; the Jews were objects of missionary efforts, the success of which would hasten the advent of the millennium, Christ's reign on earth. In the world of Islam the survival of Jewish communities was made possible by the general climate of comparative religious tolerance which prevailed in Moslem countries.

6

Since the days of enlightenment, the main motives of philo-Semitism were rooted in the principles of tolerance; the belief in liberty for all religions developed into the creed of equality for all men and evoked general humanitarian sentiments which included the Jew. Mediaeval Jew-hatreds were based on myth and mystery, envy and hate: yet these hostile manifestations were usually characteristic of the uneducated, the under-privileged and the vulgar. A fifteenth-century Jewish historian asserts that Jew-hatred is restricted to the masses and that the learned classes were relatively free of this social disease.[7a]

All these motives and attitudes, sentiments and considerations, created a massive body of philo-Semitic actions, flowing from philo-Semitic views. These enabled the Jewish community in the Western world to survive the attacks of Church and State, the envy of the commercial competitor, the fury of the bigoted mob, the hatred of the religious fanatic, the nationalist and racialist foe, all of whom considered the Jew an unwanted alien, a pariah in society, an infidel in the community of true believers. Yet prior to the advent of Nazism the enemies of the Jews recoiled from eliminating them from the body of Western humanity. Philo-Semitism and its theoretical attitude are phenomenons closely linked to the spiritual situation of Western man. The Jew in the primitive Far-Eastern world was simply tolerated, as other "non-believers" also were. There was no Toland or Lessing, neither Mirabeau nor Macaulay, to give him an integrated place in the thought and life of the surrounding world. Philo-Semitic theory and conscious practice are, like the Jewish Diaspora communities, modern Jewish culture and the State of Israel, a product of Western civilisation.

One of the motives of anti-Semitism was, curiously enough, the charge that the Jews originated the Christian religion. The Church was largely despised, if not hated, by the rationalists. The Church had cursed the Jews because they did not follow Christ while its enemies blamed them for bringing forth a tyrannous, obscurantist faith — Christianity. However, some enlightened minds, such as Rousseau, Montesquieu, Herder

7

and Lessing, did not transfer their disregard for the Christian Church to the Jewish people. On the contrary, they initiated a secularised approach to the writing of history, assigning to the Jews a place among ancient peoples who contributed to civilization. This new historical attitude gave the Jews credit for the best there is in Christianity, and established the theory of the Judeo-Christian tradition, as an essential factor in the formation of Western civilisation.[8] The enlighteners even compared the Biblical way of life with the teachings of Persian, Indian or Chinese sages. Those distant nations were the favourites of English and French rationalist thinkers because, though not Christian, they were nevertheless perhaps purer and better and even more pious than the devoutest Catholics of Paris or Rome.

The sixteenth and seventeenth centuries, following on the Reformation, were periods when some practical philo-Semitism began to make its presence felt in certain areas of Western European society. It was facilitated by the trend towards the separation of Church and State, the growth of the idea of religious tolerance, sympathetic Christian interest in Judaism and an awareness of the economic benefit to be derived from the activity of Jewish merchants. Such diverse personalities as Hugo Grotius, the Dutch jurist, John Locke, the English philosopher, gave expressions to various aspects of the new ways of thought.

Philo-Semitism, as a counter-trend to anti-Semitism, has been a vital element in the history of the Jews from the time of their dispersion among the nations until today. In the Christian world, not only anti-Semitic, but also philo-Semitic tendencies have been theologically motivated, because the Jews are chosen for a special role in the last act of the world drama. "All Israel should be saved . . . the Deliverer should come out of Zion and shall turn away ungodliness from Jacob. For this is my covenant unto them when I shall take away their sins" (Romans 11:26-27). "As concerning the Gospel, they are enemies for your sakes, but with reference to the election, they are beloved for their father's sake. For the gifts and calling of

God are without repentance" (ib 11:29). This idea of Israel's "Chosenness" is the reason for saving the Jews from extermination — the fate of innumerable heretics — and preserving them within the Christian world, even in dejection and misery. The theological element gave the Jews a measure of "security" in the days of Christian-Ecclesiastical domination and frequently created a philo-Semitic mood among popes and the highest Christian clergy. There was, until our day, a mysteriously ambivalent attitude of conflict and alliance between Israel and Christendom. The conflict created mountainous obstacles of prejudice, hatred, vilification and slander. It appealed to the basest instincts in man. The very existence of the Jew was a challenge to the Church. The Jew was on a lower level than the Christian and was to be treated as such; he did not have the benefit of the cleansing power which flowed from Christianity. On the other hand, the alliance between Israel and the followers of the Christian faith ensured physical survival and created a certain contact, an urge for a dialogue and a need for spiritual communication and mutual concern between Jews and the Christian world, which in our days has brought a marked change in the official attitude of the Church in relation to the eternally chosen people of Israel. This spiritual meeting between Jews and their neighbours is non-existent in the world outside the Judeo-Christian spiritual realm. Jews and Judaism mean absolutely nothing to Buddhists, Indians, Chinese and Japanese; even in the realm of Islam, the Jewish spiritual heritage plays an insignificant role. It was in the Christian world that, parallel to contempt, a distinct type of veneration for the Jewish people's spiritual heritage — the Bible, its heroes and sages — existed. This ultimately created a pro-Jewish climate from which flowed both the Balfour Declaration of 1917 and the Vatican Council decision of 1965. The practical implications of the new official attitude of the Catholic Church to the Jews have not yet become clear.

It is noteworthy that Jews are found amongst Christians who have preserved the ancient Hebrew documents, the Scriptures, and amongst Moslems who adhere to uncompromising monotheism and venerate "the Book", but not amongst those whose faith is not connected with Hebrew sources. In countries where there are no Christians or Moslems who are in some way spiritually related to Jews, the latter no longer exist and have been forgotten. Despite basic differences, there exists a real relationship between Jews and their Christian surroundings. With the common adherence to the Bible as the background, Jewish life among Christians is possible. It is questionable and anomalous amongst nations which do not venerate the Bible.[9]

The thought that Jewish survival in the Diaspora was only possible in Bible-conscious surroundings has recently gained strong acceptance. Professor J.L. Talmon writes perceptively on the unique relation and interdependence between the Jews and Christian civilisation.

"In the vision of history of Western-Christian civilisation, the Jew occupied a vital or at least a unique place. To the multitudes of Eastern and South-Eastern Asia, Jews are an unknown, incomprehensible and negligible quantity. The Jew in the West may be persecuted, reviled, despised, expelled and massacred. He was indissolubly connected with the central event in the history of Christendom. But he constituted a tremendous problem. He embodied a great mystery. Immense effectiveness was ascribed to him, for good or evil. He appeared a factor of significance out of all proportion to the numbers involved. We have a long, terrible and bloodstained account with the Christian world. I venture to say, however, that already now the rise of non-European powers is beginning to make the record look somewhat different and less straightforward than in the not-too-distant past. No Jewish historian, whatever his evaluation of the various factors involved in the restoration of Jewish statehood, can ignore the fact that Zionism would never have had a chance of success if centuries of Christian teaching and worship, liturgy and legend, had not conditioned the Western nations to respond almost instinctively to the words 'Zion' and 'Israel', and thus to see in the Zionist ideal not a romantic chimera or an imperialistic design to wrest a country from its actual inhabitants, but the consummation of an eternal promise and hope. No Jewish associations impinge upon the Far Eastern civilisations. Their record is clean of anti-Semitism, but it is also empty of Jews."[10]

Philo-Semitic feeling was occasionally induced by religious experience in the artistic sphere. Frances Trollope, the mother of the English novelist Anthony Trollope, in describing a trip to Austria in 1836-37, recalls a visit to a Viennese synagogue, where the musical quality of the service made a deep impact on her. After criticising the low level of the Viennese Opera of those days, she continues: "There is yet another species of music which I have heard in Vienna: of this I hardly know how to speak . . . There is in truth, so strange a harmony in the songs of the children of Israel as performed in the synagogue in this city, that it would be difficult to render full justice to the splendid excellence of the performance, without falling into the language of enthusiasm. A voice performs the solo parts of these extraordinary cantiques . . . The volume of vocal sound exceeds anything of the kind I have ever heard".

The voice which made such a deep impression on her was that of the celebrated Salomon Sulzer, Cantor of the new synagogue in the Seitenstettengasse (1826), who counted Franz Schubert and Franz Liszt among his admirers; and on whose "Shir Zion," services of many Jewish congregations are based even today.[11] Franz Liszt was deeply impressed by the services in the Viennese synagogue, particularly the rendering of the musical part by Sulzer. "Seldom", he wrote, "had we experienced in such an overwhelming manner the vibration of the chords of divine worship and of human sympathy as we did on this evening. In the light of numerous candles which glistened in the ceiling like so many stars, a strange choir began in low guttural voices. It seemed as if every breast were a prison cell from the depth of which rose praises to the God of the Ark of the Covenant in the midst of exile and distress, calling upon Him with staunch faith and the full certainty of eventual deliverance from endlessly long enslavement . . . One seemed to see the Psalms floating aloft like spirits of fire, and bowing as suppliants at the feet of the All Highest".[12] "We had the oppor-

11

tunity", writes Liszt, "to form an idea of what Jewish art might become if the Israelites would express all the intensity of the indwelling emotions in the form of their own spirit. We met in Vienna Cantor Sulzer."[13]

Historians of art emphasize that in the Middle Ages there existed co-operation between Jews and Christians in the field of writing, illuminating and binding of manuscripts, and later in the printing of books. The relations between Jews and non-Jews in the sphere of artistic creations led to a friendly intercourse which contributed to the breaching of the wall that separated Jews and Christians. It was an added means of creating an atmosphere of reconciliation, leading ultimately to Jewish emancipation.[13a] The appreciation and support of music displayed by Jews has frequently given rise to philo-Semitic emotions and utterances. Out of innumerable instances, the following remarkable passages from Pablo Casals' reminiscences may be quoted:

For me, perhaps the most frightful aspect of the Dreyfus affair was the fact that many people were against him because he was Jewish. And I found it almost unbelievable that in Paris — with all its culture and its noble traditions of the rights of man — that here, in this city which was called la ville lumiere, anti-Semitism could spread like a foul plague. What words, indeed, are there to describe this disease, which would later infect a whole nation and rationalise the massacre of millions of men, women and children on the grounds that "Jewish blood" flowed in their veins? One's mind staggers at the monstrosity! The very idea of hating Jews is incomprehensible to me. My own life has been so enriched by tender associations with Jewish fellow artists and friends.

What people on earth have contributed more to human culture than the Jewish people? Of course they make wonderful musicians. The reason is that they have so much heart — yes, and head, too! When I am conducting and tell the orchestra members, "Play Jewish," they know what I mean.[13b]

An exaggerated attitude in the sphere of philo-Semitism is adopted by Lord Snow (the novelist, C.P. Snow). To the question "Why are Jews so successful in every sphere of endeavour?" he suggests that there may be something in the Jewish genes which produces talent on quite a different scale from the Anglo-Saxon gene-pool. Lord Snow evaluates the achievements of the Jews who from the beginning of the nineteenth century had a chance to compete with Gentiles over a wide range of human activities. The record, he writes, is remarkable and quite outside any sort of statistical probabilities, especially when one remembers that there can never have been twenty million Jews alive in the world at any one time, and no more than seventeen or eighteen million just before the Holocaust. Take any test of achievement you like — in any branch of science, mathematics, literature, music, public life. The Jewish performance has been not only disproportionate, but almost ridiculously disproportionate. Run your eye down the lists of Nobel prize-winners for the past twenty-five years. You will find that between a third and a quarter have Jewish names.[14]

This is no doubt an excessive form of pro-Jewish sentiment. It is highly questionable whether Jews really display biologically conditioned superior qualities. It is inadmissible to separate the Jewish genius of Nobel prizewinners from their German or Anglo-American environment. The Jews in the backward Oriental world have created nothing remarkable in any sphere of culture during the last centuries. It is wiser to attribute the success of individual Jews to old-fashioned hard work, inspired by a host of objective factors related to home and social environment. Lord Snow would do well to rely on Toynbee's "challenge-response" historical theory, rather than absurd speculations about gene-pools.[15] However, Lord Snow's ringing declaration may serve as a motto for many philo-Semites in modern days: "While there is a single anti-Semite alive, we are proud to be on the other side."[16]

There are innumerable items of philo-Semitic content extant in all languages, testimonies to feelings of friendship for the

13

Jews, admiration for Judaism, recognition of Israel's significance in the scheme of Western civilisation. No study of the subject can claim to be complete. The theme of philo-Semitism is as inexhaustible as that of Jew-hatred, and no less important.[17]

Hopefully, in the not too distant future, the problem of the Jewish people will be, in the words of Mordechai Kaplan, to find a spiritual substitute for the defensive war against anti-Semitism as a basis for Jewish unity.

A BALANCED CONCEPT
OF JEWISH HISTORY

Leading Jewish historiographers reject the "lachrymose concept" of Jewish history;[18] the theory that the Jewish situation has always and everywhere been predominantly dark, especially in the pre-modern era. According to that concept, Jewish history is essentially a sequence of sorrows, a *Leidensgeschichte*, composed of tragedies. It is widely held today that the mediaeval story of the Jews is characterised not only by accusations, persecutions and degradation, but also sprinkled with individual good relations and mutual confidence between Jews and Christians. Popes, princes and bishops employed and trusted Jewish doctors and excluded them from decrees which bore heavily on their fellow Jews. Scholars met and discussed Biblical texts. Maimonides was always spoken of with respect by Thomas Aquinas, who found in him a fellow Aristotelian, rather than the "perfidious" Jew. Secular princes and Church rulers made use of what was a peculiar feature of Jewish economic activity — Jewish skill in dealing with money. Enlightened rulers, such as the Emperor Frederick II (1194-1250), refused to believe in the blood accusation while the popes lent the weight of their authority against this baseless libel. Pope Innocent IV proclaimed his opposition to the accusation of ritual murder in a bull to all the bishops of Germany and France, countries where that libel most frequently occurred. The refutation of the blood accusation, begun by Pope Innocent IV in 1247, was repeated by various popes as late as Clement XIII in 1763. There was a continuous stream of papal decrees in defence of Jewry, between 1120 and 1763. Although they seem to have been of limited avail in coping with popular prejudice, they must have necessarily exercised a decisive influence on the protection of Jewish life, property, even dignity, by Christian rulers, and ultimately ensured the survival of at least some sections of Jewry in those parts of the Christian world from which they were not expelled. Many papal bulls have a pro-Jewish ring and are outspoken in their condemnation of violence and forcible conversion of the Jews. Not much more could be expected in the pre-modern era when the dominant doctrine of the Church affirmed the inferiority of the Jewish community and expected the Jews to accept the ultimate truth of Christian belief.

While the general relationship of Jews and Christians was governed by the current image of the Jew, who at worst was considered an emissary of the devil, and, at best, a permanent witness to the crime of deicide, there were also recorded manifestations of friendly feelings towards Jews and signs of compassion with Jewish suffering on the part of leading Christians. When Jews suffered in the days of the second crusade, Bernard of Clairvaux, leading Christian ecclesiastic, raised his voice in protest against their persecution. In his letter, he laid down the general lines of policy, with regard to the Jews, which has guided the Roman Catholic Church. Jews are not to be persecuted or killed; they are living symbols of the Passion, and their dispersion is sufficient punishment for their sins. They will ultimately be converted, but it can never happen if they are subjected to oppression. A Hebrew chronicler of the Second Crusade (Ephraim of Bonn) termed Bernard a saviour of the Jews from the greatest distress, and praised his unselfish deeds.

"The Lord heard our supplications and had pity upon us. He sent one of their greatest and respected teachers, the abbot Bernard, from the town Clairvaux in France. And he also preached to his people according to their custom, crying 'It is good that you are ready to go forth against the Moslems; but whosoever uses violence against the Jews commits a deadly sin.' All honoured this monk as one of their saints, neither has it ever been said that he received a bribe for his good service to us. We gladly gave our possessions as a ransom for our lives. Whatever was asked of us, silver or gold, we withheld not. If our Creator in His great compassion had not sent us this abbot, there would have been none in Israel that would have escaped or remained alive. Blessed be He who saves and delivers. Praised be His name."

This portrayal of a personality, who, in the midst of fanatical passion aroused by the crusades, kept his tolerance and humanity, disproves the thesis that there was no light in the dark image of the Middle Ages. A similar incident is reported about the rescue of Rabbi Yacob Ben Meir (Rabbenu Tam) by a powerful knight who happened to ride by. The knight persuaded the crusaders to release Rabbenu Tam. They acceded to this request and the danger was averted.[19]

Christian Spain stood among the Christian states of Europe as a land of both religious fanaticism and religious tolerance. Both were natural phenomena in a country where members of all three monotheistic faiths lived and worked side by side. There was, to a certain degree, spiritual contact between Christians and Jews and in spite of the vehement controversy between the two creeds on the soil of Spain, there were frequent manifestations of genuine cordiality between members of both sides. The Infante Don Juan Manuel told of the passing of Sancho the Fourth, attended during his last hours by Jewish physicians, Isaac and Abraham Ibn Wakar. The Infante, later celebrated as a war hero and a leading exponent of chivalry in Castilian literature, advised his son always to keep in his service a Jewish physician for he had found no other physician as capable or as trustworthy. In his last will, drawn up in 1339, the Infante wrote — "Even though Don Solomon, my physician, is a Jew, and is therefore ineligible to serve as executor of my estate, yet, inasmuch as I have found him to be always

17

indescribably faithful, I request that my sons retain him in their service and entrust their affairs to him. I am confident that they will profit thereby."

In a codicil to his will he again urged his son to include Don Solomon among his advisors — "For I know well that this will serve the son to greater advantage than anything else."[20]

In the theological literature of the day such a humane note was unusual, but not utterly excluded. The great Catalonian mystic, Raymond Lully (d. 1315), who probably derived his knowledge of Judaism from Maimonides' *Guide of the Perplexed,* brings together in his *Book of the Gentile and the Three Sages* the protagonists of the three faiths in a friendly disputation. Jew, Christian and Moslem, in turn, expound their respective faiths before a pagan who has come to them in search of salvation. The sages do not interrupt one another's exposition, but the pagan sometimes interposes a question. After they have completed their discourses, the three learned men, in an inspired mood, bid farewell to the grateful pagan; they refuse to hear his decision as to the faith he has chosen, intending, as they do, to continue their discussion further on equal terms. They obtain one another's permission to prolong their remarks at the next opportunity, and beg each other's forgiveness for any possible slight inadvertently cast upon another's faith. The author strives to remain objective in his presentation of the arguments of each of the three religions. Judah Halevi's *Kusari* (1140) — a vindication of the Jewish faith — may have served as a prototype for Lully's polemic work.

The theory of *Leidensgeschichte,* the concept which depicts the existence of the Jewish people as a unique, almost unrelieved chain of suffering and contempt — a theory predominant in the emancipation era — is refuted by a number of contemporary Jewish historians. Their scholarly conscience and, subconsciously, also their pride in the Jewish heritage made them impatient with the eternal self-pity characteristic of Jewish historiography. "It is important to divorce the indubitable reality of the general insecurity of mediaeval Jewish life from the consideration of the Jews' political and legal status in those mediaeval countries where they were tolerated by law."[21] Judeo-Christian relations were characterized by an intrinsic polarity which subjected the Jews to humiliation and at the same time guaranteed their physical survival. Viewing the problem as a whole, it may be asserted that the Jewish factor in mediaeval civilisation can well serve as a criterion of the genuineness and inwardness of that civilisation. Despite the enormous Jewish sufferings which not even the staunchest opponent of the tragic concept of Jewish history would wish to minimize, there was general fairness or at least attempted fairness in the world of the mediaeval man. Numerous exceptions notwithstanding, the prevailing legislation of practically all mediaeval countries tried to safeguard the legitimate interests of the Jewish minority. A Jew could not be forced to appear before the court of his Christian opponent; the Jew could insist upon repairing to his own court, if he was the defendant, or more frequently, to a special mixed court or a generally less prejudiced superior court or appeal to its highest officials. Neither were the Jews to be condemned on the testimony of Christian witnesses alone. Their inclusion, along with clerics, women and other defenceless groups, under the safeguards of royal "peace," was intended to grant them a higher degree of protection than could be safeguarded by mere paper privileges.

One must also bear in mind, that despite the tremendous bloodshed between 1096 and 1391, in the wake of the fanatical crusaders, we find no instance of governmentally-instigated *pogroms*. It was left to the Czarist government of the late nineteenth century, and to its disciples among the Nazis, to introduce this new, anarchical feature into the relationship between the State and its Jewry. This is far from denying the Jewish role of "scapegoat" in the mediaeval as well as in the modern world. This function of Western Jewry to serve as an outlet for accumulated hatreds and as a sort of safety valve within explosive societies, is well established. Nevertheless, one may readily acquit all mediaeval governments of acting

19

in a way reminiscent of the organized Nazi Jew-baiting of November 1938, or the Nazi programme for the "final solution."

A certain measure of fairness permeated the relations between the Church and the Jews. Despite its all-embracing claim for supremacy and notwithstanding its overt attempts to penetrate all domains of public and private life, the Church imposed upon itself limitations in regard to Jews which may not be overlooked.

Notwithstanding the divergencies between Judaism and Christianity, there was a basic unity of thinking which converted all conflicts into a struggle between brethren rather than a war between strangers. Only in the light of such unity of thinking was it possible for the greatest masterminds of the Christian world to quote freely the views of Maimonides and other Jewish teachers. Only such unity made it possible for Solomon ibn Gabirol to write a philosophic work so inter-denominational in character — his Mekor Chaim (fons vitae) ca. 1150 — as to permit, thereafter, the mistaken notion that its author had been a Muslim or a Christian. The basic outlook of all Europeans was so much determined by the common Judeo-Christian heritage as to make such a mistaken identification possible.

Conditions in the Middle Ages varied from century to century. Before the year 1200, Prof. I.A. Agus affirms, the Jews were not serfs, they were the only free persons in Central Europe, while the general body of Christians were indeed servi.[22]

Opponents of the "tearful" view of Jewish history rightly assert that the life of a group in a particular age should be studied in comparison with the general conditions of life of that very period — their economic and political status should be compared with those of their immediate neighbours, their safety with the security prevailing in that time and place.[23] A realistic appraisal of the success or failure of the Jews of Central Europe, during the ninth through the twelfth centuries, reveals that the Jews of this period seemed to have fared not

20

much worse than their neighbours. "Traditional" Jewish historians were greatly handicapped by the fact that the bulk of the historical material available to them came from sources which necessarily selected for preservation only those items of information prejudicial to a balanced understanding of Jewish history. Most of the source material they used was either composed by non-Jews, or by Jewish necrologists, compilers of lists of martyred Jewish dead. This source material by its very nature pre-determined the attitude and the judgement of these historians; it forced them to see events in unrelieved darkness and thus to distort history.

This significant trend of thought in recent Jewish historiography emphasizes the fact that anti-Jewish thoughts and deeds were not the only factors determining the situation of the Jews in the pre-modern era and defining the character of Christian-Jewish relations. While no final judgement can ever be pronounced on such a complicated, multifaceted reality as the social-economic, cultural and psychological situation of the "Jewish infidel" in the age of Christian faith, the idea that the position of the Jews in Christian society was determined exclusively by unremitting and violent Jew-hatred is one-sided and therefore incorrect. The Jews could not have survived a millennium and a half, if Jew-hatred alone was the governing factor in Jewish-Gentile relationships from the time of the loss of Jewish sovereignty until the days of emancipation and national restoration. It has been correctly observed that the anti-Jewish practices of the Dark Ages were superficial. How a man was treated throughout the year was more important than how he was treated during Eastertide (reference to the practice of stoning); how he earns his livelihood is more significant than how he is to be hanged if it ever comes to that (reference to the practice of hanging by the feet). The essentials of life were not touched by the popular code of the Dark Ages. Nor, presumably, was this carried into effect systematically at any time. The picture of the honoured Jewish merchant who travelled about unmolested throughout the year, but was stoned and buffetted at Eastertide, may not be logical, but it

21

may nevertheless be true.[24] The view that Jewish history is little more than a chain of persecutions and an unrelieved story of martyrdom is being abandoned by contemporary Jewish historiographers. Such interpretation also neglects unduly Jewish achievements in intellectual pursuits, in the field of religion, in literature and centres attention almost exclusively on pain.

Modern Jewish historiography stresses the need of considering fully not only the negative, but also the positive forces in the position of the Jews in mediaeval Europe, not only the anti-Jewish feelings in the Christian environment, but also the contributions of Jews to the cultural, financial and political strength of their neighbours. These positive forces were highly significant and effective. The tiny little group, the ten thousand souls, that lived in Catholic Europe in the year 800 multiplied more than a thousand times in the following eleven centuries — in spite of strong anti-Jewish feeling and of serious persecutions in all the lands they dwelt in. Moreover, throughout this period they maintained a higher standard of living than that of ninety-five percent of their neighbours. This constitutes great success in the group's struggle for existence — probably greater than any other national group in Europe. This phenomenon, therefore, deserves serious study and detailed investigation.[25] The anti-lachrymose concept of Jewish history is emphatically stressed by Professor I.A. Agus of Yeshiva University, New York, who opposes the idea that throughout the Middle Ages the situation of the Jews was of a particularly distressing nature; at times he even paints a bright picture of their position which seems not only to mitigate the traditional concept, but to turn it into its very opposite: the Jewish situation was privileged until the end of the eleventh century.

In the pre-crusade period the Jews of Catholic Europe constituted a highly privileged class. Politically they were quite free; religiously they were uncontrolled and unrestrained; economically they were highly successful, and culturally they were by far the most progressive group in Europe.

One of the most important causes of this unusual state of affairs was apparently the fact that they were able to assure a much higher state of security for themselves than their Christian neighbors. "While the latter huddled around the strongholds and the castles of their lords and rarely dared venture abroad, the Jews were able to travel in comparative safety from one end of Europe to the other, and to trade successfully in commercial centres located hundreds of miles away from their homes. This superior state of security ... was mainly an outgrowth of the unusually fine techniques of inner organization, and the highly efficient methods of self-government, created and employed so successfully by the Jews of this period."[26]

It is worth recalling that Jewish merchants, called "Radanites", regularly undertook distant journeys from Europe to the Orient, from Franconia to China.[26a] Eldad Ha-Dani (ninth century) visited Jewish communities in North Africa and Spain and related fantastic accounts of the Ten Tribes who, he averred, were living a free nomadic existence. The most famous Jewish traveller, Benjamin Tudela (twelfth century), journeyed throughout Europe and then to Palestine, Mesopotamia and Persia. The dispersion of the Jews over the whole populated world and the comparative security and prosperity they enjoyed facilitated such travels. Jews maintained international trade almost alone in the early Middle Ages.

There was naturally a marked ambivalence in the Jewish situation until very recent days and any historian can find sufficient source material either to paint a dark image, or portray a more favourable one of the Jewish position. However, a completely gloomy picture as drawn hitherto is no longer justified; it belongs to the preconceived notions concerning Jewish history. Anti-Semitism, humiliation, expulsion and massacre, suffering and rightlessness, gravely affected the Jewish position. It is hardly possible to minimize the crimes perpetrated, the sorrows inflicted on the Jewish communities in the Christian world, or to underrate the distress and shame experienced by Israel. There was both mob violence and legalized oppres-

23

sion, massacre and rightlessness which darkened the life of the Jews.

But there is also evidence of an element of legal fairness, of humane tolerance, an occasional understanding of Judaism and respect for the indomitable Jew in his unyielding adherence to his faith. Modern Jewish historians pay rightful tribute to the role of the Polish nobility. The rulers and noblemen of Poland are frequently accused of every kind of misdeed against the Jewish population. But from 1500 to 1650 the Jewish population in Poland and Lithuania increased from fifty thousand to more than half a million. Mistaken, too, is the general assertion that the Jewish situation deteriorated because Jews were delivered into the hands of the nobility. In fact conditions for the Jews in the eighteenth century were better in the cities and towns belonging to noblemen, dependent on the gentry, where they were subject to no restrictions or to fewer than in those of the realm. Noblemen also made it possible for Jews to settle in suburbs of those cities in which Jewish residence was limited, as for instance in Warsaw. Historians taking a balanced view of Jewish history take issue with the dolorous concept of Polish-Jewish history. They oppose the cliche of great Jewish poverty in the past, which takes no account of the fact that millions of peasants in inter-war Poland had to split matches before using them.[27]

It is misleading to stress only the negative aspect in the relations between the Jewish and the Polish people. The Jewish people are bound to Poland by traditions that go back a thousand years. Recorded history testifies to the immigration of Jews to Poland as early as the eleventh century. The cruel persecutions in mediaeval Germany brought ever new waves of Jewish immigrants to the adjacent eastern country, with the result that as early as the sixteenth century the Jewish community in Poland was the largest in the world, maintaining the greatest centre of Jewish culture. Two hundred years later the Jews inhabiting the vast territories of the old Polish Republic constituted about two-thirds of European Jewry. Between the two wars the Polish Republic again comprised the largest community in Europe, ranking within world Jewry as second only to the Jewish population of the United States. In spite of anti-Jewish discrimination and propaganda, Polish Jewry, at the beginning of the Second World War, represented one of the strongest and most creative Jewish communities in the world. After the war, Poland, the satellite of Moscow, followed the pattern set by Soviet Russia, both with regard to the Jewish minority and the foreign policy towards Israel. One should see the positive side in Polish-Jewish relations, the millennial sojourn of Jews in the Polish realm until their massacre by the Nazi-Germans, the deeds of rescue which were performed by individual Poles at the risk of their lives during the Nazi occupation. It should be remembered that the Polish people demonstrated its solidarity with Israel on the eve of the Six-Day War and immediately after it. The student demonstrations throughout Poland in the spring of 1968 gave voice to this solidarity and to the people's rejection of the wild Soviet incitement against Israel, which had by its own power extricated itself from the threat of destruction which its neighbours had launched against it with the aid of modern Soviet arms.[27a]

Jewish history is more complicated than that of any other nation, because it is interwoven with the histories and destinies of many other peoples during the past two thousand years. Jewish history is part and parcel of the history of mankind. No history is so variegated and so extensive; it is a history that unfolds itself in many countries under all skies, in all climes. It is harder to write and its causes and effects are more difficult to determine than the history of other groups. It is so varied and complex that Mabillon's advice to the historian "to distinguish what was certain from what was probable, and what was probable from what was dubious, and what was dubious from what was false" becomes a formidable task. It is a fundamental requirement for a proper understanding of the factors which shape Jewish life to avoid facile generalizations and not to be carried away by sentimental group emotions, such as the affirmation of an unbridgeable gulf between Jew and Gentile.

It has been observed that young Jews growing up with the kind of curriculum which stresses pogrom, persecution and exile as the main theme of Jewish history — the Lachrymose Concept in Prof. Baron's phrase — must naturally get the impression that nothing of value was ever produced by the Jewish people, that their history is one of continuous suffering. Young people may come to the conclusion that the world cannot be altogether wrong in their condemnation of the Jews. "Where there is smoke there is fire" is a popular adage. If this is so who would want to perpetuate the tragic career of a people destined only for hate and suffering?[27b]

At this juncture of history when Jews not only live a free life among Gentile nations, but when the State of Israel has become part of the great world, and has assumed the guardianship of the holiest place of Christendom and of prominent sanctuaries of Islam, it is essential to build a bridge of understanding and mutual respect. It is vital for Israel and the Jewish people to forego the notion of a deep abyss dividing the Jews from their Gentile neighbours. Recording pro-Jewish trends of thought, patterns of behaviour and rules of conduct could play a role in the new situation which confronts the Jews in relation to the world of which they are part and in which they are destined to play a vital role. The relation of the Jew to his surrounding world was determined by both anti-Semitism and philo-Semitism. It was not only prompted by hatred but also by positive factors, tolerance, friendliness and, above all, legal protection of his life and property. These positive factors enabled the Jews to survive, to increase in numbers, to study and to teach, to attain and maintain political status, and to resist overwhelming hostile forces. It is fair to recognize that the forces making for Jewish survival in an alien environment were as strong as those which aimed at the destruction of Jewish existence. Not only spiritual contact with surrounding civilizations, but also political and economic interaction between the Jews and the nations among whom they lived had positive aspects which should eliminate the isolationist approach from the writing of Jewish history.

It has been observed that since the Second World War, a concept of historiography has been developing which, paradoxically, rejects the lachrymose theory of Jewish history. Instead of placing the main emphasis on martyrdom and persecution in Jewish history, a more positive view of Jewish life is presented, based on the dynamics of interaction with the outside world — an interaction similar to that between other religious, ethnic or economic groups. It is curious that this interpretation should become notable in the wake of Jewry's most disastrous period, the Nazi era, 1933-1945. However, the normalization of Jewish life in a sovereign state and in the countries west of the Iron Curtain appears to be the main cause for this change of attitude. Jews have entered the Western family as a sovereign nation and as full members in pluralistic societies. The consciousness of being "unique" is waning.

Contemporary Jewish scholars pay tribute to the Church for not doing what it had political and ecclesiastical power to do — to ignore the status and presence of the Jew and thus exclude him altogether from the mediaeval world. The Church did make repeated attempts to protect the Jews and to define their rights. If the Jew was excluded from Christian society, he was but one in a system of isolated groups. It is an error to conclude that in the Middle Ages only the Jewish people suffered.[28] To the credit of the papacy be it said that many of the pontiffs were more tolerant than the inferior clergy, and did not favour forced conversion. The very prohibition against social relations between Jews and Christians offers evidence that such normal relations existed; and the constant exhortations of the clergy to shun the society of the Jews are in themselves proof that not all Christians followed the example of the frenzied monks and the fanatic mobs.[29]

The indiscriminate condemnation of Christian attitudes to the Jews has given way to a certain amount of recognition for the Church's consent to Jewish survival in its midst. There was, for example, no room in Byzantium for non-believers; any deviation from the official Christian Church was severely punished, but the Jews were tolerated. The Jewish religion had been recognized in Rome; thus the Jewish community had a special legal status and was protected by law. Not all Byzantine Emperors adhered to the law, and at various times Jews were persecuted, even forced to adopt the official religion. Later, baptism was abolished and the converts were allowed to return to Judaism. The Second Council of Nicaea, held in 787 C.E., proclaimed that the Church cannot accept Jews unless they voluntarily "confess their error and turn to Christianity with willing hearts." The Council declared that the Jews may live openly according to their religion. Thus Byzantium became an important Jewish centre, drawing immigrants from the West and the Near East. Eventually it became one of the sources of the new Jewish settlements in Russia and Poland.

The Jews in the Middle Ages up to the modern days did not live in a society which showed them nothing but unmitigated hostility. The surroundings which made it possible for them — unyielding non-conformists, "Eternal Protestants" — to live, to draw on their own spiritual strength, to create values in the field of literature and thought, were, at least partly, favourably disposed, guaranteeing Jewish life, property and freedom of worship, even though their motives were socially conditioned and partly of an economic nature.

The most famous of the charters which governed the lives of the Jews in the Middle Ages was that granted by Frederick the Belligerent in July 1244, to the Jews of his Duchy of Austria. This document is important because it was soon adopted, with some changes, by most East European countries to which the masses of Jews finally drifted: Hungary, Bohemia, Poland, Silesia and Lithuania. This charter — a very favourable one — was issued to encourage money-lending among the Austrian Jews and probably also to attract moneyed Jews to migrate to this outlying German state which was in need of ready credit. Every effort was therefore made in this constitution to grant the Jews ample opportunity to sell their wares and, above all, to lend money. They were given adequate protection; they were subject to the direct jurisdiction of the Duke who guaranteed them safety of life and limb. The right of the Jews to govern themselves in communal and religious matters was not specified by the Duke, but this was taken for granted. One may assume that the Jews who lived under this charter enjoyed extensive political autonomy.

A similar sentiment pervades the enactments of Casimir the Great, "The Peasant King of Poland" (1334). He was solicitous about defending the Jews in all their rights and, to make sure that they would suffer no discrimination, took them out of the jurisdiction of the ecclesiastical courts. He made the murder of a Jew punishable by death, removed the restriction which kept Jews from entering the houses of Christians or visiting the municipal baths. So grateful were the Polish Jews to their royal benefactor that, at the marriage of his granddaughter, one of their merchants in Cracow presented her with one hundred thousand florins in gold, a gift equal to the dowry she had received from her grandfather. A similar position obtained in Lithuania under the reign of Gedimin. At the funeral of the Grand Duke Vladimir Vasilkovich "the Jews wept . . . as at the fall of Jerusalem, or when being led into the Babylonian captivity." Witold, too, who in 1389 issued a charter similar to that granted by Casimir the Great, was for a long time after his death remembered by the Jews for his tolerance and generosity. Examples of edicts and ordinances protecting the Jews could be multiplied. They prove that the usual picture of unmitigated hostility, persecution, insecurity, massacre, does not portray the complete situation. Only a balanced image of anti- and philo-Semitic fortunes conveys the correct impression. Persecution and protection issue from the same root, the ambivalent attitude of the Church to the people who gave it the Christ. The lachrymose concept of Jewish history is being superseded by a more equitable judgement of the Jewish position. Not only does an over-emphasis on Jewish suffering distort the total picture of Jewish historic evolution, but at the same time it does a disservice to a generation which had become impatient with the nightmare of endless persecution and massacres!

The status of Jews in Islamic lands prior to the contemporary emergence of pan-Arabian was fairly satisfactory in both theory and practice. Unlike Christian Europe, where the Jews were frequently the sole minority opposing the religious culture of the majority, the Moslem world was inhabited by numerous nationalities and religious sects; the Jews thus were never the only minority in the Arab world, a fact which mitigated that oppressive feeling of living alone in a hostile world, characteristic for so much of mediaeval Jewish thinking in Europe.

Contrary to the legal situation in Christian Europe, the Jews under Islam were never treated as aliens. Hence the absence of any large-scale expulsion of Jews from entire countries such as interrupted the continuity of Jewish history in many European lands. There was, within the realm of Islam, none of that feeling of personal insecurity which dominated the mediaeval Jewish mind in the West.

In peaceful times the Jew was protected by law against personal assault almost on a par with the Muslim, and his average life expectancy was probably at least as high as that of his "believing" neighbour. His economic opportunities too suffered only from relatively minor restrictions. Like his Muslim confreres, he could traverse the vast expanse of the Muslim world in search of economic or intellectual benefits. The majority of Jews undoubtedly viewed certain disabilities as but a minor price they had to pay for their freedom of conscience and their ability to live an untrammelled Jewish life within the confines of their community.[30]

The Jewish encounter with the Moslems in Spain and the resulting "Golden Age" of Jewish history are striking examples of a friendly, tolerant social structure, resulting in a markedly favourable attitude towards the Jews. This attitude manifested itself in the political, economic and cultural sphere; it gave the Jews communal autonomy, enabled them to travel across the wide areas of Islamic territory and to share with the Moslems the heritage of science and philosophy of Greece and the East. The "Golden Age" came to an end with the re-conquest of Spain

30

by the Christians in 1492, but it left an indelible imprint on the cultural quality of Jewish life in the Western world; it endowed Jewish history with a memory of spiritual efflorescence and a cultural symbiosis with the surrounding world which refuted the assumption of a persistent spiritual gulf between Jews and Gentiles and the unabating quality of anti-Semitism. Jewry in the Moslem world sank in the course of centuries into spiritual stagnation, but this was not due to anti-Semitism, but to the general decay of the Moslem world which resulted alike from the decline of Arabic philosophy and from the intolerance of Moslem sects such as the Berber Almoravides and Al-mohades.[31] The hate which divides Jews and Arabs in this era is of yesterday, while their common roots go back to the dawn of antiquity. A new vision of Jewish-Arab fraternity could possibly be grafted on that great record of co-operation and friendly co-existence attained by these two peoples in the mediaeval world.

Naturally, a much needed corrective to the "Vale of Tears" concept of Jewish history should not be made at the expense of truth. It is essential not to err in the opposite direction. The writing of Jewish history by contemporary historians is characterized by the desire not to exaggerate the martyrological concept in Jewish history; it asserts that the persecution-interpretation of Jewish history is in need of correction. It would be futile, even dangerous, to minimize the extent of anti-Jewish discrimination and the severity of persecution and oppression of which Jews were victims since the beginning of the Diaspora. Anti-Semitism and vilification of Judaism blot the pages of human history. In this age the Jews have been the victims of the greatest and most heinous crime history recalls. It revealed the hideous evil which lurks beneath the most progressive cultures. It is necessary to strike a balance between the endeavour to win the trophy of martyrdom, as claimed by Zunz,[32] and the minimizing of Jewish martyrdom throughout the ages. The persecution-interpretation of Jewish history as the sole motif governing Christian-Jewish relations

31

is not valid. It is imperative to fit the status of the Jewish community into the general tendency of religious intolerance, dominant in the pre-modern era. Though occasional persecution did take place here and there during the pre-Crusade period, all these were but sporadic actions, occasionally endorsed and generally ignored.[33]

James Parkes, the eminent Christian expert on Judaism, endeavours to mitigate the grimness of the Jewish position in Eastern Europe by citing the compassionate and dangerous rescue work done by many Christians especially during the Nazi regime.[34] The past, both in its positive and negative aspects, in its favourable and harmful interaction with the Gentile world, in anti-Semitism and philo-Semitism, contributed to the Jews' ability to survive until this day. Just as Jews should never forget Amalek, the Biblical enemy and his innumerable heirs and successors, so should they remember their friends throughout the ages.

The ambivalent attitude of the Church to the Jewish people accounts for the survival of the Jewish community in the midst of Christendom. If Judaism had been nothing but a heretic sect, Judaism would have been eliminated from the Christian world. Since the overwhelming majority of world Jewry derives from Christian Europe, there would have been left today only disparate fragments of Oriental Jewry. But, in Catholic Europe, Jews were supposed to be protected as well as scorned. Shall we remember only the episode of persecution and forget the protective arm which the Church as a whole and the Papacy in particular extended to our mediaeval forefathers? Is not such an attitude the very reverse of the Mosaic injunction — thou shall not scorn an Egyptian, for a sojourner were ye in his land? Jews always maintain that they today ought not to be blamed either for the crucifixion of Jesus, or for the persecution of the Apostles and the early Christians, or for any actual or imaginary crimes of the past. Should we now turn around and blame Christians for all the horrors of fanaticism in the mediaeval and modern world? To regard the Nazis as lineal descendants of "the Council of Nicea" is as vicious as to treat

Trotsky and the Jewish Bolsheviks as descendants of the Jewish tradition.[35] Even in the Christian Western world which became the centre of Jewish life after the decay of the Eastern countries, the prevailing understanding, at least up to the Crusades, was that Jews could live their independent life as a sheltered minority in accordance with their own tradition. Even the church recognized the Jews' claim to continued existence as a separate and distinct ethnic group, enjoying fundamental safeguards for the security of their persons and property, considerable freedom of movement and worship and autonomy in religious and cultural affairs.

Jewish historians oppose the theory that Gentile-Jewish hostility is due to a unique cause, namely the anti-Jewish techniques and actions of the Christian church.[36] It is unfair to blame the church for its evil deeds and not acknowledge the positive side of its attitude to the Jews in their midst. Having been taught by Hitler that the physical extermination of the Jews is entirely feasible, and by the Soviet Union that their destruction by cultural genocide is also possible, the Jewish historian cannot but note that while the pagan religions did not survive the establishment of Christian hegemony over all of Europe, Judaism did. The Jewish historian therefore must conclude that if Judaism survived, one reason was certainly a decision by the Christian Church, when and where it had power, to permit it to survive. Chrysostom, who preached that the Jews have become worse than wild beasts, certainly belongs to any history of the Jewish-Christian symbiosis; but so does Pope Gregory the Great, who said that the Jews must not be expelled, deprived of their rights, or converted by force, but rather that they must be brought into the fold by reason and mildness. Gregory, more than any other priest, established the institutional basis of the Jewish-Christian symbiosis wherever the Catholic hierarchy was in power. If anti-Semitism was condoned and furthered by the Church, the Church also made sure to uphold a minimal Jewish status. The practical alternative to this kind of anti-Semitism was genocide — which, indeed, the same Pope Gregory failed to condemn in regard to the pagans. Genocide against the Jews, whether practiced by Hitler or by the crusading rabble, arose from the breakdown of church authority vis a vis the Jews.[37]

There is of course a danger in historical iconoclasm, such as the undermining of the hitherto generally accepted lachrymose concept of Jewish history. Those who deny absolute validity of that concept hesitate to face the danger of such a destruction of a traditional interpretation of the Jewish past. Professor S. Baron recalls the shock he received when, after the publication of a preliminary essay of this subject, the representative of a leading publishing house in New York warned him that his book is "debunking" the Jewish Middle Ages. The lachrymose concept of Jewish history has served as an eminent means of social control; its repudiation now might help to weaken further the authority of Jewish leadership.[38]

The lachrymose interpretation of Jewish history has been satirized in the famous story *The Sermon* by the celebrated contemporary Hebrew novelist Chaim Hazaz. In this ironical description of Jewish attitudes bred in exile, Hazaz derides the Jewish love of suffering and affirms that Zionist history commenced a new chapter in Jewish existence, a history of action, of glory, of heroes and conquerers, discontinuing the past tale of suffering and martyrdom. He describes the Jews' intense consciousness of persecution and oppression which have become their second nature; some are proud of their woes, an attitude which Hazaz calls "nocturnal psychology."[39]

A balanced view of Jewish history affirms that, side by side with age-old anti-Semitism, fanaticism and bigotry, shame and agony, there exists a notable tradition of philo-Semitism which may enable Jews and Gentiles, Jews and Christians, to confront each other without guilt, suspicion and envy, in an atmosphere of mutual acceptance and recognition.

PHILO-JUDAIC TENDENCIES
IN CLASSICAL ANTIQUITY

The statements of Graeco-Roman writers concerning Jews and Judaism are generally of an unfriendly nature. The Jews appeared in the ancient world as an odd people, refusing to participate in pagan culture, holding fast to their peculiar rites, and separating themselves persistently from the general body of the community. Four things in particular were responsible for the Jews becoming a popular target of antagonism and ridicule among the educated people of the time: the rite of circumcision; the strict observance of the Sabbath; the abstention from eating pork; the adoration of God without images. There is no doubt that the religious and racial peculiarities of the Jews, their contempt of Hellenic cults, pageants, and gymnastic displays, their refusal to take part in all that constituted the very essence of Greek culture, contributed to their unpopularity in the ancient world. The main motive of Greek and Roman anti-Semitism was undoubtedly the dislike of the unlike.[40] Those features of Judaism which repelled, led, especially in Alexandria, to an anti-Semitic literature, to the levelling of vicious charges, such an enmity to the State and even scurrilous accusations such as the ritual murder libel. On the Jewish side, anti-Semitism created a vast apologetic literature, refuting accusations and extolling the virtues of the Jewish people, both as a nation and as citizens of their countries.

Apologetic efforts frequently led to missionary endeavour and to an active search for converts.

At the same time, some of the qualities of Judaism attracted the heathen and caused profound admiration. The Jewish oddities did not only repel; on the contrary, to many members of the Greek intellectual classes, they seemed interesting and attractive. In many instances dislike of the unlike turned into love and admiration for the dissimilar; strange customs and ideas caused not only feelings of antipathy, but frequently gave rise to sympathetic reactions and new insights. Aristotle's disciples, Clearchus[41] and Theophratus[42], were the first Greek writers to come into contact with the Jews. The little Jewish State, established under its high priest in the highland of Palestine, appeared to Clearchus as being inhabited by descendants of philosophers. The Jews seemed to spend their time conversing on divine matters and observing the stars at night, calling upon them as divine in their prayers. As they were philosophers by race, they discussed the nature of deity among themselves. There was, it seemed to Greek writers, nothing like that in the worship of the Greeks; there was no conversation on divine matters in the Greek temple. The nearest thing known to them was a debate in the Philosophical School. Indeed, the Jews were apparently a "Race of Philosophers".

The amazing intellectual quality of Jewish worship created the belief that the Jews possessed a very profound and very special body of thought and doctrine. Megasthenes, the third century BCE Greek historian, the Ambassador of Seleucus Nicator to the Indian King Chandragupta, declared that all that had been written on natural science by the old Greek philosophers may also be found written by the Hindu Brahmins and the Jews in Syria (Palestine). Observation of Jewish life attracted large numbers of pagans who found in Judaism a rule of life for every occasion, furnishing, as it does, something that appealed to a disintegrating society. The purity and simplicity of its theology captivated the intellectuals; the mystery and quaintness of its customs, its exotic rites, its Sabbath rest, the antiquity of its lore, recommended the Jewish faith to large masses in the heathen world. While Jewish customs repelled some members of Gentile society, it attracted others. There were the fully-fledged converts who, in Philo's words[43], saw fit to worship the Creator and Father of the Universe and embraced the idea of One ruler instead of many. There were those who accepted all the customs and rituals of Judaism. They revered, in the words of Juvenal, the Roman satirist, the Sabbath, worshipped nothing but the clouds and a heavenly spirit, ate no pork, were circumcised, learnt, observed and honoured Jewish lore alone.

During the period of the Second Temple there was a vigorous missionary movement in Judaism, both in the Diaspora and in Palestine. Converts were eagerly sought and obtained in large numbers.

Philo-Semitism in the ancient world, leading to full conversion to Judaism, or to a semi-proselyte state of attachment to the Jewish community — a kind of associate membership — or frequently to non-committal admiration of Jewish beliefs and moral teachings, without accepting the burden of ceremonial law, was motivated by close observations of Jewish creed and life.

Classical sources frequently reflect admiration for the imageless cult of the Jews, the belief in one invisible God, Lord of Heaven and Earth. Varro[44], the Roman historian, quoted by Saint Augustine, declared that the ancient Romans had worshipped without images for one hundred and seventy years; if this condition had continued, the gods would have been worshipped more purely. He cited the Jews to prove this point and asserted that those who erected the first images of God deprived people of reverence and led them astray. Strabo[45], the famous Greek historian and geographer, spoke of Moses with a certain degree of sympathy, depicting him as a genuine stoic philosopher. Moses, he informed us, taught that the Egyptians had erred in making the divinity to resemble animals; that such a thing was not done by the Libyans, or even by the Greeks, who represented Him under a human form. For that alone is God which embraces us all as well as the earth and the sea, which we name heaven and world, and the nature of things. But what man in his senses would venture to make an image of that, an image only resembling something around us? Rather must the making of images be given up altogether, and a worthy temple be consecrated to Him; let Him be worshipped without any image whatever. Hecataeus of Abdera[46], the Greek historian, even then declared with a ring of admiration that Moses had not made any images of God, because he believed that the heavens, embracing the earth, are God and master of all. Dio Cassius, the Roman historian, stated that God worshipped in Jerusalem without images was unutterable and invisible; and yet the Jews devoted to Him a more fervent service than all other men.[47]

Tacitus, the Roman historian (first century C.E.), shows an ambivalent attitude. He emphasized that the Jews conceive through their mind their only God; they consider as ungodly those who fashion figures of divinities in the human form. Their God is the supreme being and eternal, who cannot be imitated and is immortal. Tacitus' feeling for national tradition would have precluded the acceptance of any novel or wholly foreign creed. This prejudice led him to condemn all oriental cults and apparently explains his unfriendly attitude towards Judaism and Christianity. These were called "abominable superstitions", but the tenets of Christianity were never touched on, and only one passage suggested any knowledge of Jewish beliefs. There, surprisingly, Tacitus' tone implied sympathy with the strict monotheism of the Jews.[48]

Julian, the Roman Emperor, known as the Apostate (331-363), rebuked the Christians of his days for giving up the belief in God's unity, by adopting the doctrine of the Trinity; whilst the Jews, educated in the teachings of Moses and the Prophets, kept the teaching of God's Unity.[49]

The belief in one, all-embracing, imageless God served as the main source for the sympathetic, even admiring attitude of enlightened heathen thinkers towards the Jews. It was this type of philo-Semitic mood and thought which drew numerous converts to Judaism and ultimately helped the growing Christian faith to displace not only the religions of classical antiquity, but also to overcome the oriental creeds attracting the minds of men in that era, such as the Persian Mithras cult.

Another reason for the rise of philo-Semitic sentiments in the ancient world was the austere morality of the Jewish community in contrast to the dissolute way of living, common among the upper classes in large cities, like Rome and Alexandria. Jewish morality no doubt played an important part in winning Gentile converts to Judaism. It was the ethical message of the Hebrew prophets, with its profound sense of God's righteousness, holiness and ethical demands, that evoked enthusiasm for the teachings of Judaism. Strabo mentioned that the successors of Moses observed justice and piety with great sincerity and only later became influenced by superstition.[50]

Furthermore, Jewish religion with its stress on instruction must have appeared to the Greek intellectuals as a kind of philosophy. Some classical texts affirm that Pythagoras had derived his philosophy from the Jews.[51] Arrian, the pupil of Epictetus, the stoic philosopher, used the word "Jew" as synonymous with philosopher. It is not important to appear to be a philosopher but it is important to *be like* a true philosopher; if a man calls himself a Jew without living as such, he is not recognized as a Jew. Practice must be in accordance with principles.[52]

Even in the generally hostile atmosphere of the Greco-Roman world, certain aspects of Judaism and Jewish life evoked admiration. The saying of Hecataeus of Abdera, quoted in the letter of Aristeas, that poets and writers refrained from quoting Jewish sources because they were too pure and holy, may be apocryphal. However, the decline of heathen religions left room for a new faith, free from the secret magic features of the mystery cults.

All these utterances of Greek and Roman writers are imbued with respect for, though not with understanding of the Jewish belief in God. While the anti-Semites objected to the exclusive character of Jewish monotheism and condemned the Jews for refusing to worship local divinities and to offer sacrifices to the emperor, admiration for the imageless concept of God, as taught by Judaism, emerged in classical thought, as well as for Jewish morality and intellectual striving. Philo-Semitism in the ancient world is thus seen as an intellectual homage to the pure Jewish concept of a supreme deity, raised above the material images of contemporary heathendom.

The attitude of the outside world towards Judaism showed peculiar characteristics in the Hellenistic-Roman period. Judaism as a living creed possessed a power of attraction and drew proselytes in great numbers, while classical literature is largely imbued with anti-Jewish feeling. This ambivalent attitude of the ancient world towards Judaism — both strong sympathy and violent antipathy — is due mainly to Jewish monotheism which explains both the success of Judaism and the enmity towards it; similar factors were later manifest in the reception accorded to Christianity. While the anti-Semitism of the ancient world has been adequately studied, the sympathy which Judaism evoked should not be overlooked. The ethical teachings of Judaism, the belief in one Holy Deity, the austere story of creation caused many intellectually groping individuals to attach themselves to Judaism. Reports of Church fathers reflect appreciation of the Bible, when first read by Greeks and Romans. Tatian (second century, C.E.), recorded the convincing impression which the Old Testament made on him "through its lucid expression, its easily comprehensible account of the creation of the world, its foreknowledge of the future, the excellence of its laws, and its teaching of the sole rule of God." The proselytizing effort of Judaism, which, as it is known, showed remarkable success, was based on strong pro-Judaic tendencies prevalent in the ancient world.[53]

FRIENDLY POPES

The Second Ecumenical Council in 1965 and its concern with the Church's responsibility for anti-Semitism have aroused new interest in the papcy and in its relation to the Jews. It has also been responsible for a significant improvement in the atmosphere conducive to Jewish-Christian dialogue. Pope John XXIII (d. 1963), one of the most illustrious figures in modern ecclesiastical history, was animated by an earnest desire to build bridges of friendship between the Christian denominations, as well as between the "two voices of Judea," Judaism and Christianity. A few days before he died he composed a prayer asking God's forgiveness for the sufferings caused to the Jews over the centuries by the Roman Catholic Church. Pope John is reported to have considered that this prayer should be recited in all Roman Catholic churches. The text of the prayer reads: "We are aware today that, for many, many centuries, our eyes were so blind that we were no more in a position to see the beauty of Thy Chosen People, nor to recognise in their countenance the feature of our privileged brethren. We understand that the sign of Cain is marked on our forehead. For centuries our brother Abel lay in blood and tears for our errors, because we had forgotten Thy love . . . . Forgive us the curse we have unjustifiably inflicted on their Jewish name. Forgive us for crucifying Thee in thy flesh a second time, for we knew not what we did."

Pope John was not a solitary figure in his friendly attitude to the Jewish people. He represented a definite tendency of philo-Semitism, never entirely absent from Christian life and thought. What was the policy of the popes towards the Jews? On the one hand, the Church of Rome safeguarded the religious privileges which the Jews traditionally enjoyed, including the full practice of Jewish customs and protection against violence. On the other hand, Jews as "infidels" were denied any improvement in their status and barred from any possibility of exercising authority over Christians. The fact that Jewish communities always existed under papal rule proves the existence of favourable aspects in the papal policy towards the Jews. In the papal city of Rome the principle of toleration meant the continuous preservation of the Jewish community without a single interruption through expulsion or massacre.[54] The Jews were tolerated out of "Christian love" or as "living witnesses of the truth of Christianity." Beyond this two-fold general tendency of physical toleration and spiritual humilation, the actions of the popes were expressions of personal attitudes and political expediency. Individually many popes employed Jewish physicians and befriended Jewish scholars, at a time when Jewish scholarship was severely restricted throughout Christendom. The special Papal Edicts, called Bulls, relating to the Jews, were mainly of a repressive character. They enacted anti-Jewish legislation, condemned the Talmud, instituted the ghetto, and occasionally were responsible for persecution. Some decrees were motivated by fairness, even humane considerations, and defined Jewish privileges in a friendly manner. Some popes denounced solemnly the vicious blood accusation levelled against the Jews, others issued strong declarations against forcible conversion and the holding of religious disputations which frequently led to mob violence. There were popes who favoured the Marranos — Jews converted to Christianity by force — and used their influence to mitigate the harshness of the Inquisition in its dealings with alleged backsliders and heretics, especially its gruesome method of exacting confessions by torture.

One of the most notable personalities in ecclesiastical history is Pope Gregory the Great (590-604), whose tolerant attitude towards the Jews became the official policy of the Catholic Church. Gregory, though himself most eager to bring the Jew to Christianity, expressed sharp disapproval of forced baptism. Worth of record is the pope's effort to do justice to the Jews of Palermo in Sicily. The bishop of that city had seized and occupied a synagogue; when he saw that Gregory objected, he quickly consecrated it as a church, making its return to Jewry impossible. Gregory attempted to correct this injustice by restoring to the Jews the value of the buildings and by instituting a search for the vessels of the synagogue that had been carried off.[55] The principle of tolerance which Gregory had taken over from the later Roman Empire, became, at least in theory, basic in the relations between Catholicism and Judaism. The Church, highest authority in the Christian world, frequently issued decrees in defence of Jewry. Beginning with Pope Calixtus II (1119-1124), a series of Bulls appeared, threatening Christians with excommunication and other penalties, if they converted Jews by force, illegally exercised violence against them, robbed them of their possessions, attacked them at their religious devotions, desecrated their cemeteries, or dug up and carried off their dead. The list of these offences is important because it is typical of the vexations to which the mediaeval Jew was exposed.

One of the most famous bulls in favour of the Jews is the one issued by Pope Innocent IV (1243-1254) against the ritual murder accusation, the most senseless and untruthful charge ever levelled against a human group. Innocent's edict is a notable document of humane feeling, breathing actual sympathy with the unfortunate Jews, as indicated in the title "Concerning the Tearful Complaint of the Jews in Germany." The basic motive for the Pope's friendly sentiments towards the Jews is his view that it is from the writings of the Jews that the testimony of the Christian faith has come forth.

"We have received the tearful plaint of the Jews of Germany that some princes, both ecclesiastical and lay, and other nobles

43

and rulers of your districts and dioceses are plotting evil plans against them and are devising numerous and varied pretexts so as to rob them unjustly and seize their property, without stopping to consider that it is from the archives of the Jews, as it were, that the testimony for the Christian faith has come forth. Despite the fact that Divine Scripture pronounces the law "Thou shalt not kill" and despite the fact that it prohibits the Jews, while solemnizing the Passover, to touch any dead body, nevertheless they are falsely accused that during this very festival they share the heart of a murdered child. This it is believed their law enjoins, although it is clearly contrary to the law. No matter where the dead body is found, their persecutors wickedly throw it up to them . . . . Now, since we do not want the said Jews to be unjustly harrassed whose conversion our Lord in His mercy expects, therefore, we command that you show yourself favourably disposed and kindly towards them, and that you shall not permit the Jews to be molested undeservedly any further by anyone with regard to the matters mentioned above or with regard to similar ones."[56]

Another friendly Pope whose attitude had a profound influence on the situation of the Jews in the Christian world was Gregory X (1271-1276). Gregory decreed that the testimony of a Christian against a Jew had no validity, unless it was confirmed by a Jew. Of historical importance was his vigorous denunciation of the ritual murder charge. This refutation of the malicious blood accusation, begun by Innocent IV in 1247, was repeated by various Popes as late as Clement XIII in 1763. However, continuous streams of Papal decrees for over six centuries seem to indicate that they were only moderately effective in combating prejudice. Two remarkable utterances by Gregory X deserve to be recalled. "We decree that no Christian shall compel a Jew to come to baptism unwillingly. But if any of them shall take refuge of his own accord with Christians, because of conviction, then, after his intention will have been manifest, he shall be made a Christian without any intrigue. For, indeed, that person who is known to have come to Christian baptism not freely, but unwillingly, is not believed to possess the Christian faith . . . ." "Inasmuch as the Jews are not able to bear witness against the Christians, we decree that the testimony against Jews shall not be valid, unless there is among those Christians some Jew who is there for the purpose of offering testimony."

Gregory X emphatically opposed the charge of ritual murder and condemned Christians who falsely accused the Jew of this crime. "Since," he wrote, "it happens occasionally that some Christians lose their children, the Jews are accused by their enemies of secretly carrying off and killing these same Christian children and of making sacrifices of the heart and blood of these very children. It happens too, that the parents of these children or some other Christian enemies of these Jews, secretly hide these very children in order that they may be able to injure these Jews, and in order that they may be able to extort from them a certain amount of money by redeeming them from their straits. And most falsely do these Christians claim that the Jews have secretly and furtively carried away these children and killed them, and that the Jews offer sacrifice from the heart and the blood of these children, since their law in this matter precisely and expressly forbids Jews to sacrifice, eat, or drink the blood, or to eat the flesh of animals having claws. This has been demonstrated many times at our court by Jews converted to the Christian faith: nevertheless very many Jews are often seized and detained unjustly because of this. We decree, therefore, that Christians need not be obeyed against Jews in a case or situation of this type, and we order that Jews seized under such a silly pretext be freed from imprisonment, and that they shall not be arrested henceforth on such a miserable pretext, unless — which we do not believe — they be caught in the commission of the crime. We decree that no Christian shall stir up anything new against them, but that they should be maintained in that status and position in which they were in the time of our predecessors, from antiquity till now."

Other Popes have shown understanding and sympathy for the people of Israel: Clement VI (1342-1352), who protected

Jews at the time of the horrors of the Black Death; Leo X (1513-1521) who permitted a Christian, Daniel Bomberg, to print the first edition of the Talmud and thus helped to inaugurate the flowering of Hebrew literature; Clement VII (1523-1533), the Pope who refused his sanction to the divorce of Henry VIII from Catherine of Aragon, was called the "Patron of Israel." He protected Solomon Molcho, the famous Marrano, and established friendly relations with David Reubeni, the alleged emissary from the lost ten tribes, who considered himself a forerunner of the Messiah.

According to the temper of their times, they were all predecessors in spirit to Pope John XXIII. Cecil Roth, the well known Jewish historian (1899-1969), never tired of accentuating the fact that the Jew is under a distinct debt of gratitude towards the Popes, almost his only protectors, and frequently his patrons in a barbaric age. The later period of persecution was induced by external circumstances, and should not blind our eyes to the long tradition of tolerance which lay behind it. Nevertheless, one should not be oblivious of certain forms of persecution at which some popes connived, such as forced baptism of children[57] and the spirit of hostility of the Jews which pervaded many papal pronouncements and enactments. But the picture was by no means entirely bleak.

In modern days the powerful voice raised in favour of the Jews was that of Pope Piux XI (1922-1939). The Pope spoke out vigourously against the anti-Jewish campaign and racialist measures inaugurated by the fascist Italian ruler, in imitation of the Nazi decrees. Piux XI rejected the Nazi race theories as ill-conceived nationalism "which we have already had painful occasion to denounce as erroneous and dangerous." "Such racial theories," he declared, "are detestable, and because they are not Christian, they end by being not human." True Catholicism, he affirmed, is universal, not racist, not nationalist, not separatist, but catholic. To the German concept and word *Rasse* he opposed the ancient Latin ideas of *gens* and *populus,* the connotation of which belongs much more to the moral, than to the biological order. When Pope Piux XI learned that racialism had been introduced into Italy, he defined the Catholic standpoint in an address on July 15, 1938. "The universality of the Catholic Church," he said, "certainly does not exclude the idea of race, of descent, of nation, of nationality; but the human race, the whole human race, is but a single and universal race of man. There is no room for special races. We may therefore ask ourselves why Italy should have felt a need to imitate Germany." The inspiration for much of the Catholic resistance to Nazism derived from the celebrated 1937 Encyclical of Pius XI *Mit brennender Sorge,* a scathing attack on Hitler's racism. It may be assumed that the Pope issued that Bull in German to be sure it was understood in Germany.

The following passages of a discourse delivered on September 6th, 1938, before the directors of the Belgian Catholic Radio Agency, during the height of the Nazi persecution of the Jews, have won world-wide fame and admiration. Commenting upon the words of Mass, "The sacrifice of our father Abraham," Pope Piux XI said: "Note that Abraham is called our Patriarch, our ancestor. Anti-Semitism is incompatible with the thought and sublime reality expressed in this text. It is a movement in which we Christians can have no part whatsoever. Anti-Semitism is unacceptable. Spiritually we are Semites."[58] "Spiritually we are Semites," repeats the illustrious Catholic philosopher Jacques Maritain. "No stronger word has been spoken by a Christian against anti-Semitism, and this Christian is the successor of the apostle Peter." The Pope gave lofty expression to the glorious descent of Jews and Christians and claimed a "Semitic" affiliation of the Christian nations.

A source of deep concern for a fruitful Jewish-Christian confrontation is the ineffable pain resulting from the murder of millions of Jews in the Nazi era and the problem of the silence of Pope Piux XII. The question whether Piux XII should have condemned the evils of Nazism more clearly and vigourously lies at the centre of one of the sharpest post-war controversies which, until now, has been conducted on the basis of general assertions and fragmentary testimonies. A careful analysis of documentary evidence, particularly the reports of German representatives at the Vatican[59] shows that no definite answer can be given to the question raised by the war-time policy of the Holy See because the documentation is still incomplete. The Pope seemed to have cherished a sympathy for Germany, as he knew it in pre-Nazi days; he hated Bolshevism and observed with fear its progress in Central Europe. It appears that he considered Nazism a lesser evil than Communism; he was also convinced of the utter futility of negotiating with the German authorities. In a letter dated April 20, 1943, to the Archbishop of Berlin, Msgr. Preysing, known for his courageous anti-Nazi stand, the Pope referred to the refusal of a confidential petition, addressed by the German Episcopate to the Government of the Reich. He frequently mentioned the material aid given to the Jews during the first years of the war and explained his restraint, by calling attention to the anxious pleas for all those persecuted whose interest demanded that all evidence be weighed and measured carefully, lest, contrary to the Pope's intention, he made their situation worse and more unbearable. In a secret address to the College of Cardinals the Pope asserted that "the Vicar of Christ," who asked no more than pity and a sincere return to elementary standards of justice and humanity, found himself facing a door that no keys could open.

It appears that the Pontiff resigned himself to silence because other church leaders had approached the German authorities without the slightest results. An examination of the documents reflect the depth of confusion arising out of an unprecedented problem: would intervention aid or harm the interests of groups suffering a most appalling fate? The Pope, relying exclusively on moral persuasion, was the victim of a human predicament, similar to that of members of the unfortunate *Judenrate* in Eastern Europe. The situations were too complicated for facile condemnation. "Such are the limits beyond which this investigation may not go. Even as a political personage, Pius XII cannot be studied solely on the basis of the diplomatic documents to which we have had recourse. These

48

texts throw light only on certain aspects of a policy and only on some traits of personality."[60]

And yet, Pope Pius XII too must also be listed among the friendly popes, in spite of the severe criticism levelled against him for not having intervened with sufficient vigour, when the brutal extermination of European Jewry was brought to his notice. The personal motives for his hesitation can no longer be established with certainty, but nobody in Rome accused the Pope of lack of compassion on a personal level. Italian Jews generally prefer to emphasize what Pope Pius XII did for them rather than what he did not do. The Pope established several offices devoted to rescue work among the victims of Nazism and throughout the war made energetic efforts to ease the lot of the Jews. French and Dutch, Polish and Ukrainian bishops acted on behalf of the Jews on instructions from the Pope. In 1943, when Chief Rabbi I. Herzog appealed to Pope Pius XII from Jerusalem, the Pontiff answered that he would to "all in his power to end the persecution of the Jews." Rabbi Herzog, who went to Istanbul to obtain funds and assistance for Jewish rescue migrations, found another sympathetic friend in Cardinal Roncalli, the late Pope John XXIII, the Papal Nuncio there. As the ultimate phases of the "final solution" were being applied throughout Europe, Jewish refugees poured into Vatican City; others sought shelter in basilicas and convents outside the Vatican wall. At one time, no fewer than 15,000 were sheltered in Castel Gondolfo, the Pope's summer residence outside Rome. The Pope sent a letter to the bishops instructing them to remove the fences of convents and monasteries so that they could become refuges for Jews. On June 4, 1944, when the Allies entered Rome, the News Bulletin of the Jewish Brigade (which fought with the British Eighth Army) declared: "To the everlasting credit of the people of Rome and the Roman Catholic Church, the lot of the Jews has been made easier by their truly Christian offers of assistance and shelter. Even now, many still remain in places of worship which opened their doors to hide them from the fate of deportation to certain death.

For obvious reasons the full story of the help given by the Church to our people cannot as yet be told."[61]

There is a tendency abroad to marshall evidence in favour of the Pope and Christian leaders, to understand the tremendous difficulties which they faced in their confrontation with the unutterable evil of Nazidom, to evince some sympathy for their dilemma. This judgement is motivated by the desire to narrow the gulf between the Jewish people and the Church. The creation of the State of Israel has awakened a new concept of Judaism among Christians: they have come to recognize that the eternal wanderer, doomed to perennial homelessness, has now found a permanent place of rest — the State of Israel. Since the Vatican Declaration of 1965 on the Jews, there has been a favourable change in the Church's attitude; but hostility and misunderstanding stretching over millennia cannot be easily erased. It is today of vital importance to highlight the positive aspects in the Jewish-Christian encounter. There was both good and evil in what is probably the darkest period of human history, the shameful period of Nazi ascendancy. It cannot be forgotten that many members of the German Catholic hierarchy supported Hitler's anti-Semitism or at least failed to oppose it actively. But the fight of enlightened church leaders throughout Germany and the world against the evils of racism and anti-Semitism should be neither omitted from descriptions of the confrontation between the Church and the Reich, nor minimized.

History proves that there was a humane side in the dealing of the Papal Court with the Jews, from the edict of tolerance of Gregory the Great to Pope John XXIII's sincere endeavour to rectify some of the injustices perpetrated by the Church against the people of Israel. Especially notable is his elimination of the word *perfidi* which prefixed *Judaei* in the Good Friday prayers for the conversion of the Jews.[62]

There is a friendlier spirit discernible in the attitude of the Catholic Church to the Jews. The Vatican Council Declaration made the first step towards eliminating hostility and replacing

it with sympathetic understanding. Cardinal Bea, architect of
the Declaration on the Attitude of the Church towards non-
Christian Religions, which was passed by the Vatican Council
in its final session, presents a full account of the Roman
Catholic Church's attitude towards the Jewish people from the
early days to the present.[63] As to Judaism, the Declaration
affirms the bond which spiritually ties the people of the New
Covenant to the offspring of Abraham. The Church acknowl-
edges that the beginnings of her faith and her election, according to God's saving design, are found already in the patriarchs,
Moses and the Prophets. She professes that all who believe in
Christ — Abraham's sons according to the faith — are included
in the same Patriarch's call and that the salvation is symboli-
cally prefigured in the exodus of the chosen people from the
land of bondage. The church, therefore, cannot forget that she
received the revelation of the Old Testament through the
people with whom God in His inexpressible mercy made the
ancient Covenant. Since the spiritual patrimony common to
Christians and Jews is so great, the Council wishes to foster
and commend mutual understanding and esteem. This will be
the fruit, above all, of biblical and theological studies and of
brotherly dialogues. Whosoever benefits from Christian teaching owes a debt of gratitude first and foremost to God; but,
Cardinal Bea affirms, he also owes something to the people
which God has been pleased to make the instrument of His
activities. For this reason, Christians who today visit the Holy
Land in their desire to venerate the soil where Christ lived and
journeyed, worked and suffered, should show respect for the
people to whom they are bound by so many spiritual bonds and
whose election and history served as a prelude to their own
selection and history, their own faith and salvation. In her
rejection of every persecution against any man, the Church,
mindful of the patrimony she shares with the Jews and not
motivated by political reasons, but by the Gospel's spiritual
love, decries hatred, persecution and manifestations of anti-
Semitism, directed against Jews at any time and by anyone. As

51

far as Christian dogma allows, the relationship between the Catholic Church and the Jewish people should be established on a new basis.

In his elaborate commentary on the Declaration, Cardinal Bea endeavours to minimize and explain away all sayings of the New Testament which imply or express hostility to the Jews, while stressing and amplifying those teachings which serve to glorify and exalt the Jewish people. In this desire there lies a sincere effort to eliminate tension and hostility between Jews and Christians and create a new favourable atmosphere for a Jewish-Christian confrontation. There exists a strong tendency to foster sympathy between the Jewish people and the Church. Some aspects in the relationship between Church and Synagogue are still disquieting, but the task of promoting understanding and appreciation between the two daughters of Judea remains imperative.

The official attitude of the Roman Catholic Church to the non-Christian religions, as adumbrated in St. Peter's Church, Rome, on October 28, 1965, was outlined in *Die Brug* (July 1968), the Catholic Afrikaans monthly. The statement condemned all discrimination on the grounds of race, colour, status, or religion, and rejected nothing in these creeds which was true and holy. As regards the Jews, the Church remembered that it had received the revelation of the Old Testament from them and that the apostles, the foundation and pillars of the Church, were born from the Jewish people, as were many of the first disciples who preached the Gospel of Christ to the world. The statement said that Paul had testified that God still felt the greatest love for the Jews for the sake of the Patriarchs. The Church was the new people of God, but the Jews must not be presented as a people rejected or cursed by God, as though this flowed from the scriptures. The Church also condemned anti-Semitism not for political reasons, but because of the spiritual love of the gospels and bearing in mind the heritage it shared with the Jews.

In the course of the Robert Waley Cohen Memorial Lecture (1966), Archbishop Igino Cardinale, Apostolic Delegate to

Britain, declared that no sincere Catholic historian can deny that there have been many regettable instances of religious intolerance, which went far beyond dogmatic intolerance, in the life of the Church. However, while admitting Christian guilt in the persecution of the Jews, the Archbishop also appealed to Jews to respond to the spirit of conciliation and goodwill expressed in the new Vatican Declaration on the Jews. He further declared that the Church now exhorted her children to acknowledge, preserve and promote the spiritual, moral and cultural values found in non-Christian religions. The Jewish origins of Jesus and his disciples were now emphasized. It was stressed that, though the Jews did not accept the Gospel and in many cases opposed its spreading, they still remained dear to God, and must remain so to every Christian. A very important part of the declaration, the Archbishop added, dealt with the problem of Jewish involvement in the arrest and death of Jesus. The supposition that all the Jewish people, from the earliest Christian times to the present, were guilty of the crucifixion had been pushed to extreme consequences, creating prejudice and contempt which had caused the Jews much suffering. Anti-Semitism was undoubtedly a complex crime, with psychological, economic and political as well as religious components. But it could not be denied that this painful phenomenon had its primary origin in the religious context, by which it was sustained and from which it continued to draw some of its dynamics even today.

The charge of a collective guilt on the part of the Jewish people — the chief source of bitterness from the earliest Christian era — was unequivocally repudiated by the Declaration, and Catholics were instructed to eliminate from their teaching and preaching all other false views concerning the Jews.[64]

A new era in Jewish-Christian relations has been witnessed in the past years, since the Second Vatican Council issued a Declaration on the Church's Relations with non-Christian Religions. A Commission to implement the Declaration on the Jews was set up in Britain. It has prepared a booklet setting out the Commission's achievements to coincide with the fifth anniversary of the Declaration. In an introduction, the editor states that the New Testament shows that Christianity has a special relationship to Judaism. "The re-discovery of this has led to a great enrichment in the understanding of our faith . . . In the immediate future we hope that this appreciation will be shared by a greater number of Catholics."[65]

As an instance of the "New Spirit" it may be noted that the new nineteenth edition of the official Spanish dictionary has been purged of expressions offensive to Jews after talks between leading Spanish and Jewish scholars. The Royal Academy of the Spanish Language has eliminated the previous definition of "Jew" as meaning "usurer" or "miser." Spain, with about 9000 Jews, has erased derogatory references from Catholic textbooks in compliance with the Vatican Council's 1965 ruling in favour of better relations with the Jewish faith.[66]

It will take a long time to eliminate age-old prejudices from the thoughts of the Christian community. But a significant beginning has been made by the Proclamation of the Vatican Council and subsequent developments within the Catholic Church to right some of the ancient wrongs and create a new climate of a better understanding between those who uphold the eternal verities of religious faith, drawn from Hebraic sources.

CHRISTIAN FRIENDS OF RABBINIC TRADITION

The Talmud was generally considered by the Christian world as a symbol of Jewish separatism, legalism and obstinacy; mysterious and inexplicable to the Christian reader, replete with trivialities and superstitions. Christian theologians rejected the "sterile subtleties" of rabbinic exegesis. The Talmud has been proscribed, burnt and subjected to ceaseless calumny since the days of Justinian, who, as early as 554 C.E., issued a special interdictory novella (no. 146) against it. Throughout the centuries secular and spiritual powers hurled anathemas and bulls against it and decreed wholesale confiscation of this book. Christendom looked on the Talmud as the expression of that post-prophetic Judaism which was superseded by the Church; rabbinic writings thus became the chief target of anti-Judaic charges, which were generally inspired by prejudice, ignorance and fanaticism.

On the other hand, the gigantic many-faceted work of the Talmud manifested a remarkable power of attraction. It became an object of concern and interest to many Christian scholars and thinkers who were fascinated by the vast and varied literature, represented within its pages. The Talmud drew to itself various types of Christian readers. Scholars saw in rabbinic writings the prime source for traditional exegesis of the Holy Writ and thus a possible key to the true meaning of

Hebraica veritas. Lovers of literature found in the unique literary quality of rabbinic writings an impetus for rewarding study. Other students were impelled by a romantic recognition of the vital quality of the Talmud as the chief source for the power of survival, inherent in the mysterious, yet indomitable Jewish people.

There were those Christians who were inspired by a sense of justice to defend the Talmud against baseless accusations and, in the name of freedom of thought, to oppose any control of the mind through the destruction of literature. Some friends of the Talmud in the pre-modern age were motivated by feelings of admiration for Jewish literature, particularly the Bible, rabbinic lore and mystic writings, while at the same time evincing little sympathy with the denizens of the Ghetto whose sordid fate reflected their denial of the truth of Christianity.

Some Christian scholars studied Rabbinic literature in a spirit of sympathy, yet were ultimately concerned with the conversion of the Jews as the final consummation of the Christian mission. In modern times the study of the Talmud is frequently motivated by the desire to understand the sphere of life and thought from which Christianity arose, to become acquainted with the "background of the gospels." Occasionally the personal contact between Christian scholars, who sought instruction from Rabbinic experts, especially since the days of the Reformation, tended to create a deeper understanding for post-biblical Judaism, even sympathy with the literary treasures of Israel.[67]

The first staunch defender of the Talmud was *Johannes Reuchlin* (1455-1522), the illustrious German humanist and Hebraist, one of the most celebrated scholars of the sixteenth century. Reuchlin endeavoured throughout his life to be an impartial servant of learning; he thus became an intrepid champion of the Talmud against the attacks of the fanatical Dominicans. As a man of intellectual honesty, Reuchlin placed truth above all other values; in his passion for intellectual fairness he championed genuine scholarship as against biased knowledge. It was Reuchlin who disclosed to European scholars the existence of Rabbinic literature and opened up new approaches to the study and evaluation of post-biblical Jewish writings. When in 1509, as a result of the accusations of a Jewish apostate, the notorious Pfefferkorn, the Talmud was condemned to destruction by Emperor Maximilian, Reuchlin rose in defence of Hebrew literature in the following memorable words: "The Talmud is not there for any scurvy fellow to run over it with unwashed feet and say he knows it all . . . Christ himself ordained that the Talmud be preserved. This is the plain meaning of his words: 'Search the Scriptures; for in them ye think ye have eternal life: and they testify for me' (John 5:39) . . . The homilies and hymnodies of the Jews are not to be interfered with, in accordance with the edicts and decrees of Emperors and Popes — that the Jews be not disturbed in their synagogues, their religious worship and customs. None of these books, as is claimed, contain statements hostile to Christians. For the Jews have their writings for the purpose of their own inspiration and the preservation of their faith in time of persecution by pagan, Christian or Mohammedan, but not to inflict harm on or cause shame to anybody . . . It is obvious that they do not recognise Christ as God. That is their faith, but they do not intend to cast aspersions on anybody." In a letter written in Hebrew which Reuchlin sent to Bonetto de Lattes (whose Hebrew name was Jacob ben Immanuel Provinciale), the Jewish physician to Pope Leo X, Reuchlin writes ". . . it was due to me that all the Talmudic writings were not burnt in Germany. I am convinced and believe that whatever slander was spread about these books, was spread in order to gain notoriety."[68]

An interesting phenomenon in the history of Christian interest in Hebrew literature is the family of the Buxtorfs, Johannes the Elder (1569-1629) and Johannes the Younger (1599-1664). For more than seventy years they occupied, in succession, the Chair of Hebrew at Basle, published Hebrew grammars, and lexicons, translated Jewish authors of the Middle Ages and taught rabbinic lore to their contemporaries. The Elder Buxtorf prepared the first important bibliography of rabbinic works, while his son rendered into Latin, for the benefit of the learned Christian public, the Jewish philosophical works, Maimonides' *Guide of the Perplexed* and Yehuda Halevi's *Kusari*.

While the Buxtorfs, like most of the Christian Hebraists of their days, were motivated partly by the desire for the conversion of the Jews, the humanistic atmosphere of the post-Renaissance period led to the exploration of knowledge for the sake of widening man's intellectual horizon. There can be little doubt that in the course of a life-long study of Rabbinic literature the Buxtorfs, especially the Elder, acquired sympathy for and understanding of rabbinic learning. The Talmud, declares Johannes Buxtorf, is a learned work, a large corpus of erudition; it contains manifold learning in all sciences; it teaches the most explicit and the most complete civil and canonical law of the Jews, so that the whole nation, as well as their Synagogue, might live thereby in a state of happiness in the most desirable way. It is the most luminous commentary of the scriptural law, as well as its supplement and support. It contains much excellent teaching on jurisprudence, medicine, natural philosophy, ethics, politics, astronomy and other branches of science, all of which makes one think highly of the history of that nation and of the time in which the work was written.[69]

The famous German author and humanist Johann Gottfried Herder (1744-1803) was a great admirer of the aesthetic qualities of the Hebrew Bible and created an entire school of thought which fostered the literary appreciation of the Holy writings. Herder also gave attention to rabbinic lore and rendered a number of Jewish legends found in the Talmud into German, thus creating, for the first time, contact between the world of Western enlightenment and the age-old traditions contained in the Haggadic (narrative, non-legal) elements of the Talmud.[70]

One of the staunchest defenders of Rabbinic literature in the face of consistent anti-Semitic condemnation was the German Protestant theologian and Biblical scholar *Franz* Delitzsch, (1813-1890). Delitzsch exalts the Talmudic attitude to labour. Ancient Judaism, Delitzsch affirms, honored labour and handicraft. When the Holy One, says a passage in the Talmud (Pesachim. 118a), pronounced his sentence on fallen Adam, he burst into tears at the words, "Thorns also and thistles shall it bring forth to thee . . ." But when God added, "In the sweat of thy face shalt thou eat bread," he was comforted. "Love Labour," was a maxim of Hillel's teacher, Shemaya (Aboth.1.10). "Great is labour," says another (Nedarim 49b), "for it honours its master." "The Talmud," (Rosh Hashana 1:9) he declares, "puts the usurer on the same level with the gambler, and considers both to be vicious men, unfit to bear testimony in a court of justice."

Domestic servants were treated as members of the family. Kindness and consideration for them is recommended both by precept and example. "Beware," it is said, "to eat fine bread and to feed thy servant upon black bread; to sleep on cushions while he lies on straw" (Kiddushin 20a). Righteousness was already then understood by the better class in the same sense in which St. Matthew describes Joseph, the husband of Mary, as a "just" or, as Luther translates, "pious man," that is, they held righteousness to consist, not in strict adherence to the law, but in following the law of kindness.

In his evergreen work *Zur Geschichte der Jüdischen Poesie* (Leipzig, 1836) Delitzsch devotes a remarkable chapter to poetry in the period of the Mishnah and Talmud with a profound sense of understanding for rabbinic moods and expressions. Delitzsch deals with the poetic elements in rabbinic literature — fables, parables, allegories, religious lyrics, prayers — with an emphasis on the aesthetic sense of that literature rarely found among Christian students of rabbinics. He singles out and translates the passages from Baba Metzia 84 where the physical beauty of Rabbi Yochanan is described. As further evidence of aesthetic feelings among the rabbis he quotes the poetic description of the beauty of Rabbi Abahu, of the women of Jerusalem and of the Nazirites, and offers other instances of rabbinic aesthetics.

The rabbinic Aggadah* is for Delitzsch the essence of "thinking in terms of beauty." "Der Midrash ist an sich schon gewissermassen eine poetische Exegese, er enthalt aber gewohnlich auch noch eine Fülle von Parabeln, Sinnsprüchen und Sagengeschichten. Der Midrash knüpft die alterthumliche Sage und die Geschichte der nächsten Vergangenheit an das ewige Wort der Schrift. *Schriftverse sind die goldenen Rahmen, in welche er die buntesten Gemälde volkstümlicher Geschichten einfasst.*"[71]

Among the Christian friends of the Talmud in Germany special mention should be made of Hermann L. Strack (1848-1922). Strack, though probably not immune to conversionist motives, has gained undying fame as a valiant fighter against the blood libel, but even more so by his *Introduction to the Talmud and Midrash* and his *Commentary on the New Testament in the Light of Talmud and Midrash* (1921-1928), a truly monumental opus, published in collaboration with *Paul Billerbeck*. One cannot over-estimate the merit of Strack's *Introduction*. It has been reprinted several times and has become the key to the knowledge of Rabbinic literature in both Jewish and non-Jewish circles. The spirit which moved Strack to open the gateway to the Talmud to the wider public of scholars and laymen emerges from his prefaces to the first (1887) and fifth editions (1908) of his *Introduction*.

Strack asserted that his *Introduction to the Talmud* was the first attempt to give objective and scientific information concerning the whole of the Talmud and was designed to lead to the study of this literary monument, equally remarkable for its origin, encompassing contents and the authority which has been accorded to it. In writing his appraisal of the Talmud he

---

*The non-legal contents of rabbinic literature, including ethical teachings, legends, folk-lore, stories, sayings of the wise, expressions of Messianic faith and longing.

strove honestly to allow himself to be influenced neither by polemical nor by apologetic considerations, but only to serve the truth. He would consider himself amply rewarded for his laborious work, if he succeeded in removing "many a prejudice, whether with those who are unconditionally hostile to the Talmud, or with its over-zealous admirers, and to pave the way for a more just and calm appraisal."

There are, Strack declared, certain ignorant agitators (most of them are, at the same time, malevolent) who seek to make the Christian-German people believe that the Jews are solicitous, employing every possible means at hand, to keep the Talmud a secret book, for fear its contents should become known. "The Talmud," Strack solemnly affirmed, "contains no report or utterance which, assuming of course that it is to be found there, any Christian scholar, who is at home in the language and the subject-matter, is not able to find . . . . In the entire Jewish community there is not a single piece of literature nor an oral tradition which is inaccessible to learned Christians. The Jews make no efforts whatsoever to conceal anything from the Christians, nor could they if they would. The Talmud, the *Shulhan Aruk,* and other Jewish literary works are secret books only for those Jews no less than Christians — who have not acquired the necessary knowledge for a reading of the original texts nor know anything about the translations that are in existence. For such people, Caesar's *Bellum Gallicum* will be an equally secret book." Strack expressed the hope that his *Introduction to the Talmud* would help to further the knowledge of truth and thereby also a just judgement.

Strack based the rabbinic commentary on the New Testament on the following considerations: By his physical descent the Lord belonged to the Jewish people and was a descendant of David. Likewise, Mark, Matthew, John, Paul and Peter and the other authors of New Testament writings (except Luke) were Jews. For a right understanding of their utterances it is necessary to be acquainted with the life and thought of Judaism in that period.[72]

In this context the name of a worthy Christian Hebraist should be placed on record, August Wünsche (1839-1913). As a student of Franz Delitzsch, he was instrumental in bringing the contents of rabbinic writings to the notice of the Christian world. Wünsche excelled as translator of several Midrashim and Haggadic elements of the Talmud into German; his work, *Aus Israels Lehrhallen,* in five volumes, containing translations from *A. Jellineks' Bet Hamidrash,* was a pioneering venture in rendering rabbinic material into a Western language. Wünsche wrote many books and articles on the Bible and the Talmud and collaborated with a rabbinic scholar, Rabbi Dr. J. Winter, in editing a classical *Anthology of Jewish Literature since the Completion of the Biblical Canon (Die Jüdische Literatur seit Abschluss des Kanons),* a model for later selections from Jewish literature.

Many friends of the Talmud were genuine students of rabbinic literature and motivated in their sympathies by familiarity with rabbinic sources and an interest in Talmudic lore and legends. There were others who considered themselves friends of the Talmud, but they cannot be claimed as students of rabbinic writings. However, in the face of anti-Semitic accusations, they used such extracts of quotations from rabbinic texts as were known to them from Jewish or Christian sources, in order to prove the nobility of rabbinic teachings, and thus they manifested their friendship for the Jewish people.

Count Henry Coudenhove — Kalergi (1859-1930), Austrian diplomat and social reformer, was the author of a classic treatise on anti-Semitism, in which he professed the highest admiration for Judaism. In particular, he contrasted the theory of salvation developed in Catholicism, Protestantism and the Orthodox Church with the one prevalent among the Jews. The Christian churches teach that there is no salvation outside the Church of Christ without faith in it. Islam holds that all those who do not believe in the Divine Message of Mohammed will be damned. The Talmud, Coudenhove recorded, considers all just and pious men worthy of inheriting the world to come; the Jews therefore no longer make proselytes. People who desire to accept Judaism are usually dissuaded from doing so, and the above Talmudic passage is quoted to them, while Christians and Moslems are zealously endeavouring to win proselytes from other denominations.[73]

One of the leading Philo-Semites of modern days, the German liberal and humanitarian, representative of ethical pacifism, Friederich Wilhelm Foerster (1869-1966), evaluated the Talmud with profound sympathy. "We must never lose sight of the fact that the study of the Talmud demands great concentration of thought, a detachment from all worldly things during the time of study and a religious devotion to tradition. We are indeed reminded of certain scholastics of the Middle Ages with whom the mere process seemed to be an end in itself." The moral teachings of the Talmud, Foerster wrote, often reveal a lofty spirit. "Sometimes the moral teachings of the Talmud attain heights that surprise the Christian reader, who is, on perusing it, bound to recognize a close approximation to Christian teachings on forgiveness and love of one's enemies — in passages where those who are insulted, but refrain from any insult in return, and who suffer willingly and not murmur are praised. The Talmud tells of the rabbi, who every evening on retiring to rest, said: 'I forgive all those who have wrought evil against me,' while another rabbi is reported to have answered the question 'What man is strong?' with the words: 'He is strong who can turn an enemy into a friend.' Yet another rabbi thought: 'If a friend needs thy help in loading up, first help thy enemy, so that the evil impulse may be mastered.' Elsewhere in the Talmud we read that the righteous among all people have a portion in the world to come, and also a heathen who does good out of the fullness of his heart is worth as much as a High Priest in Israel"[74]

Foerster's book is one of the most remarkable manifestations of philo-Semitic thought and sentiment in modern days; it is a moving tribute to every positive aspect of Jewish life and history, especially to the well-springs of Jewish piety, the faith of the Talmud and the religious emotions of the Chassidic movement. Foerster stresses the invaluable Jewish contributions to

Western civilization. Foerster's attitude arose no doubt as a reaction against the brutal racism of the Nazi writers who exalted anti-Semitism into a complete system of thought. His praise of Israel's incomparable spiritual greatness, of its wonderful gifts and achievements, is a remarkable manifestation of pro-Jewish feelings which one may hope will direct the thinking of contemporary Germany.

There is a notable tradition of rabbinic studies in the English-speaking world. *John Selden* (1584-1654) published learned studies on the laws of the Hebrew. *John Lightfoot* (1602-1675) issued his *Hebraic and Talmudic Hours,* offering rabbinic parallels to the gospels. *Edward Pocock* (1604-1691) displayed impressive Rabbinic knowledge, as evidenced in his translation into Latin of six sections of Maimonides' commentary of the Mishnah, the first book printed in Oxford in Hebrew characters. It has been rightly remarked by the late Chief Rabbi Dr. J.H. Hertz that "scholars of no other land than England have been so much more under the spell of Talmudic studies for their own sake, and have more clearly recognized the indispensableness of these studies for the elucidation of fundamental problems in the world of religion and culture."[75]

Christian Hebraists in the sixteenth century, participated in the Authorized Version of the Bible in 1611: Edward Lively, Regius Professor of Hebrew at Cambridge, wrote scholarly works showing a very competent knowledge of Hebrew and a wide range of reading. One may mention his annotations to five of the minor prophets with a Latin interpretation. For points of grammar and vocabulary he frequently referred to David Kimchi's Book of Roots. His work which is distinguished by humility reflects an Anglican rather than a Puritan temper. There is about his work a suavity and a tolerance which is not to be found in the Puritan theologians. His writing has at times an almost eighteenth-century flavour. It has to be noted that tolerance was the basis of philo-Semitism in pre-emancipation Europe. Next to Edward Pocock, Lively was considered as the "greatest of Hebraists."

A famous critic of the authorized version was Dr. Hugh

Broughton, a distinguished scholar, described by his fellow-scholar, John Lightfoot, as "the Great Albionean Divine, renowned in many Nations for Rare Skills in Salems and Athens Tongues and Familiar Acquaintance with all Rabbinical learning." Familiarity with Rabbinic writings which necessitated consultation with Jewish teachers points to interest in post-biblical Jewish thought, and indicates some understanding for contemporary Jewry. This cannot be assumed with regard to scholars who were familiar with the Hebrew Bible only, unless philo-Semitic thoughts or actions can be adduced. Broughton seems to have had friendly relations with Jews which would account for his Jewish learning and his knowledge of traditions. Though he joined in the usual attack on the Jews for deliberately corrupting the text of the Hebrew Bible, yet he derived a great deal from Jewish sources and was on friendly terms with Jews throughout his life.[75]

A special interest in rabbinic literature was shown by a Dutch scholar, Wilhelm Surenhuys, whose translation of the Mishnah, with two commentaries on it, into Latin was printed between 1698-1703. Surenhuys applied himself with love and diligence to his work and sat at the feet of Jewish teachers from whom he imbibed the conviction that the oral law, the Mishnah, in its main contents is as divine as the written words of the Bible. He intended to acquaint Christian youth, who trained for theology and the clerical profession, with the contents of the Mishnah, thus receiving "ordination" before becoming Christian priests.

"He who desires to be a good and worthy disciple of Christ must first become a Jew, or he must first learn thoroughly the language and culture of the Jews, and become Moses's disciple before he joins the Apostles, in order that he may be able through Moses and the prophets to convince men that Jesus is the Messiah."

In the case of Surenhuys it is clear that admiration for Israel's literature prompted active sympathy with the people who created it. He cordially thanked the Senate of Amsterdam for the protection it afforded to the Jews: "In the measure in which this people once surpassed all other peoples, you give it preference, worthy men! The old renown and dignity, which this people and the citizens of Jerusalem once possessed, are yours. For the Jews are sincerely devoted to you, not overcome by force of arms, but won over by humanity and wisdom; they come to you, and are happy to obey your republican government."

Surenhuys opposed those Christians who, basing their knowledge on the Scripture of the Jews, reviled the people of Israel "like highwaymen, who, having robbed an honest man of all his clothes, beat him to death, and send him away with scorn." Surenhuys intended to make the whole of rabbinic literature accessible to the world through the Latin language.[76] This interest in rabbinic literature signified a new pro-Jewish approach, an emphasis on tolerance, based on admiration for historic Judaism. Although the missionary motive cannot be quite excluded from the thought of some Christian Hebraists, their enthusiasm for rabbinic learning paved the way for a new attitude of the Christian world to the Jews, leading ultimately to emancipation from the ghetto.

In modern days one of the outstanding Christian Hebraists in the English-speaking world was *Canon Herbert Danby* (1889-1953). Danby belonged to the small group of Christian scholars of Judaism who, in addition to their knowledge of Biblical language and thought, were also familiar with Rabbinic idiom and literature; they entered into the heart and soul of Rabbinic thought, contributed to the understanding of post-Biblical Judaism by scholarly dissertations on Rabbinic themes.

Danby's chief contribution to the furtherance of Rabbinic knowledge is his monumental translation into English of the Mishnah (1933). This classic of the oral tradition of Judaism ranks as the second great book created after the Biblical era by the Jewish people.* Danby's English version of the entire text

---

*Mishnah (teaching), legal codification containing the core of the Oral Law, compiled by R. Judah Ha-Nasi, c. 220 C.E. The Mishnah is divided into six orders, the orders into tractates.

of the Mishnah is considered today as a classic in its sphere, distinguished by the fact that, in both translation and notes, Danby endeavoured to enter into the spirit of Hebraic tradition. "Considering," he writes in his introduction, "the centuries of intensive study devoted to the Mishnah and its associated literature by Jewish commentators from the time of the Talmud to the present day, to neglect or ignore their results is as presumptous as it is precarious."

Danby's English Mishnah opened to the English-speaking people one of the most important sources of traditional Jewish life and thought and acquainted them with many noble examples of Rabbinic morality such as the teaching in the tractate in Sanhedrin: "Only one single man was created in the world, to teach that, if any man has caused a single soul to perish, Scripture imputes it to him as though he had caused a whole world to perish; and if any man saves the life of a single soul, Scripture imputes it to him as though he had saved the whole world. Again, but a single man was created for the sake of peace among mankind, that none should say to his fellow: my father was greater than your father."

In assessing Danby's work, one must realize the difficulties that beset the path of a Gentile scholar who attempted to enter the world of Rabbinic thought and master the secrets of Talmudic literature, without having the advantage of a training in the traditions of Rabbinic learning enjoyed by Jewish scholars. The greater is his merit, if he succeeds in making Rabbinic literature accessible in some degree to Gentile readers.

Danby's outstanding quality in rendering rabbinic texts into English is also manifested in his translations of the two books of the Code of Maimonides, the Mishnah Torah, one of the basic sources of Judaism, entrusted to him by the editors of the Yale University Judaica Series. His renderings of the *Book of Offerings* (1950) and the *Book of Purification* (1953) are distinguished by painstaking scholarship and remarkable awareness of the nuances in rabbinic terms.

Though a Christian, Danby did not subscribe to the common Christian prejudice against the Jewish insistence on practical observance of religious precepts, but was fully aware of the intrinsically moral aim of Jewish legalism. He emphasized Maimonides' closing paragraph in the *Book of Offerings* in which the great Jewish codifier points out that the purpose of the law is to thwart man's innate avarice, to suppress his natural immoral tendencies, and to keep him straight in all his doings.[77]

Among English Christian friends of the Talmud the name of Travers Herford (1860-1950) stands out as one of the "Righteous among the Gentiles." Deeply imbued with a love of Jewish learning, Herford devoted his life to a well-nigh impassioned study of rabbinic literature; in his numerous books and essays he succeeded in formulating the distinctive characteristics and the historic justification of rabbinic Judaism. Herford, a Unitarian Minister, was the first Christian scholar to present a positive evaluation of the contribution of the Pharisees to the spiritual development of both Judaism and Christianity, and to give a true estimate of their characteristics and achievements.

When his first book, *Aim and Method of Phariseeism,* appeared in 1912, it created a veritable sensation. It was epoch-making for a Christian scholar to vindicate the much-maligned Pharisees by asserting and proving that they were wrongly accused of hypocrisy and unspiritual formalism. Herford expounded the traditional Jewish position with regard to the gospel narrative; not only with scrupulous fairness, but with a warmth and sympathy that has never yet been bestowed by a Christian writer on the religion of the men who have been regarded traditionally as narrow bigots, practising a stereotyped ceremonial and professing a lifeless creed.

Herford was one of the few Christian scholars who understood that the Pharisees succeeded in keeping the religion of the Torah as a living principle, capable of being adapted to the everchanging conditions of life, while their opponents, the Sadducees, who would not abandon the literal meaning of the Scriptures, failed to devise means for the perpetuation of Judaism after the fall of the state, and disappeared from the scene of history. The Pharisees saved Judaism from becoming petrified, and by developing the oral law gave it the means of preserving its vitality for all times. The leading teachers of rabbinic law knew as well as Paul did, and long before him, that the letter killeth but the spirit giveth life. The precise purpose with which they formulated the Halachah (the law) was to prevent the letter from killing and to open the way for the spirit to give life. And this is what actually followed from their labours on the Halachah.

Hereford's unique achievement consists in his successful endeavour to understand, as a Christian, the Judaism of the rabbis, and to grasp what Phariseeism meant from the inside, to its own devotees and not merely what it appeared from the outside, to its opponents. He strove to ascertain the real significance of the word Torah, the keyword of Judaism. No Christian had ever before comprehended the inner meaning of Torah and done justice to its purpose with such insight as Herford. He rightly affirms that the term Torah cannot be adequately translated; it does not and never did mean simply "law," a code of legal enactments. It means and always has meant "Divine Teaching" in the widest sense of the word. To its faithful followers Torah was neither a spiritual nor physical burden, but a limitless opportunity for serving God in reverence, love and joy. Far from consisting merely of a catalogue of tedious requirements, rabbinic Judaism "comprised the knowledge of God Himself, and His providence and righteousness and fatherly love, of the way of Communion with Him, the assurance of forgiveness to the penitent, the means of grace and the hope of glory."

To an astonished Christian world, and to not a few surprised Jews, Herford revealed the Judaism of Jesus' contemporaries as a vital religion in which inner motives counted just as much, and more than external form and as a living faith that inspired and sanctified its adherents. Herford emphatically affirmed that the ethics of the gospels are very largely the ethics of the Pharisees and that everyone who reads the Sermon of the Mount and kindred passages knows that the teaching there given is substantially Jewish, that the ethical teaching of Jesus is to a considerable extent identical with that of the Pharisees, and that it passed directly into Christianity. Whatever, therefore, may be deemed the importance and worth of the Christian ethics; however it may be exalted as the priceless treasure which it surely is, so great is the measure of what the world in general and Christendom in particular owes to the Pharisees.[78]

On the death of Herford in November 1950, the Jewish Chronicle (London) published an obituary by Chief Rabbi Dr. J.H. Hertz which contained the following passage: "Jewish scholarship throughout the world will mourn the passing of Dr. Travers Herford, truly one of the pious men of the nations. His objective, and consequently sympathetic studies on the character, teaching and significance of the ancient teachers of the Talmud and Midrash, will ever remain as a memorial to a singular soul, deeply religious, and one who dissipated false opinion and prejudice by the light of truth and informed conviction."[79]

Few Christian scholars have made such a profound impression on the world of Jewish learning as *George Foot Moore* (1851-1930), the American Orientalist, whose splendid presentation of Judaism in his monumental opus *Judaism in the First Century of the Christian Era* (1927) earned him a permanent place in the pantheon of the Christian friends of the Talmud. It is an entrancing exposition of Jewish doctrine and ritual, arranged under such headings as "Revealed Religion," "The Idea of God," "Man, Sin and Atonement," "Observances," "Morals," "Piety," "The Hereafter." Moore gave a complete picture of Judaism as it had developed since the return of the Jews from Babylonian captivity. There is nothing in it of the usual prejudice, that of contrasting the "legalism" of Judaism with the "Gospel of Love" in Christianity. Moore entered the spirit of Judaism and made himself completely at home in it. He studied it from within with profound sympathy and appreciation. He was fair and just to the achievements of the scribes, the pharisees and the Tannaim, the teachers of the Mishnah. He was one of the most eloquent champions of Judaism and sincere friend of Talmudic expressions of piety.

Moore stressed that Judaism, while clinging to its national character, never abandons the personal and universal quality of prophetic religion. Judaism thus made religion in every sphere a personal relation between the individual man and God. In bringing this into clear consciousness and in drawing its consequences, lies Judaism's most significant advance beyond the older religion of Israel. It was, Moore emphasizes, a relation of the individual to God, not in isolation, but in the fellowship of the religious community and, ideally, of the whole Jewish people, the "Keneset Israel." Not only the synagogue, but also the entire communal life — even in its secular aspects — knit together by its peculiar beliefs, laws, and observances, was the expression and the bond of this fellowship. Thus Judaism became in the full sense a personal religion, without ceasing to be a national religion. Moore's work may be rightly considered as the most comprehensive and correct presentation of the Judaism of the time and every educated Jew and Christian should study this superb work.[80]

The man who brought about a fundamental change in the traditional anti-Jewish attitude among Christians was the Rev. James Parkes (born 1896), one of the most illustrious contemporary Christian scholars in the field of Jewish studies, who in a number of publications has endeavoured to disprove the traditional Christian affirmations concerning Judaism.

The traditional Christian theory of the relation between Judaism and Christianity asserts that the Christian faith completely and finally superseded Judaism, which had lost its vitality and worth as a living religion. Having given birth to Christianity, Judaism was left a worthless remnant whose subsequent history was of no significance to the development of religious ideas or the creation of ethical values. All truth had passed from Sinai to Calvary and the promises made to the older faith were fulfilled in the New Covenant, the triumphant Gospel of Christ. But not only had Judaism lost its divine authority, its adherents were under a curse as a result of the crime of deicide. The Jews having voluntarily called down on their heads the punishment for their perfidy, were justly suffering divine vengeance and had become the proper object of Christian scorn and hatred.

Parkes considers himself a member of a "minority movement" among Christians who are prepared to revise the traditional hostile attitude of Christianity to Judaism and to recognize the function of the Jewish faith as a normal vital religion of a living people.

Parkes investigates the relations of the two faiths from the revolutionary standpoint of equal validity and relevance of both Judaism and Christianity. The two great prophetic religions which sprang from the soil of Palestine, the revelation on Sinai and of Calvary, the salvation through Torah and the Christ, are of equal authority and permanence. Parkes refutes the familiar views that the Judaism of the Pharisees was a formal, exclusive, legalistic religion and that the law burdened its adherents. Rabbinic religion which has sustained the Jewish people during its long martyrdom was a living, creative and fascinating spiritual system which opened to its adherents the way to God, through the gates of prayer and the doctrine of good works. Pharisaic Judaism was for the Jews not merely an instrument of survival but an overflowing source of happiness, peace and spiritual splendour.

Parkes denies the traditional Christian view that the Jews were God's chosen people until the advent of Christ, and then forfeited their title which was inherited by the Church. Parkes believes that the title "Chosen People" applies to both the Jewish community and the Church. The Christian religion is an individualistic faith, a mystery of personal salvation, offering a doctrine of man. Judaism is a way of life, a collective religion, presenting the image of a true community. Christianity expresses the personal aspect of religion, while Judaism emphasizes the social aspect, through which the whole of human life comes within the religious domain, with no distinction between the religious and the secular. Neither Judaism nor Christianity must lose their essential nature, for the world needs both aspects. Judaism and Christianity must both continue to fulfil their mandate from God; their permanent co-existence is God's will. Consequently Parkes refuses to contemplate any superficial merger of Judaism and Christianity and opposes the conversionist activities of the Church. Christianity without the cross is as empty of meaning as Judaism without Torah. A religion made out of patches and compromises and superficial syntheses would be a monster lacking the very qualities which gives each religion its permanent value to humanity. Judaism and Christianity are two kinds of religion; the two voices of Judea which can never blend without the surrender by one or other of the fundamental purpose.

It should be noted that Parkes's evaluation of Judaism and Christianity as religions of equal worth and significance is not motivated by the ideas of enlightenment, according to which each religion has its status and justification in society, as long as it proves itself to be useful, and succeeds, in the spirit of Lessing's parable of The Three Rings, to make its confessors "beloved of God and Man." Parkes is an Anglican clergyman who is committed to the truth of Christian revelation and the belief in God's supreme manifestation in history through Incarnation in Christ. Yet he is prepared to assign to Judaism a continuous function in the realm of the religious spirit, on a basis of equality with Christianity. The covenant between God and Israel on Sinai has never been annulled; both religions derive from one stem and both divide the inheritance into equal parts. Both religions are of equal value as revelations of God. Calvary, Parkes asserts, stands beside Sinai without cancelling the latter. Judaism and Christianity are not rivals but two aspects of one truth. Within the Jewish world similar views were held by Franz Rosenzweig (1886-1929), the noted German-Jewish philosopher. Both Judaism and Christianity, he taught, were true revelations of God, Judaism as the everlasting life, Christianity as the everlasting way; both are parts of the great truth.

Parkes is perhaps the only Christian theologian who considers Judaism not as the mother religion of Christianity, but as a sister faith. It is on this basis that he postulates Jewish-

73

Christian understanding, while remaining faithful to his own religion. Parkes's identification with the spirit of the rabbis is revealed in the following passage which gives abiding expression to the essential quality of rabbinic life:

"The life which the rabbis of Yavnah and all their successors were offering and which the Jewish people came to accept, was a fascinating combination of burdens and privileges all related to daily living; for the vast literature of rabbinic Judaism is entirely devoid of systematic theology such as one meets in the Christian writers. The character of God was assumed, and neither described nor argued; all the interest was in the human response to a divinely initiated covenant relationship. The response was both ethical and ceremonial; and if the non-Jewish reader stands astounded before the immense mass of discussion of what seem to him minor points, especially of the ritual of a non-existent temple, he easily overlooks the fact that the standard of living prescribed, domestic, social, commercial, and in relation to the Gentile world, was high. Perhaps the most interesting development in a society, in which voluntary acceptance played so large a part, lay in the conceptions of the importance of sanctifying and not dishonouring the name of God (Kiddush ha-Shem and Hillul ha-Shem) in relations with the Gentile world. A Jew must accept martyrdom and avoid dishonesty in dealing with a Gentile."[81]

Parkes remarks perceptively that any Jew automatically suspected an interested Christian of having missionary motives, and deeply resented the Christian attitude of superiority, whilst his Christian colleagues resented his endeavour to lay the chief blame for mediaeval anti-Semitism on the Christian Church and making no reference to the necessary conversion of the Jews. He concludes, "I learned very early that to evolve a new attitude to Jewish-Christian relations was to be a lonely job."

The section of the Talmud which was most popular among Christian students of rabbinic literature was the tractate *Pirkei Avoth,* the *Chapters of the Fathers,* which played a notable role in building bridges of understanding between the Christian world and the rabbinic mind. The contents of the Chapters are easily accessible to the reader; its ethical maxims are of universal interest and application. *Charles Taylor* in the introduction to his edition of *Pirkei Avoth* (1877) described the work as consisting of maxims of the Jewish Fathers whose names are mentioned in its pages, and is chiefly valued as a compendium of practical ethics. "Its simplicity and intrinsic excellence has secured for Avoth a widespread and lasting popularity."

French Catholic scholars have made a notable contribution to the understanding of that decisive turning point in human civilization, the rise of Christianity and its separation from its Jewish mother faith. *Charles Guignebert* (1867-1942) in his classic work *The Jewish World in the Time of Jesus*[82] offered to the French reader a fair appreciation of both Judaism and Christianity and a sympathetic evaluation of the role of Judaism in the religious development of the Western world. Jesus, he wrote, was born among Jews on Jewish soil, and his message was for Jews alone. In its origin, therefore, Christianity must be considered a Jewish phenomenon. Jews first carried it into Greek soil, where an extraordinary success awaited it, and there, too, it found its first home in the hearts of Jews, or of those who were already influenced and prepared for its reception by Jewish propaganda.

Guignebert introduced, among French students of Judaism, a note of just appraisal of Talmudic literature, a body of writings commonly regarded as replete with superstitions and tedious legalistic requirements. Guignebert also correctly emphasized the decisive role of the Talmud in the preservation of the Jewish people throughout the ages. The Talmud is to be regarded as a monument, witnessing to the religious vitality of Israel after the catastrophe which shattered and dispersed the Jewish nation in A.D.70: It is a repository of all traditions and hopes of Judaism and of all the interpretations and thoughts of its learned men which might survive that bitter experience with its hateful memories. In the anguish of their terrible disillusionment, the vital elements of Judaism which are contained therein were revised and determined. They were brought together into an organised system for the sustenance, consolation and instruction of the scattered people. To present a friendly unprejudiced picture of Talmudic literature is a prominent tendency among philo-Semitic scholars.

The master of Jewish studies in Catholic France was Father *Joseph Bonsirven*, S.J. (d.1958). What Travers Herford achieved for England and G.F. Moore for America, Bonsirven accomplished for French Catholic studies of Judaism. Like these two great masters of Jewish lore in the English-speaking world, he too endeavoured to explain the fundamentals of the religious position of rabbinic Jews from the inside, to look at their creed and deed with their own eyes. Bonsirven even displayed a fair measure of understanding for that aspect of Judaism most obnoxious to Christian theologians and frequently condemned as arid formalism — the passionate Jewish insistence on ritual. The Jews, Bonsirven affirmed, are an essentially religious people who wish to permeate their whole life with religious gestures. They see in God not only their Father and their King, but also the Holy One, whose holiness must be emulated and reproduced. In order to reach these goals, the Jewish mind likes to use visible rituals. Spiritual realities are thereby translated and established. This attitude does not prevent an increasingly powerful tendency to a more inner worship and a more ethical concept of holiness.[83]

Father Bonsirven has to his credit a number of profound and comprehensive studies on rabbinic Judaism in the era of the Parting of the Ways. He also established a school of French Catholic students who have made significant contribution to the study of that period. Bonsirven, though naturally upholding the Christian doctrine of the divinity of Jesus and the consummation of Judaism through the rise of Christianity, succeeded in maintaining a warm-hearted attitude towards Palestinian Judaism, the matrix of Jesus' ministry and teaching. Bonsirven's major works endeavour to strengthen the awareness of the Jewish background of the New Testament and to instil a proper understanding for that Jewish *milieu* from which sprang both the Talmud and Christianity. Bonsirven, a

Jesuit Priest, upheld the creed of Christianity as an absolute verity. For him Judaism, which he calls the most perfect of all natural religions, has entered history for the sake of Jesus. Nevertheless, a profound admiration for the Jewish faith was displayed by that devout Catholic. Memorable is Bonsirven's glowing tribute to the ardent piety of Israel and to the Jewish belief in God, who to Bonsirven, unlike to most Christian theologians, was not only a God of fear, but also a God of love. Christians must recognize the greatness and purity of Jewish beliefs concerning God. It is genuine and strict monotheism with a profound sense of divine grandeur; this leads to a very humble adoration, together with childlike and unlimited trust in the inexhaustible goodness of the Father. It is a belief in the Creator who alone has brought the universe into being, and preserves it with loyalty and love. "There is an awareness of the domination exercised by the Lord which extends over all things. These convictions inspire a deeply religious sense: an absolute submission which implies a faithful observance of the commandments: a loyalty which would lead, if necessary, even to martyrdom; a worship imbued with both fear and love; a reverence sometimes excessive but coupled with a touching familiarity towards the Father and Spouse of Israel . . . these convictions and this piety surpass everything that contemporary philosophies have to offer, not only because of their purity but especially because they are not the prerogative of a small *elite;* they inspire a whole people."

A remarkable praise of the Talmud is found in a book written by a contemporary Russian orthodox priest, *Lev Gillet,* who became an admirer of Jewish spiritual values under the influence of Aime Palliere (1875-1949), author of *Le Sanctuaire Inconnu*[84], a Christian convert to Judaism and one of the most interesting characters in modern Jewish history. Gillet, though not entirely free from conversionist motives, is sincere in his hatred of anti-Semitism and genuine in his admiration for the Talmud. "I am a Priest of the Russian Orthodox Church. The Orthodox Churches have a heavy historical guilt towards Judaism; in the persecutions of the Jews, chiefly in Russia and

Rumania, they have often sinned either by their silence or by their acquiescence or by their incitements. I would here, as far as an individual can do it, atone for this guilt."

What is the permanent value of the Talmud? Gillet asks. The Talmud, he declares, aims at the penetration of the whole of human life by God's presence. It does not confine worship to the hours of prayer, but sanctifies the home and its daily round of duties. So wide is its range that arts and sciences, agriculture and cooking, medicine and worship, jurisprudence and building are equally inspired by its spirit, which is the hallowing of life. This universality of the Talmud, this interconnection of religion and every phase of life, saves the Talmudic student from stagnation and keeps him freshminded. The Talmud bears the mark of a supreme originality, for the Jewish people and that culture are above all theocratic. It expressed all the dreams and hopes, all the pangs and joys of Israel. As such it is not only a masterpiece of Jewish literature, but, Gillet affirms, one of the summits in the history of the human mind.[85]

Profound understanding for the Pharisees and their teachings has been shown by Professor Kurt Schubert, an Austrian Catholic, who teaches Judaica at the University of Vienna. The Pharisees, he holds,[86] were able to invest the Mosaic law with a new actuality in conformity with the needs of the Jewish Diaspora. They combined the Messianic idea with the idea of election, and thus found a meaning and a purpose in Judaism in a world which, from a purely external point of view, is still in a desperate condition. Schubert declares that there is hardly another phenomenon in the history of religions which has been as frequently misunderstood as pharisaism. As a rule Christians know the Pharisees only through the New Testament, which presents a derogatory image of pharisaism, and this became the common property of Christendom. Schubert rightly declares that the Pharisees should be judged in fairness from the sources of the Talmud, which is neither hostile like the New Testament and the Qumran texts, nor apologetic, like Josephus. Schubert endeavours to understand the attitude of the Pharisees in their polemics against Jesus and to assess the adverse statements of the New Testament fairly. The Pharisees are wrongly blamed for commanding the people to hate their enemy, as stated in Matthew 5:43. Schubert rightly states that nowhere in rabbinic literature is such a commandment to be found. Such an attitude is reflected in the Qumran texts, where the Qumran Essenes prepare for a final eschatological war of vengeance against their and God's enemies. The statement in Matthew 5:43 probably refers to a saying of the Qumran Essenes, not of the Pharisees. For pharisaic teaching one should recall the dictum of Hillel, who lived approximately one generation before Christ. His admonition has, in the meantime, become the property of many cultures: "What is hateful unto thee, do not do unto others." For Hillel the whole Torah is contained in this command to love your fellow-man. The ritual commandments and other ordinances of the law are only interpretations and practical applications of this central injunction.

Another Austrian Catholic scholar, Dr. Wolfgang Beilner, in his work *Christus und die Pharisäer* (Vienna, 1961) refutes the poisonous *cliches* current in the Christian world about the Pharisees and demonstrates how they endeavoured to safeguard the integrity of Israel's faith against every foreign influence — a commendable task.

Mention should be made of a tract called *The Pharisees* offered as the first fruit of the Centre of Biblical and Jewish Studies, recently set up by the Congregation of our Lady of Zion, a Roman Catholic religious order for women. The tract by Sister Marie-Louise Gabriel, a member of the order and active in a new centre, sets out to rectify the traditional Christian attitude of contempt for Judaism, and of disregard for the whole body of Jewish tradition and teaching, which "has been a constant strand in the Christian tradition from its very beginnings to the present day." A "Pharisee" has, beginning with the Gospel according to St. Matthew and right up to the latest edition of the *Oxford Dictionary,* been synonymous with "hypocrite," "formalist," "self-righteous person." It was not until Travers Herford's erudite and sympathetic studies in the first half of this century that a Christian scholar acknowledged Pharisaism and Rabbinic Judaism to be codes of religion and ethics, valid in their own terms, the direct linear descendants and organic development of Prophetic Judaism.

The great significance of the little tract is that it reveals for the first time that this point of view enjoys the toleration of the Roman Catholic hierarchy. It is accepted as the expression of a legitimate view, even though still of a minority. The concluding paragraph of the pamphlet affirms that in fairness to the Pharisees it is important to emphasize not only their negative role in the New Testament, but also the positive part they played, first, in preparing the fervent spiritual life in the midst of which Christianity was born, and later, in saving for their people the inheritance which contains the first revelation of God to man.[87]

Sister Marie-Louise Gabriel is a Secretary of the Commission charged with publishing a book about Jews in a series of Catholic text-books in English. Another project of the Commission is an educational kit for Catholic Schools containing reproductions of Jewish religious articles, such as Tefillim, Tallaithim and Haggadoth. The object of all these activities is "to try to eliminate existing prejudices" against the Jews. All these projects are being followed up in order to implement the Vatican council's declaration on the Jews.

It is premature to judge the probable outcome of these Catholic activities with regard to actual Christian-Jewish relations. But dominant Christian attitudes reflect a strong philo-Semitic tendency and an endeavour on the part of the Christian Church to right the wrongs perpetrated against the Jews, to create a climate of opinion which would make it possible to conduct a fruitful Jewish-Christian dialogue or, at least, to continue to differ in matters religious, in a spirit of tolerance, harmony and perhaps even understanding. It is regrettable that large sections of the Jewish people are unaware of these activities which are not motivated by conversionist motives. Sister Marie-Louise Gabriel reports that she could not

CHRISTIANITY'S DEBT TO JUDAISM

The Bible

Christianity owes to Judaism the Hebrew Bible: if Judaism had given it nothing but the Book of Psalms, its debt would still have been inexpressibly great. Christians acknowledge that the greatest Jewish gift to world civilization is the Hebrew Scripture. Whoever, in the course of history, affirmed the spiritual inferiority of the Jewish people was refuted by friends of the Jews, who point to the superb spiritual and literary quality of the Hebrew Bible. In the imperishable literature of the Old Testament, Israel has offered to the Church and to the world a magnificent and enduring contribution. So long as human speech endures, writes Prof. H.H. Rowley, this collection will be treasured and will continue to minister to the spirit of man. Of its range and variety its superb literary value and its robustness of spirit nothing need here be said. It is a record of human experience and is relevant to human need in every situation and through it all there is a spiritual penetration of the deepest value. It tells how man heard God speaking in all that they passed through and how they came to understand the nature of God and the meaning of life.[91]

The specific indebtedness of the Church to the Synagogue as House of Prayer was emphasized in the work of modern Christian scholars, who endeavoured to evaluate Judaism on its merits, without reference to Christian dogmatism. The synagogue was a place for instruction in the truths and duties of revealed religion; and in imparting and receiving this divine instruction, no less than in praise or prayer, they were doing honor to God — it was an act of worship. It determined the type of Christian worship, which in the Greek and Roman world of the day might otherwise easily have taken the form of a mere mystery; and, in part directly, in part through the church, it furnished the model to Mohammed. Thus Judaism gave to the world not only the fundamental ideas of these great monotheistic religions, but the institutional forms in which they have perpetuated and propagated themselves.[92]

The glory of the Hebrew Bible, its profound morality, the wisdom of its laws, its moral grandeur and literary beauty, served as a continuous source of inspiration for lovers of the Bible and admiration for the people which gave this priceless treasure to the world.

Philo-Semites considered ancient Israel, whose political life was dominated not only by the absolute power of the King, but was shaped by the moral conscience of the Prophets, as a model of justice and liberty. Neither their kings, nor their priests, writes J.S. Mill, nineteenth-century English philosopher and economist,[93] ever obtained, as in other countries, the exclusive power of moulding the character of the Jews. Israelite religion which enabled persons *of genius* and a high religious tone to be regarded as inspired from heaven, gave existence to an inestimably precious unorganized institution — the *Order* (if it may be so termed) of *Prophets*. Under the protection generally, though not always, effectual, of their sacred character, the prophets were a power in the nation, often more than a match for kings and priests, and they kept up, in that little corner of the earth, the polarity of influences which is the only real security for continued progress. Religion there was consequently not what it has been in so many other places — a

84

consecration of all that was once established, and a barrier against further improvement.

John Stuart Mills considered the Jews, next to the Greeks, as the most progressive people of antiquity, and, jointly with them, the starting-point and main propelling agency of modern civilization.

Philo-Semites emphasized the racial nobility of the Jews and the fact that Judaism is the seed-bed of Christianity. The very spirit of Christianity is derived from Judaism; every thoughtful Christian must gratefully acknowledge his spiritual indebtedness to the Hebrews. Christians have inherited the ethical and religious insights of Israel, declares the Federal Council of the Churches of Christ in America (1939). "Though a Christian holds them with a difference, he should never forget that the historic roots of his faith are in the Hebrew people. From Israel he inherits the Ten Commandments, which are still our basic moral standards. From Israel he inherits the priceless treasure of the Psalms, which are an essential part of Christian worship everywhere in the world. From Israel he inherits the vision of social justice which has come to us through Amos and Isaiah and Micah. From Israel he inherits even the unique Christian classic, the New Testament, nearly all of which (if not all) was written by Jews. A Christian who faces the modern world must also be conscious of a present spiritual kinship with his Jewish neighbours to whom their religious heritage is still a vital force. That kinship is grounded in the common faith in the ultimate spiritual foundations of the universe. Over against those who adhere to a materialistic philosophy of life and a mechanistic concept of human destiny, Christians recognize themselves as at one with the Jews in the first sublime affirmation of the Pentateuch, 'In the beginning God.' Over against current disillusionment and despair, Christian and Hebrew stand together in their belief in the one Holy God who is the Creator of all and whose righteous will gives meaning and direction to life."

In the days of the Nazi persecutions, the opponents of Nazism pointed to the greatness of the Hebrew Bible as an incontestable argument against the anti-Jewish campaign which asserted Jewish inferiority as an inherent racial quality. Cardinal Faulhaber, in his celebrated sermons, delivered in Munich, Christmas 1933 after Hitler's advent to power, based his anti-Nazi orations on the need of Western man to revere the sacred Scripture of the Old Testament, implying the direct link between the heroes of the Hebrew Bible and their contemporary Jewish descendants. He declared from the pulpit, "It is a fact in the history of civilization that among no people of the pre-Christian era do we find so great a number of intellectually prominent men, who, by their words and by their whole personality, have devoted themselves to the religious guidance of their nation as among the people of the early Bible. Among no other people do we find a series of writing in which the fundamental truths of the religious life are presented with such clarity, such distinctness and such harmony as in the Mosaic Pentateuch with the simple beauty of its biblical stories; in the books of Kings, classical models in the art of historical writing; in the books of the Chronicles with their liturgical prescriptions; in the Book of Job with its treatment of the problem of suffering; in the wisdom books with their maxims of conduct; in the books of the four major and the twelve minor prophets, with their national sermons; in the books of the Maccabees, where the ancient heroism of the faith is once more resplendent. In these days, when the history and the literature of other pre-Christian peoples are being investigated, the science of religions is able to make the comparison; and to the people of Israel it will award this certificate. You have excelled them all by the sublimity of your religion; among all the nations of antiquity you have exhibited the noblest religious values . . . . Let us venerate the Sacred Scriptures of the Old Testament."[94]

One of the main causes of attack against Judaism was the alleged particularist tendency of the Hebrew Bible. The Jews claim to be God's "Chosen People," the God of the Old Testament is mainly concerned with His own nation, the Biblical laws aim chiefly at separation. Philo-Semitic writers explain the particularist tendency of the Old Testament as rendering an immense service to mankind by preserving the heritage of Israel which otherwise would have been lost in the general process of assimilation, prevalent during the Hellenistic period of history. The doctrine of election signifies that God chooses those who respond to His choice; it is therefore not a form of arbitrary favouritism; the freedom of the response is as firmly maintained as the assurance that the initiative in electing is with God. Christians are accustomed to condemn the Hebrew spirit of particularism out of hand, but are rarely willing either to understand it or to consider the conditions which produced it. "They forget," Rowley emphasizes, "that they have entered into a great inheritance for which they did not labor." Particularism was the shell which sought to preserve the religious essence of Israel. It sought to shut in the Jewish community and to protect it from outside influence that its feeble life might continue. Particularism was not born out of disloyalty to the wider vision of Deutero-Isaiah and his fellows, but of necessity, and its aim was not to confine Judaism to Jews, but to preserve Judaism for Jews. It was not inconsistent with a real interest in the pagan world or with a deep desire to lead men of alien race unto God and to receive them into the fellowship of his people.[95]

Another motive in defence of chosenness, advanced by philo-Semites, was the recognition of the unique quality of Israel's loyalty and perseverance in the face of persecution. Dean Ralph William Inge, English philosopher, Dean of St. Paul's, extols the unique Jewish virtue of faithfulness. *"What we were to look for was the secret of the unique greatness of the Jewish people.* In what sense, and for what reason, were they 'the Chosen People?' Shall we not say it was because of their indomitable faith? They worshipped a God who revealed His name, that is His character, as 'I will be with you.' What will He be to them? They did not know. They guessed. They staked their lives, their fortunes, their hopes, on their guesses, and they guessed wrongly again and again."

Philo-Semitic scholars defended the religious value of Pharisaic Judaism against the image of hypocrisy as pictured in the famous passages of the New Testament (Matthew 23). They sympathetically asserted the spiritual quality of Pharisaic religion and its innate ethical bent. These scholars also pay due regard to the innate value of particularism. When Christians are inclined to depreciate the Pharisees in the light of what they read of them in the New Testament, let them not forget, admonished Rowley, that they were far preferable to the Sadducees; and when they wish to call particularism hard and narrow, let them not forget that it was vastly more serviceable to the world than the laxity of its opponents. Phariseeism in its essence was not self-righteousness and hypocrisy, but loyalty, utter loyalty to the faith of Judaism and to the Will of God, as Judaism understood it.

There can be no doubt that knowledge of the Jewish past, understanding of the teachings of Judaism and an appreciation of the cultural, literary and ethical values, created by Israel, ultimately engenders a pro-Jewish sentiment. It leads to a positive attitude to the Jewish people, the bearers of these values, and serves as an antidote to anti-Semitism. Jacques Maritain, one of the most influential of contemporary Catholic philosophers, admonishes the Christian not to hate the Jews. "It is no little matter for a Christian to hate or to despise or to wish to treat degradingly the race from which sprang his God and the immaculate mother of his God. That is why the bitter zeal of anti-Semitism always turns in the end to a bitter zeal against Christianity itself."[96] Leon Bloy (1846-1917),[97] French novelist and essayist, author of *Le Salut par les Juifs* (1892), exhorted his fellow Christians to respect the Jews and to oppose anti-Semitism, in the following words: "Suppose the people about whom you spoke continually with the greatest contempt and you had for them only insults or outrageous sarcasms, were your father and mother, what would be your sentiments? Well, that is exactly what is happening to our Lord Jesus Christ. We forget or rather we do not wish to know that as a man, our Lord was a Jew, the epitome par excellence of the Jewish nation, the lion of Judah; that his mother was a Jewess the flower of the Jewish race; that the apostles were Jews, along with all the prophets; finally that our whole liturgy is based on Jewish books. How, then, can we express the enormity of the outrage and the blasphemy involved in vilifying the Jewish race?"

One of the most powerfully arguments of philo-Semites in favour of the Jewish people and its special role in the scheme of Divine Providence is the survival of the Jews in the face of unparalleled suffering. This fact, of a nation unflinchingly preserving its national existence without a home, is advanced as being of special significance. "The preservation of the Jews is really one of the most signal and illustrious acts of divine Providence," wrote Thomas Newton, eighteenth-century English clergyman, Bishop of Bristol.[98] "The Jews can go up higher than any other nation, they can even deduce their pedigree from the beginning of the world. They may not know from what particular tribe or family they are descended, but they know certainly that they all sprung from the stock of Abraham. And yet the contempt with which they have been treated and the hardships which they have undergone in almost all countries, should, one would think, have made them desirous to forget or renounce that origin; but they profess it, they glory in it; and after so many wars, massacres, and persecutions, they still subsist, they are still very numerous; and what but a supernatural power could have preserved them in such a manner as none other nation upon earth hath been preserved? Nor is the Providence of God less remarkable in the destruction of their enemies, than in their preservation . . . . We see that the great empires, which in their turns subdued and oppressed the people of God, are all come to ruin; because though they executed the purposes of God, yet that was more than they understood; all that they intended was to satiate their own pride and ambition, their own cruelty and revenge. And if such hath been the fatal end of the enemies and oppressors of the Jews, let it serve as a warning to all those, who at any time or upon any occasion are for raising a clamour and persecution against them."

In the eyes of philo-Semites, God's Providence seemed to watch over the fate of the Jewish people, save them from the pit of destruction and guide them in the path of eternity.

Gotthold Ephraim Lessing, the celebrated German dramatist and champion of enlightenment, put the following beautiful words into the mouth of the Jew, extolling the perennial quality of Jewish faith and fidelity. "Our God has so far from forsaken us that He has rather remained our protector even amidst His Judgments. If He had not watched over us, would we not long since have been swallowed up by our enemies, would they not long since have exterminated us from the face of the earth and wiped our name from the book of the living? Scattered to all corners of the globe, oppressed, maligned and persecuted everywhere, we are nevertheless the same today as we were a thousand and more years ago. Recognize His hand, or else name us another people that have met sorrow with such invincible powers, and amidst all their afflictions have worshipped God, from whom their afflictions have come, have worshipped even after the manner of their forebears upon whom He showered his blessing."[99]

Philo-Semites singled out a number of qualities, by which, in their view, the Jews distinguished themselves and rendered particular service to mankind. One of these qualities which render Jewish persistence particularly valuable is that of being the Eternal Protestant, the Great Dissenter, the upholder of the right to be different. This aspect is stressed emphatically in an essay by *Ernst Moritz Arndt,* famous German patriotic poet and nationalist historian (1796-1860). He seems to be the first who referred to the Jews as Protestants, a theme later developed by modern Jewish thinkers.[100] "There, in the Mediterranean lands, life, liberty, morality, science and art being their higher development. There we find first and foremost the children of Israel, a people still mocked by the nations and, in some countries, treated as outcasts. Yet they were the benefactors of us all. Here, among the Hebrews, we come to the scene of original beauty, where mortal man communicated directly with God and His angels, and where yet those with the highest gifts, an Abraham, a Moses, a David, an Isaiah, remain firmly rooted in the ground of reality. Here we find, for the first time in history, personality endowed with divine rights, the full majesty of the human figure and of a moral world. Here in the Old Testament, there flourished a Protestantism that preceded the Protestants, a Lutheranism that antedated Doctor Luther. And while I mention the subject, I may add — for the comparison is certainly correct in many points — that Judaism is the Protestantism of the ancient world, while Hellenism is its Catholicism."[101]

The concept of the Jews as Protestants was taken up by Arnold Toynbee, the contemporary British historian. In refusing to be *gleichgeschaltet* by either of the two deviationist Judaic world and word religions, and in surviving as a persistent minority in a Christian and a Moslem environment, the Jews have made a deep mark on both Christian and Islamic history as living Jews, and not merely as dead Jewish forerunners of Christianity and Islam.[102] In our contemporary world, which seems to be growing more and more irreligious, the strength of the Jews lies in the resistance which they, together with Christians, offer against the new paganism.

Opponents of Judaism frequently affirm the superiority of Christianity over the Jewish faith, stressing that the Old Testament represents justice, while the New Testament preaches love. Love is a higher virtue than justice; it is more divine than mere righteousness. In the measure, as love stands higher on the scale of values than righteousness, the New Testament surpasses the Old and Christianity is nobler than Judaism. Philo-Semites, however, deny this contrast between the two faiths. They point to the exhalted ethical ideals of the prophets.

One of the greatest Christian admirers and expositors of Biblical prophecy was the German theologian *Karl Heinrich Cornill* (1856-1920). His works are imbued with appreciation of Old Testament religion and admiration for its unique religious quality. Cornill was one of the most illustrious representatives of philo-Semitism among Christian theologians in Germany. The whole history of humanity, he asserts, has produced nothing which can be compared in the remotest degree to the prophecy of Israel. "Through prophecy, Israel became the prophet of mankind. Let this never be overlooked nor forgotten: the costliest and noblest treasure that man possesses he owes to Israel and to Israelite prophecy," affirmed Cornill.[103]

One of the main aims of pro-Jewish thought in the sphere of the Christian-Jewish encounter is to record the immense debt which Christianity owes to Judaism, to demonstrate the supreme quality of the Hebrew Bible and to prove that the highest thoughts of the New Testament are already contained in the Hebrew Scriptures. Christians, affirmed H.H. Rowley, are accustomed to think of the characteristic teaching of Christianity about God as lying in the thought of His fatherhood and love; but the fatherhood of God is taught in the Old Testament as well as the New. And now, God, thou art our Father, is the cry of Isaiah. Like a father pities his children, so God pities them that fear him, proclaim the Psalmists, while Hosea declared the same truth from God's side: when Israel was my child, then I loved him and called my son out of Egypt. "And if 'God's love' is a new Testament text, its truth was perceived by Hosea and the author of Jonah and many other Old Testament writers. . . . Judaism contained much that was unique and of the deepest value to all men and while it has become normal and natural to Christians, because it was taken over into their faith, they would do well to remember that it was first achieved in the experience of Judaism. And one of the greatest of her gifts was her ethical religion. . . . We think of the virtue of sympathy as specifically a Christian virtue and certainly in Christianity it has produced fruits unparalleled elsewhere; but where did Christianity get this great virtue which it has striven so largely to express; whence, but in the heritage from Judaism? . . . that men were summoned to display a like spirit."[104]

The ethical and universal quality of prophetic religion is particularly stressed by Rudolf Otto (1869-1937),[105] the celebrated German theologian and author of *The Idea of the Holy,* who analyses the non-rational, numinous element in religion in contrast to the rational concept. The prophets represent the moralizing process which leads from the merely numinous to the "holy" quality in religion. The venerable religion of Moses marks the beginning of a process which from that point onward proceeds with ever-increasing momentum, by which "the numinous" is throughout rationalized and moralized, i.e., charged with ethical import, until it becomes "the holy" in the fullest sense of the word. The culmination of the process is found in the Prophets and in the Gospels. And it is in this that the special nobility of the religion revealed to us by the Bible is to be found, which, when the state represented by the Deutero-Isaiah is reached, justifies its claim to be a universal world religion.

Herman Gunkel, the renowned German scholar (1852-1932), paid homage to the unique quality of the Hebrew Bible which alone justifies the appellation of Chosen People, and the hope that salvation is of the Jews. Gunkel worked particularly in favour of an aesthetic appreciation and interpretation of the Hebrew Bible, in the spirit of Herder. The Old Testament presents a rich and varied gallery of personalities. This is the real greatness of the Hebrew religion. For this reason, Gunkel holds, it is an insult to the historical spirit even to name Babylonians and Egyptians in one breath with Israel. Israel was never great in works of external civilization; but in the sphere of the spirit it produced the highest that was achieved anywhere through the East — human personality living its own life in the presence of God. And because of that achievement, Israel is "the chosen people" and "salvation is of the Jews."[106]

Moses

The towering figure of Moses evoked profound admiration among lovers of the Bible and frequently led to a sincere esteem for the people from whose midst Moses sprung. Moses, the prophet, the legislator, the nation-builder, was an ideal figure whose unique, well-nigh superhuman stature cast its bright light on the people of Moses. Though the link between the man who spoke face to face with God and the contemporary "Moses of the Jew Street" seemed to be tenuous, yet those thinkers and writers who tried to rise above religious or national prejudices, saw a hidden bond between the great Moses and Moses, the pedlar. "Were I of Jewish blood," wrote *Robert Louis Stevenson,* "I do not think I could ever forgive the Christians; the ghettos would get in my nostrils like mustard or lit gunpowder . . . were he of mine, I should not be struck at all by Mr. Moss of Bevis Marks; I should still see behind him Moses of the Mount and the Tables and the shining face. We are all nobly born; fortunate those who know it; blessed those who remember."[107]

The Mosaic legislation, affirms *Johann Gottfried von Herder,*[108] German writer and philosopher, champion of Enlightenment, aimed to constitute a free people, that should be subject to no one but the Law; and in order to ensure that none would rob them of liberty, God Himself became law-giver, law-keeper, and king. He dwelt in the midst of His people. The entire people was a priestly kingdom; every one was the servant of this King and His Law. "And ye shall be unto Me a

94

kingdom of priests!" (Exodus 19:6) was the cardinal principle according to which Moses conceived his legislation. To the great spirit of Moses, to his legislation and covenant, we owe a series of excellent works in poetry, history, science and wisdom — literature which no other people possess. Prophets, sages, teachers, priests, even good kings followed in his footsteps. His theocratic code was the first bulwark against cruelty and idolatry, inhumanity and oppression and likewise a nursery of the purest conceptions of God, of sublime hymns, psalms, precepts and doctrines. How happy we would have been, if it were fulfilled completely!

Friedrich von Schiller, celebrated German poet, shared some of the popular prejudices of his environment against the Jews, and yet paid homage to the founder of the Jewish religion, the exalted status of ancient Israel among the nations and the universal significance of the Jewish nation. He wrote, "The establishment of the Jewish state by Moses is one of the most memorable events recorded in history. It is important as a manifestation of the intelligence with which it was consummated, and even more so because of its abiding effect on the world. The two religions which control the larger portion of the inhabited globe, Christianity and Islam, are both based on the religion of the Jews. Yes, in a certain sense it is indisputable that we are indebted to the religion of Moses for a large share of the culture which we now enjoy. Through it, a precious truth became known, the doctrine of one God, which, if left to the intellect alone, would have been discovered only after a slow process of evolution. The Hebrew system enjoyed this extraordinary advantage, that the religion of its sages and the religion of its folk were not in direct mutual contradiction, as was the case among the enlightened pagans. From this standpoint, the Jewish nation must appear to us historically as of universal significance. All the evil which has been imputed to them, all the efforts of literary men to disparage them, will not prevent us from doing them justice."[109]

Philo-Semitic writers affirm that the Mosaic law is distinguished not only by its sublime justice, its profound concern for the weak and oppressed, but also by its universal quality, its applicability to mankind as a whole. *Francois Rene de Chateaubriand,* French romantic writer and statesman, pointed to the noble quality of Judaism in the words: "There are only two beautiful names and memories in history — those of the Israelites and the Greeks." "Such are the laws which the Creator has engraved, not only upon the marble of Sinai, but also upon the heart of a man. What strikes us, in the first place, is that character of universality which distinguishes this divine code from all human codes that precede it. Here we have the law of all nations, of all climates, of all times. Pythagoras and Zoroaster addressed the Greeks and the Medes; Yehova speaks to all mankind."[110]

The universal character of the Mosaic legislation is also stressed by the great seventeenth century German philosopher and mathematician *Wilhelm Leibnitz.* "Among all ancient peoples," he affirmed, "the Hebrews are the only ones known to have had public principles regarding their religion. Abraham and Moses established the belief in the one God, the Source of all good, the Author of all things. The Hebrews speak of it in the manner worthy of the Supreme Being, and it is astonishing to see the inhabitants of an insignificant territory more enlightened than the rest of the human race. The sages of other nations have perhaps said as much occasionally, but they did not have the good fortune to have their teachings assume the force of law."[111]

Harriet Beecher Stowe, the American novelist, author of *Uncle Tom's Cabin,* extolled the compassionate quality of Mosaic legislation and placed it at the side of Jesus' gentle words: "The strongest impulse in the character of Moses appears to have been that of protective justice, more particularly with regard to the helpless and down-trodden classes. The laws of Moses, if carefully examined, are a perfect phenomenon; an exception among the laws of either ancients or modern nations in the care they exercised over women, widows, orphans, paupers, foreigners, servants and dumb animals. No so-called Christian nation but could advantageously take a lesson in legislation from the laws of Moses. There is a plaintive, pathetic spirit of compassion in the very language in which the laws in favour of the helpless and suffering are expressed. Not the gentlest words of Jesus are more compassionate in their spirit than many of the laws of Moses."[112]

The famous American economist and social reformer *Henry George* (1839-1897) found inspiration for his social ideals in the Mosaic law. In a lecture on Moses delivered in 1878, he paid glowing tribute to Moses and his legislation which did not aim at the protection of property, but the protection of humanity. George praised the free spirit of the Mosaic law from which sprang the intensity of family life that amid all dispersions and persecution has preserved the individuality of the Hebrew race; that love of independence that under the most adverse circumstances has characterized the Jew; "that burning patriotism that flamed up in the Maccabees and bares the breasts of Jewish peasants to the serried steel of Grecian phalanx and the resistless onset of Roman legion; that stubborn courage that in exile and in torture held the Jew to his faith. It kindled that fire that has made the strains of Hebrew seers and poets phrase for us the highest exaltations of thought; the intellectual vigour, that has over and over again made the dry stuff bud and blossom. And passing outward from one narrow race it has exerted its power wherever the influence of the Hebrew Scriptures has been felt. It has toppled thrones and cast down hierarchies."[113]

Winston Churchill, in his essay "Moses," glorified Moses and described him as "one of the greatest of human beings with the most decisive leap forward, ever discernible in human history." He placed the leader of the Jews in the highest possible historical position as the man who was the greatest of the prophets, who spoke in person to the God of Israel; he was the national hero who led the Chosen People out of the land of bondage, through the perils of the wilderness, and brought them to the very threshold of the Promised Land: he was the supreme law-giver, who received from God that remarkable code upon which the religious, moral, and social life of the nation was so securely fastened. Tradition lastly ascribed to him the authorship of the whole Pentateuch, and the mystery that surrounded his death added to his prestige. "We reject with scorn all those learned and laboured myths that Moses was but a legendary figure upon whom the priesthood and the people hung their essential social, moral and religious ordinances. We believe that the most scientific view, the most up-to-date and rationalist conception, will find its fullest satisfaction in taking the Bible story literally."[114] Churchill's admiration for Moses is to be understood in the context of his labours in the cause of Zionism, the re-establishment of the Jews in the Promised Land towards which they wandered under the leadership of Moses.

Jesus

One of the strongest motives in philo-Semitic feeling is the consciousness of the Jewish origin and Jewish background of Jesus and the Apostles. Already St. Augustine, the Latin Church father, affirmed that the promise of the Lord, that He will not cast off His people (Psalm 94:14), refers to the Jewish people, "the people where were the prophets, where were the patriarchs, the people begotten according to the flesh from the seed of Abraham." Martin Luther set the tone for this consideration in his memorable declaration: "And though we boast of rank, we must admit that we are but of pagan stock, while the Jews are of the blood of Christ. We are brothers-in-law and strangers; they are blood relations, real cousins and brothers of our Lord. Therefore, if it were proper to take pride in flesh and blood, the Jews belong to Christ more than we, as St. Paul asserts in Romans 9. Even God has demonstrated it by His acts, for He did not such great honours to any of the Gentiles, as He did to the Jews. No patriarch, apostle or prophets came of the Gentiles, and very few of them have been elevated as right Christians. Though the Gospels were made known to the whole world, the Sacred Scriptures, that is, the Law and the Prophets, were commended to no people but the Jews, as St. Paul says in Romans (3:2), and as Psalm (147) has it: He declareth His word unto Jacob, His statutes and His ordinances unto Israel. He hath not dealt so with any nation; and as for

99

His ordinances, they have not known them. Therefore Jews must not be disdained today, for the glory came from them, and not from us. They were the first Christians, and to them were addressed and commanded the words of God."

Luther expected the Jews to accept the Christian faith and so add weight to the new Protestant creed as having accomplished a task the Catholic Church never managed to fulfil — the conversion of the Jews. "I hope that by treating the Jews in a friendly manner and expounding to them the real Gospel, many of them will become true Christians and come over to the faith of their ancestors, the prophets and the patriarchs. If the apostles, who also were Jews, had adopted the same barbarous methods in dealing with the pagans as we adopted in dealing with the Jews, not a single pagan would have become a Christian . . . They are blood-relations, of our Lord; therefore if one were to boast of blood, the Jews belong to Christ more than we . . . I beg my dear Papists when they have become tired of calling me heretic, to call me Jew."[115]

One of Luther's remarkable sayings, on the Jewish origin of the Christian faith, is contained in his preface to the Old Testament. "Here you will find the cradle and swaddling clothes in which Christ lies to which the angel directs the shepherds. They are poor and mean swaddling clothes, but precious is the treasure, Christ, who lies in them."

While anti-Semites derived support from Luther's violent Jew-hatred, manifested in his later writings,[116] philo-Semites throughout the ages have echoed Luther's thought of the blood kinship between Jesus and the Jewish people. They insist that Jesus' Jewish extraction makes it impossible for Christians to harbour anti-Semitic feelings.

Hugo Grotius, the eminent seventeenth century Dutch jurist and statesman, evinced great interest in Judaism, stressing the Jewish fundaments of Christianity, "The Jews," he declared, "should not look upon Christians as adversaries. Christians know very well that they are offspring of holy men, whom God often visited by His prophets and His angels; that the Messiah was born of their nation, as were the first teachers of

Christianity. They were the stock into which we were grafted; to them were committed the oracles of God, which we respect as much as they."[117]

G.E. Lessing, the famous German champion of Enlightenment, puts the following words into the mouth of the lay brother, who represents "simple-minded faith" in Lessing's celebrated drama *Nathan the Wise.* It does not matter in what religion a child is brought up, children need love before all other things, "and if the maid (Nathan's daughter) but grew before your eyes healthy and good, then in the eyes of God she still remained as precious as before. And was not Christianity itself built up in Jewry? It has vexed me oft, and cost me many a bitter tear that Christians should so utterly forget their own redeemer was himself a Jew."[118]

"As a Christian," writes *Vladimir Soloviev,* nineteenth-century Russian philosopher and poet, "I perceive that I am deeply indebted to Judaism; was not my saviour after the flesh a Jew? The prophets and apostles too were Jews. The foundation stone, the basis of a universal church, was taken from the House of Israel."[119]

Ellen Key (1879-1926), the famous Swedish author and social reformer, derides, together with other philo-Semites, the attempt to make Jesus descend from Aryan origins. "Everyone knows — and many acknowledge — the intellectual gifts, creative force, thirst for knowledge, and persevering, clearsighted energy of the Jewish people. But too little is said of the qualities which nevertheless appear most characteristic to those who have seen Jewish women and men at close quarters; their strength in love, their sense of fraternity, their helpfulness and self-sacrifice. It was not an accident that Jesus came of the Jewish people. The attempts now made to prove that he was an Aryan are a waste of labour for those who — as in my case — have more readily found his qualities in those of Jewish than in those of Germanic descent."[120]

Jesus was a Galilean Jew, affirms, *F.C. Grant,* mentioned before, one of the leading American theologians of today. "The advocates of the foolish Aryan theory, thirty years ago, denied that Jesus was a Jew; this strange theory formed a part of the lunatic dream of Nazi racial superiority; the 'Jewishness' of Jesus, should never have been questioned. The reasons for doing so are obviously derived from anti-Semitic prejudice. The New Testament everywhere takes it for granted that Jesus was both a Jew and a Galilean."[121]

The theme of Jesus' Jewish — "Semitic" — descent, as a leading motive against anti-Semitism, has been one of the main weapons in the arsenal of the friends of the Jews and made its way felt in days of crisis. It emphasized both the physical and in some mystic way the spiritual link between Christians and the people of Israel.

As an example of philo-Semitic action aroused by the consciousness of Jesus' Jewish origin, the following occurence during the Nazi period may be adduced: When the Nazis occupied Croatia, they encountered strong opposition from the clergy, particularly from Archbishop Alois Stepinac, who in other respects failed to show any opposition to German-Croatian collaboration. The Bishop's ire was aroused when the Nazis ordered two priests and six nuns in his arch diocese to wear the Star of David because they were of Jewish descent. Even after the Germans had rescinded the order, Archbishop Stepinac declared from the pulpit: "I have ordered the priests and nuns to continue wearing this sign, belonging to the people from whom the Saviour came."[122]

Jesus, affirms Godfrey E. Phillips, contemporary English theologian, was a human person, a true Jew, and his devotion to the Old Testament and the revelation of God which is enshrined, determined the very pattern of his life and his performance of the work God had given him to do. The studies of H. Strack and P. Billerbeck show that the gospels are more characteristically Jewish than has been hitherto realized; their central figure, Jesus, was much more definitely Jewish than was commonly thought.[123] It has taken nearly two thousand years, observes Nathan Soderblom, Archbishop of Upsala, Nobel prize winner, before we now begin to realize how Jesus not only drew from the prophets and psalmists, but also continued the deeper religious channel of contemporary Judaism.[124]

Friends of Judaism and the Jews emphasize the Jewish character of Christianity and point to the role of the Old Testament within the spiritual realm of Christian civilization. This observation was especially relevant in counteracting any propaganda about Jewish depravity and spiritual sterility as conducted by "Nordic" fanatics.

It is astonishing how thoughtless are those Christians who imagine that they can be anti-Semites and do not realize that the very spirit of Christianity is derived from Judaism, writes Nicholas Berdyaev, nineteenth-century Russian philosopher, celebrated existentialist theologian, one of the foremost exponents of Russian philo-Semitism. It is incompatible with Christianity, which teaches that every human being is created in God's image. In the German racial theory there is no salvation for the "lower races." Hatred towards Jews has also an economic and social background. The Jews serve as scapegoats for all the misfortunes and calamities which befall humanity. Curiously enough, the Jews are also accused of the diametrically opposed evils; they are the alleged builders of capitalism and originators of socialism. "The Jewish problem at present implies therefore the conversion to Christianity, not of the Jews, but of the Christians. A purification process of the Christian world, based on the defence of truth and human dignity, is now taking place, and the Jewish question is part of it. Jews and Christians are rapidly changing their attitudes towards one another. They are now entering a totally new phase of mutual understanding. In our contemporary world, which seems to be growing more and more irreligious, the strength of the Jews lies in the resistance which they offer, together with Christians, against the new paganism."[125] That Jews and Christians are allies in the battle against materialism and irreligion, is a favourite argument with Christian philo-Semites.

A philo-Semitic trend in Dutch Calvinism is stressed by Professor A. van Selms, formerly of the University of Pretoria. The answer to the question of who killed Christ is given by the Dutch poet and theologian *Jakobus Revius* (1568-1658) in a remarkably beautiful poem which should find its place in this context (English translation by Henrietta Ten Harmsel).

No, it was not the Jews who crucified,
Nor who betrayed you in the judgement place,
Nor who with buffets struck you as you died.
No, it was not the soldiers fisted bold
Who lifted up the hammer and the nail,
Or raised the cursed cross on Calvary's hill
Or, gambling, tossed the dice to win your robe.
I am the one, O Lord, who brought you there,
I am the heavy cross you had to bear,
I am the rope that bound you to the tree,
The whip, the nail, the hammer, and the spear,
The blood-stained crown of thorns you had to wear:
It was my sin, alas, it was for me.

Revius and another poet and theologian, *Johannes Vollenhove* (1631-1708), echoed and sentiments of Dutch Calvinism concerning the universal responsibility for the death of Christ, and thus implicitly denied the accusation of deicide raised against the Jews. The Netherlandish churches' courageous protests against the anti-Semitic measures taken by the German occupation forces are well known. Dutch Calvinism has always condemned anti-Semitism as a sin against God and mankind.[126]

Dr. Arthur Michael Ramsey, Archbishop of Canterbury, declared: "It is always wrong when people try to lay the blame upon the Jews for the crucifixion of Jesus Christ. The crucifixion," he said, "was the clash between the love of God and the sinfulness and selfishness of the whole human race. Those who crucified Christ are, in the true mind of the Christian Church, representatives of the whole human race. It is for no one to point a finger of resentment at those who brought Jesus to His death, but rather to see the crucifixion as the Divine Judge-

104

ment upon all humanity for choosing the ways of sin rather than the love of God."[127]

In the contradiction to the anti-Jewish theological tradition, there exists another philo-Semitic interpretation in Christian thought; this interpretation views the Jewish people as God's elect, dearest and closest. It is because of the Jews that the Gentiles were recipients of the Gospel, and it is to them that Christians should be ever grateful.

Who looks to Jesus as his Master, cannot be anti-Semitic, J.G. Masaryk affirmed, for all times and for all Christendom.[128]

The Hebrew Truth

The Christian Hebraists of the Middle Ages were concerned with the "Hebrew truth," revealed in the Hebrew Bible. They were not only impelled by a scholarly quest for a correct text; by promoting an accurate understanding of the Hebrew Bible, they hoped to further the truthful exposition of the New Testament. Their main object was to refute the Jews' denial of Christ and, through a right understanding of both Testaments, to prove that Jesus was the expected Messiah. Nevertheless, the scholarly interest of Christian Hebraists in the Hebrew language, even though partly prompted by missionary interests, promoted personal contact with Jewish exegesis and a closer acquaintance with contemporary Jews. Christian Hebraism was thus conducive to the development of philo-Semitic sentiments in scholarly Christian circles. Christian Hebraists turned to the original sources of Judaism, thereby creating an intellectual climate more favourable for a just appreciation of the Hebraic faith and its bearers; and bonds of friendship were forged between Jewish scholars and Christian theologians. "God revealed philosophy," declared R. Bacon, thirteenth-century English philosopher, "first to His saints, to whom He also gave the Law . . . because philosophy was indispensable to the understanding promulgation . . . and defense of the Law. Hence it was delivered, complete in all details, in the Hebrew language."[129]

The chief movement leading to a change of feeling towards the Jews was the Reformation, with its intense interest in the Hebrew Bible, Hebrew and Biblical studies. Being steeped in Hebraic subjects, many theologians and scholars developed sympathies for the people of the law; their interest was directed to the Jews as the people of the Patriarchs and prophets, not as members of the deicidal race. Active contact with Jewish teachers, to whom many Hebrew scholars appealed in order to perfect their knowledge of the sacred language, facilitated this change in attitude. In the days of the Renaissance, knowledge of Hebrew became one of the essential elements of the new learning, the ideal humanist being master of three languages: Hebrew, Greek and Latin. The mediaeval Christian Hebraists were torn between their opposition to Jewish claims in the field of theology, and their own vital interest in the rabbinic interpretation of Scripture. Recognition of the excellence of Jewish exegesis, which leads the diligent enquirer to a true recognition of the *Hebraica veritas,* characterizes the mediaeval Christian student of Hebrew.

Sebastian Muenster (1489-1552), the German theologian and Hebraist, who studied with the famous Hebrew grammarian *Elia Levita* (1468-1549), had frequent recourse to Jewish interpretation as a sure guide to a better understanding of the plain meaning of Scripture. He quotes not only the Targum, the Aramaic translation of the Bible, but also values highly the mediaeval Jewish commentators, Rashi, Ibn Ezra, Nachmanides, Gersonides and David Kimchi. Although for Sebastian Muenster all the prophecies of the Old Testament pointed to Christ in whom they were fulfilled, he could not but end his Latin translation of the Bible with an enthusiastic praise of Moses. Nobody could improve upon his summary of Rabbinic opinion on the father of prophecy, the greatest and unequalled of all prophets. Muenster described his task as an effort "to show to everybody the beauty and excellence of the Torah" and affirms that he undertook the translation *Leshem Shamayim,* "for the sake of Heaven and for the benefit of the Christians."[130]

107

Hebrew was taught in Bologna and Rome, a factor which brought about a remarkable social intercourse between Rabbis and Christian scholars. Moreover, interest in Jewish mystical doctrine, Kabbalah, was awakened, and Hebrew was the key to its understanding. The Netherlands too were renowned for their Hebrew studies, and the cultivation of friendly relations between Christian Hebraists and Jewish teachers. Many professors at Leiden were men of Hebrew learning, with sympathy for Jews. The chair of Hebrew at the University was occupied from 1585 till 1597 by Raphelengius, who knew Hebrew, Syriac, Aramaic, Arabic and Persian. He was succeeded by Junius, a good Hebraist and well acquainted with Judaica. Jacob Alting, professor of Hebrew at the University of Groningen, had two rabbis as his teachers, and translated with one of them the last chapter of the tractate Sanhedrin of the Talmud.

Hugo Grotius, the great Dutch jurist, mentioned above, had studied at Leiden with Raphelengius and Junius and had acquired their spirit of tolerance. The government entrusted him to write a regulation for the Jews of Holland in which he cited the contact with Jewish scholars and access to Hebrew learning as one of the benefits deriving from a Jewish community.

There was of course also an anti-Jewish conversionist trend among the Hebraists in the Christian world; the Christian attitudes ran the gamut from crude anti-Semitism to humane understanding of the Jewish situation. Whether out of sincere interest in Judaism and Jews or out of a desire to convert them into Christians, the golden age of Holland was truly "Hebrew flavoured," as the Dutch writer Busken Huet once said; both Jews and Christians were the richer for the vast scholarship which flowered during that age.[131] Concern with Kabbalistic teachings was partly motivated, like all theological studies in those days, by the desire to prove the truth of Christianity; but it necessarily created a new scholarly link between Jew and Christian and gave rise among the scholarly class to genuine regard for the Jews and their lore. Noted Hebrew grammarian and lexiconographer Elia Levita, in replying to some rabbis

108

who blamed him for teaching the law to a Christian and thus possibly providing Christian scholars with weapons against Judaism, gave the following remarkable answer: "Cardinal Egidio de Viterbo came to me and kissed me with the kisses of his mouth, and declared: Blessed be the Lord of the Universe who has brought thee here! Now abide with me and teach me, and I shall be to thee as a father .... Thus we took sweet counsel together, like iron sharpening iron. I imparted my spirit to him, and from him I learned excellent and precious things."[132]

Pico della Mirandola, leading Italian humanist, introduced the Kabbalah into the Christian world. Through Pico, Hebrew knowledge reached Reuchlin, famous German humanist and Hebraist. It is through the interest in the Kabbalah that Pico and Reuchlin restored the Hebrew language to the academic world on an equal basis with Greek, thus giving Hebrew a status, which, in some measure, affected the attitude of the humanists to the people who created the Hebrew language. Pico also received his Hebrew training from Jewish teachers, a contact which was bound to implant regard for the Jews themselves. It is certain that Pico and Reuchlin were led by their belief in the value of the Kabbalah to an interest in Hebrew which crowned the learning of the Renaissance. Reuchlin loved the Hebrew language ardently and was enthusiastic about its simplicity and music. He put into practice what Erasmus of Rotterdam had postulated, declaring that Hebrew should rank with Greek and Latin and be taught in all institutes of higher learning. The light of the *hebraica veritas* should no longer be withheld from the world. The inclusion of Hebrew as a subject of academic exertions held out a new hope for the Jews. For although they had no access to the universities yet, there was a chance for them to maintain contact with the world of scholarship, as the advice of learned Jews on Hebrew grammar and rabbinics was always sought. The underprivileged dwellers of the Ghetto could take courage from the knowledge that the barrier separating Jew and Christian was beginning to weaken.

The distinguished French orientalist and historian J.E. Renan (1823-1892) emphasized the significance of mediaeval Jewish scholarship for the understanding of the Bible in the Christian world. Besides the immense service which the Jews rendered to the world in the matter of religion by converting it to the belief in one God, one cannot deny, he affirmed, that they have also been of the greatest service in the matter of knowledge. Renan declares that but for the Jews, the Hebrew Bible, one of the most important monuments of history and philology, would have ceased to exist. It is certain that had Christianity completely absorbed Judaism in the first centuries of our era, the Hebrew text of the Bible would have been lost. In the Middle Ages again the Synagogue furnished the Church with the only creditable Hebrew scholars it possessed — Raymond Martini, Nicolas de Lyra, Paul of Burgos. Lastly, the Renaissance applied to Jewish masters for the grammatical instruction which, long after, became so fruitful in the hands of European scholars. The preservation of the original monuments of Hebrew literature thus appears to have been exclusively due to the Jews. Do we appreciate what would have been the enormous loss to the sum of human knowledge, if the text of the Hebrew writings had disappeared through the neglect of Christian scholars?[133]

It should be recalled that Renan's position was ambivalent. He was influenced by Gobineau's notorious theory about the inferiority of the Semitic races in comparison with the Germanic races; and at times fell prey to the current racial theories. But he cautioned his readers against applying the theory to the Jews of his period. The latter, in spite of their direct descent from the former inhabitants of Palestine, had lost, under the influence of modern civilization, all traces of a "Semitic" character. However, Renan's generalizations about Indo-Germanic and Semitic races added to the anti-Jewish racial literature and lent a "scientific" argument to the prevailing anti-Jewish tendency. Renan, like so many of his contemporaries, stood for friendship with Jews and admiration for Judaism and at the same time could not quite resist the current theories of racial inferiority attributed to Semitic races.[134]

Puritanism

In the seventeenth century a Puritan preacher, Nathaniel Holmes, wished, according to the letter of many prophetic verses, to become the servant of Israel, and to serve him on bended knees. The more the tension increased, the more public life and religious thought assumed Hebrew colouring. The only thing wanting, to make one think oneself in Judaea, was for the orators in Parliament to speak Hebrew. One author proposed the seventh day as the day of rest, and in a work showed the holiness of this day, and the duty of the English people to honour it. This was in the beginning of 1649. Parliament, it is true, condemned this work to be burnt as heretical. But the Israelite spirit among the Puritans, especially among the Levelers, or ultra-republicans, was not suppressed by these means. Many wished the government to declare the Torah to be the code for England.[135] There is a strong philo-Semitic motivation in the puritanic type of Christianity. The Puritans had a particularly strong attachment of the Old Testament and its people. The Puritanism of New England was a kind of New Judaism, a Judaism transposed into Anglo-Saxon terms. These Protestants, in returning to the text of the Bible, had concentrated on the Old Testament and some had tried to take it as literally as any orthodox Jew. "When the Puritans came to America, they identified George III with Pharoah and themselves with the Israelites in search of the Promised Land. They called their New Country Canaan and talked continually of the

111

Covenant they had made with God."[136] They considered the Christian Church as only a continuation and extension of the Jewish Church. They believed that if they kept the covenant, they would find that the God of Israel was among them. Hebrew was to become a major subject, not merely in the colleges, but even in the schools. Harriet Beecher Stowe related that she had always felt in her childhood that the very ground of New England she stood on was consecrated by some special dealings of God's Providence. She said that her ancestors were Hebrewistic in their form; they spoke of Zion and Jerusalem, of the God of Israel and the God of Jacob, as if they were veritable Jews, and, except for the closing phrase "for the sake of Thy Son, our Saviour" their prayers might well have been uttered in Palestine by a well-trained Jew in the time of David. Santayana in the *Past Puritan* made one of his New England characters say, "We were always a circumcised people, selected for a unique role by God," and that New England somehow shares their destiny. American thinkers were particularly aware of the fundamental influence which ancient Hebrew literature had on the life and thought of New England. "At a time when there was as yet no English literature for the common people," wrote John Fiske, American scientist, philosopher and historian (1842-1901), "this untold wealth of Hebrew literature was implanted in the English mind as in the virgin soil. Great consequences have flowed from the fact that the first truly popular literature in England — the first which stirred the hearts of all classes of people and filled their minds with ideal pictures and their every-day speech with apt and telling phrases — was the literature comprised within the Bible. To its pages they went for daily instruction and comfort, with its strange Semitic names they baptized their children; upon its precepts, too often misunderstood and misapplied, they sought to build up a rule of life that might raise them above the crude and unsatisfying world into which they were born. So far as possible the text of the Holy Scriptures should be their guide in weighty matters of general legislation and in the shaping of the smallest details of daily life. The impulse by

which they were animated was a profoundly ethical impulse —
the desire to lead godly lives, and to drive out sin from the
community — the same ethical impulse which animates the
glowing pages of Hebrew poets and prophets and which has
given to the history and literature of Isreal their commanding
influence in the world. The Greek, says Matthew Arnold, held
that the perfection of happiness was to have one's thoughts hit
the mark; but the Hebrew held that it was to serve the Lord
day and night. It was a touch of this inspiration that the Puritan caught from his earnest and reverent study of the sacred
text and that served to justify and intensify his yearning for a
better life, and to give it the character of a grand and glorious
ideal."[137]

"The Hebrew nation," wrote Ralph Waldo Emerson, "compensated for the insignificance of its members and territory by
its religious genius, its tenacious belief; its poems and histories
cling to the soil of this globe like the primitive rocks. In
Puritanism, how the whole Jewish history became flesh and
blood in those men, let Bunyan show."[138]

Puritan writers and thinkers passionately believed in a new
Advent and assigned to the Jewish people a special role in the
glorious epoch of a millennium. There was in the minds of
seventeenth-century mystics a romantic identification with
everything that flowed from the Hebrew Scriptures.

In 1655, Menasse Ben Israel, the Rabbi of Amsterdam, addressed Oliver Cromwell, the Lord-Protector, and asked that
Jews should be allowed to settle again in England, three
hundred and fifty years after they had been expelled from that
country. Jews and Puritans were at one in the belief that the
return of the Jews to the British Isles would speed the advent
of the age of messianic redemption which, according to
Deuteronomy 28:64, had to be preceded by the dispersal of
Jews to all ends of the earth. Menasse Ben Israel's *Humble
Address* was, politically, a document of distinction, giving a
realistic quality to the mystical expectations of the century. It
was a time when Christians did not hesitate to join hands with
Jews in the belief that each common action would hasten the

coming of the Kingdom of God.[139] Menasse's appeal prepared the way for the resettlement of the Jews in England where they found a peaceful home until today.

The Puritans accepted Jewish history as their own, identified themselves in many respects with the Jewish people and gave their children Hebrew names. It is of central significance to realize that the identification of broad masses of Englishmen with the people of the Old Testament could not but have a decisive influence on the attitude of at least a section of the English people to the Jews. Cromwell and his followers sought in the heroes of the Bible the true prototypes of their virtues. Cromwell placed the Bible in the hands of his soldiers in order to fashion them into the invincible army, whose brave deeds history records.

There was a Christian theory affirming that the Jewish exile was a divine punishment for the Jews' failure to accept the true Messiah; on the other hand it was believed that the Jews must be scattered into every country before the Messiah would come. It was this belief combined with economic consideration which provided the impetus for the decision to allow Jews to return to England. Many devout Christians regarded a return as a preliminary to the coming of the Messiah, bringing peace to all mankind. Cromwell himself allayed a fear of the merchants of the competition of the Jews by pointing to the super-historical quality of the Jewish people. "You (English merchants) say that they are the meanest and most despised of all people. But in that case what becomes of your fears? Can you really be afraid that this contemptible and despised people should be able to prevail in trade and credit over the merchants of England, the noblest and most esteemed merchants of the whole world. Great is my sympathy with the poor people whom God chose, and to whom He gave the law."

The characteristic attitude of English philo-Semitism, based on veneration for the Hebrew Bible and esteem for the contribution which the Jewish people had made to Western civilization, is clearly expressed by W.E. Gladstone (1809-1898), British Prime Minister: "But indeed there is no need, in order

114

to give a due appreciation of our debt to the ancient Greeks, that we should either forget or disparage the function which was assigned by the Almighty Father to His most favoured people. No poetry, no philosophy, no art of Greece ever embraced, in its most soaring and widest conceptions, that simple law of love towards God and towards our neighbour on which 'two commandments hang all the law and the prophets,' and which supplied the moral basis of the new dispensation. There is one history, and that the most touching and most profound of all, for which we should search in vain through all the pages of the classics — I mean the history of the human soul in its relation with its Maker; the history of its sin, and grief, and death, and of the way of its recovery to hope and life and to enduring joy.... All the wonders of the Greek civilization heaped together are less wonderful, than is the single Book of Psalms."[140]

An important phenomenon of the seventeenth century was the partial "Judaization" of Protestant England through the channel of the Old Testament. What the revival of Hebrew learning, especially in Italy, had done for a small intellectual minority, Puritanism accomplished among the English masses. England became the people of a book — the Bible. The Puritans found an analogy between their fortunes and those of ancient Israel. The Lord of Hosts would help them to smite the Amalekites and Philistines; they rejoiced in the punishment and plagues of the "idolaters"; they had a strong feeling of their own election. The Psalms became their spiritual food. Milton knew Hebrew and blended the Greek and Hebraic genius. They were on the side of the Prophets, rather than of the Kings, the institutions. The grounds of self-respect their fathers had lost in England, they found afresh in Palestine. The great men of Israel were but farmers like their own cousins and ancestors. David had been a shepherd, Amos a herdsman, Christ himself a carpenter. For the more imaginative the gorse bushes on Old Lodge could be on fire with the flames that do not consume.[141] Puritans played a noble part in shaping the history and moulding the character of the English people. The legacy of Judaism was to them a real inspiration, and they have handed it on to their posterity in an intensity of religious devotion and a passion of moral fervour for which the whole world is still in their debt.[142]

There is, of course, no immediate connection between veneration of the Hebrew Bible and friendly attitudes to the living Jews or between pro-Hebraism and philo-Semitism. Some Hebraists emphasized the difference between the noble people of Scripture and their degraded descendants, the hapless denizens of the ghetto; between the people of the Patriarchs and the deicide race.[143] Others displayed humanitarian concern for their Jewish fellow men, while vehemently criticizing both the beliefs and ethical tenets of Hebrew Scripture. But there is no doubt that in Anglo-American thought, reverence for Hebrew Scripture, esteem for the language of the Bible, veneration for Israel's kings and prophets and admiration for Israel's ancient glory exercised an influence on the Christian attitude to the contemporary Jew; it generated sympathy for the aspirations of the descendants of the Biblical heroes who sought to regain their sovereignty and rebuild a new nation on the soil from which Scripture grew. Gentile Zionists in the English-speaking world of the modern era are spiritual heirs to the Anglo-American admirers of the Bible and of the people who gave the treasures of Scripture to the world — the Jews. The Puritan attitude to the Hebraic heritage and to the legacy of Israel, as contained between the covers of the Hebrew Bible, no doubt formed a powerful factor in modern pro-Semitic thinking and decisively fashioned that trend of thought which led, first, to the toleration of Jews in the English-speaking world, then, to their emancipation as fully-fledged citizens, and, ultimately, to official support in their longing for a reestablished nationhood in their ancient homeland. While a judgement on the merits and faults of Puritanism lies outside the concern of this chapter, the Puritan element in shaping pro-Jewish attitudes cannot be minimized.[144]

HEBREW HISTORIOGRAPHY

One of the recurring motives in higher philo-Semitism, the philo-Semitism of scholars and thinkers,[145] is the appreciation of the Biblical contribution to the writing of history. Philo-Semites stress the role which the Jews played in the formation of the historic consciousness of mankind. They were, wrote *Nicolas Berdyaev,* the famous Russian philosopher, mentioned above, the first to introduce the principles of the "historical," and a keen feeling for historical destiny in the life of mankind. The Jews have played an all important role in history; they are pre-eminently an historical people and their destiny reflects the indestructibility of the divine decrees.[146] Tribute is paid to the writing of history in the Old Testament authors by numerous Christian theologians who acknowledge that a sense of history was predominent in the religious ideas of the Jewish people. The Hebrews, according to Professor William Irvin, contemporary American scholar, produced the first real history that the world knows. "Their history possesses amazing qualities of excellence and at its best is one more of the seemingly miraculous achievements of this original people. Here we meet for the first time history on a world scope; the tenth chapter of Genesis is an astonishing document, revealing the writer's knowledge of the world of his time, and even more remarkable, his recognition of the essential unity of the entire human process. And this was ages before the notion of universal history dawned on the West; and when it did arrive there, the best achievements of Western writers were a direct result of the work of the Biblical historians. Yet one further astonishing quality of Hebrew historiography calls for emphasis. These writers were fully in accord with most recent thought in their repudiation of a theory of objective history. They wrote frankly and avowedly from an assumed point of view, which is but another way of saying that they believed that history has meaning ... The Hebrews were also the first to develop a philosophy of history; and when at length this area of speculation was taken up seriously by Western thinkers, it was in direct succession to and dependence upon Biblical accomplishments."[147]

It was particularly the Second Isaiah who perceived the whole course of history as being under the control of God who alone is Creator and Lord. This prophet may be considered as originator of a theology of world history. For the first time the vision of history's unity under the purpose of one God was made the basis of an appeal to all mankind. God's revelation is the source and ground of the meaning of all history. Israel is God's agent to be a "light to the nations." Through Israel all the families of the earth will know divine blessing. This is the true meaning of Israel's election.[148] Circumscribed though this theology of history may be, it is a noble attempt to see the course of events not as chaotic, but as duly planned by the Supreme Creator.

Another aspect stressed in praise of Israel is the symbolic and ethical value inherent in the Jewish writing of history. The view of history as a help to life has a respectable ancestry. Livy, the Roman historian, wrote: "The study of history is particularly salutary and fruitful because in it you can see, in a brilliant record, illustration of every possible type and from it you can take for yourself and your state examples to imitate and others disgraceful in their origin to avoid."[149] Biblical history, one of the greatest histories of the world, had been written from this angle and with this aim and so had become the heritage and school of a whole people. Now all the things, says Paul (1 Cor.10:11) speaking of events in Jewish history, hap-

118

pened to them for examples and they were written for our admonition. In this spirit the Hebrew Bible was written. "Hence," writes Sir Richard Livingstone, well-known English educationist, "it was and is as fascinating to the child as to the adult, to the uneducated and even the illiterate as to the scholar . . . . Its writers knew one side of history, the art of telling a story, and the mere narrative attracts any reader — the excitement of the stories of Saul and David, of the deaths of Jezebel and Ahab, of the wanderings of the patriarchs. The Bible is a philosophy of history as well as a collection of stories, and in general, if not in detail, it is the best philosophy yet written for the ordinary man. It is significant that no history has ever entered so deeply into the common mind or affected human conduct so strongly as the history of the Jewish people as conceived and written by the writers of the Bible."[150]

The historic consciousness of the prophets and the connection which they established between religion and history are singled out by philo-Semites as a peculiar quality of the genius of Israel. The prophetic attempt to search for an interpretation of history which would embrace the catastrophe and transcend the immediate tragedy is praised as the greatest and most deliberate attempt ever made to wrestle with destiny. It was the grand prophetic mission to interpret history and discover meaning in the human drama; to grapple with the moral difficulties that history presents to the religious mind. According to the eminent contemporary British historian, H. Butterfield, "one of the most significant and revealing chapters in the history of human thought is provided by the ancient Hebrew prophets in their insistence upon the judgement of God and their vindication of the moral element in history, during an age of cataclysm." Among the ancient Hebrews the doctrine of judgement provided a basis for an ethical view of history. Butterfield stresses the magnificent Jewish belief that there is morality in the processes and the course of history. The Jews recognized that if morality existed at all, it was there all the time, and was the most important element in human conduct; also that life, experience, and history were to be interpreted in terms of morality. "Everything that happened in human history had to be capable of being construed into morality, everything that happened was to be capable of translation into terms of moral benefit. What was unique about the ancient Hebrews was their historiography rather than their history — the fact that their finer spirits saw the hand of God in events, ultimately realising that if they were the chosen people they were chosen for the purpose of transmitting that discovery to all other nations."[151]

The famous German historian and statesman, B.G. von Niebuhr, praised the sincerity and reliability of the historical records of the Old Testament. "The Old Testament is the single exception (among all the other historical works) to patriotic mendacity. It never veils or hushes up an adversity of the people whose history is told in it. Its truthfulness is the most distinguished in historiography, also for him who does not believe in inspiration. At the same time, I must claim for the Old Testament besides absolute veracity, the strictest accuracy among all the historical sources."[152]

The blending of historical judgement with an ethical worldview in the writings of the prophets is a constant source of admiration on the part of historians and theologians. The sense of God's finger discernible in history is considered one of Israel's noblest contributions to the world. The prophets constantly represent history as the sphere of God's activity. He controlled its movements and made it serve His purpose. The Hebrew Bible shows a noble attitude to history that has never been transcended. It holds the firm faith that through all the policies of man, for which man alone, and not God, is responsible, God is yet speaking.[153]

The prophets' belief in God's moral purpose effective in history is beautifully expressed by the English historian and essayist, J.A. Froude (1818-1894). "One lesson, and only one, history may be said to repeat with distinctness, that the world is built somehow on moral foundations; that in the long run it is well with the good: in the long run that it is ill with the wicked. But this is no science; it is no more than the old doctrine taught long ago by the Hebrew prophets."[154]

SUFFERING AND HEROISM

The courage and heroism of leaders of the Hebrew people, particularly the spiritual fidelity of the Maccabees, have inspired men in all generations to deeds of bravery; they have never ceased to imbue posterity with admiration. Martyrs and heroes of all ages found the Maccabean martyrdom a supreme example of devotion to faith. The unfaltering loyalty to their beliefs, exemplified in the actions of Jewish heroes, has served as a constant source of inspiration to men in similar situations. Savonarola, the fifteenth-century Italian reformer and martyr, comforted his mother, before his execution, by pointing to the example of the Hebrew women of the Old Testament, "so that you may be enabled without shedding a tear to look upon your children martyred before your eyes" — a reference to the story of Hannah and her sons in the Book of the Maccabees. A modern Christian scholar, Edwin R. Bevan, has given the following glowing description of the heroic spirit of the Maccabees and the example they set to later generations of martyrs. "There shone in the moment of the Maccabean rebellion uncompromising fidelty to an ideal, endurance raised to the pitch of utter self-devotion, as a passionate clinging to purity. They were qualities for the lack of which all the riches of Hellenic culture could not compensate. It was an epoch in history. The agony created new human types, and new forms of literature, which became permanent, were inherited by Christendom. The figure of the martyr, as the Church knows it, dates from the persecution of Antiochus; all subsequent martyrologies derive from the Jewish books, which recorded the sufferings of those who in that day 'were strong and did exploits.'"[155]

The Dutch poet Isaac da Costa (1798-1860), himself of Portuguese-Jewish descent, once called the Netherlands "The Israel of the West." The emergence of the Republic of the United Provinces after the Eighty Years War for freedom from Spanish domination was likened at that time to the "Dutch War of the Maccabees," with the House of the Prince of Orange playing the role of the Jewish fighters for national independence. Joost van den Vondel, Holland's greatest poet of the Golden Age, actually used the symbol of the *pascha* (Passover) and the liberation from Egyptian slavery to describe his country's struggle for independence.[156]

Giuseppe Mazzini, Italian patriot, leader of the *Risorgimento,* compares the fate of the Italians with that of the Jews in the days of the Maccabees.[157] He admonished Italian mothers to teach their children the whole of the Book of the Maccabees, which appears as if written for Italians. Italians frequently derived inspiration from Jewish heroes in their struggle for liberty. The marvellous statue of Judith and Holofernes, sculptured by Donatello for the Medici, was placed on the platform in front of the Palazzo Publico in Florence, as a symbol of the triumph of freedom over tyranny. Verdi's opera *Nabucco,* based on the Biblical story of Israel's oppression by the Babylonians, symbolizes the Italian struggle against Austrian tyranny. The famous song of the Israelite slaves, *"Va Pensiero,"* from Verdi's opera *Nabucco* (1842) became the national hymn of Italian liberation, an anthem against foreign rule and oppression.

In the darkest hours of the Second World War, after the retreat from Dunkirk, Winston Churchill roused Britain and the freedom-loving world with words spoken by Judas Maccabeus in 165 B.C.E. on the eve of the battle of Emmaus: "Arm yourselves and be men of valour, and be in readiness for the conflict, for it is better for us to perish in battle, than to look upon the outrage of our nation and our altars. As the Will of

God is in Heaven, even so let Him do." Speaking for the American soldiers in the Caribbean, the Attorney-General Robert Kennedy, said: "They are there for the same reason that the Maccabeans stood their ground for human dignity and freedom."

Philo-Semites are impelled by a variety of motives to adopt a friendly attitude to the Jewish people, to appreciate their cultural achievements and to show concern with their destiny as a nation. Some philo-Semites are moved by a spirit of pity for all victims of persecution and are prompted by compassion for all under-privileged and oppressed. These champions of the Jewish cause are not particularly concerned with the Jews as such, but include in their humanitarian concerns all individuals who suffer unjust treatment. This humanitarian impulse often triumphed in people, who, like Charles Dickens, the creator of Fagin, the criminal Jew, were not above pandering to popular Jewish prejudice. Yet he recalls with sorrow that in the reign of Edward, the Jews were most unmercifully pillaged. They were hanged in great numbers, on accusations of having clipped the king's coin — which all kinds of people had done. They were heavily taxed; they were disgracefully badged; they were, on one day, thirteen years after the coronation, taken up with their wives and children and thrown into beastly prisons, until they purchased their release by paying to the king twelve thousand pounds. Finally, every kind of property belonging to them was seized by the king, except so little as would defray the charge of their taking themselves away into foreign countries. Many years elapsed before the hope of gain induced any of their race to return to England, where they had been treated so heartlessly and suffered so much.[158]

In describing the suffering of mediaeval Jews, David Hume, the celebrated eighteenth-century Scottish historian and philosopher, expressed poignant sympathy with the victims of bigotry and avidity. "In 1250," he wrote, "Henry III renewed his oppressions, and Aaron (of York) was condemned to pay him thirty thousand marks upon an accusation of forgery. The high penalty imposed upon him and which, it seems, he was thought able to pay, is rather a presumption of his innocence than of his guilt." In 1255, the king demanded eight thousand marks from the Jews and threatened to hang them, if they refused compliance. Hume was deeply shocked by the fact that, in order to have a better pretext for extortion, the improbable and absurd accusation of the crucifixion of a child in derision of the sufferings of Christ, advanced against the Jews at different times, was revived in England. Eighteen of them were hanged at once for this crime — though it is nowise credible that even the antipathy borne them by the Christians, and the oppressions under which they laboured, would ever have pushed them to be guilty of that dangerous enormity. Though these acts of violence against the Jews proceeded much from bigotry, they were still more derived from avidity and rapine.[159]

Philo-Semites consider the suffering of the Jewish people as particularly unmerited and scandalous; it is not only a sign of man's inhumanity to man, but evidence of deep ingratitude to one of the most illustrious bearers of human civilization. "The fate of the Jewish people," wrote *Paul Painleve* (1863-1933), French statesman and scientist, "is the scandal of history. Like Hellenism, Judaism is one of the deep sources of our occidental civilisations; it gave them its Bible, its God, its unquenchable thirst for Justice, the majestic poetry of its old prophets hurled like an outcry to the Deity. That such a people could, for eighteen centuries, be massacred, quartered, dispersed like a vile band over the face of the earth . . . condemned to endless exile and blamed for this very exile in order to justify new persecutions against them, is an iniquity which has disgusted all generous hearts for many years."[160]

A moving expression of Gentile admiration for Jewish persistence in the face of persecution, a primary source of philo-Semitic sentiments, was given by H.W. Longfellow in his celebrated poem "The Jewish Cemetery at Newport:"

. . . How came they here? What burst of Christian hate,
What persecution, merciless and blind,
Drove o'er the sea — that desert desolate —
These Ishmaels and Hagars of mankind?

Pride and humiliation hand in hand
Walked with them through the world where'er they went;
Trampled and beaten were they as the sand,
And yet unshaken as the continent.

For in the background figures vague and vast
Of patriarchs and prophets rose sublime,
And all the great traditions of the Past
They saw reflected in the coming time . . . .

Pity for the persecuted Jew led to an understanding of the tragedy of Jewish homelessness and to the first glimmering of the Zionist argument for a National Jewish Home, prompted by philo-Semitism, not political consideration. "There is no place on earth," wrote Jean Jacques Rousseau, the French philosopher, "where they can express their thoughts freely, without fear of Christian envy." Rousseau, who frequently pleaded for religious toleration and opposed missionary activities, injected into his philo-Jewish argument the theory of the Enlightenment. Religious truth is relative. What is true for Christians may be false for the Turks (Moslems). He regretted that he had never heard the arguments of the Jews as to why they should not have a free state, schools and universities, where they could speak and argue without danger. "Then alone can we know what they have to say. At the Sorbonne it is plain that the Messianic prophecies referred to Jesus Christ. Among the Rabbis of Amsterdam, it is just as clear that these prophecies have nothing to do with Jesus. At Constantinople the Turks state their arguments, but we dare not give ours; Then it is our turn to cringe. Can we blame the Turks if they require us to show the same respect for Mahomet, in whom we do not believe, as we demand from the Jews with regard to Jesus Christ in whom they do not believe? Are we right? On what grounds of justice can we answer this question?"[161] There is a direct line from this argument to the romantic Zionism of George Eliot and the sympathies and efforts of Christian Zionists on behalf of Jewish Restoration in Palestine-Israel.

PHILO-SEMITISM IN THE MODERN ERA

The protagonists of Enlightenment regarded the Jew as a fellow man, demanding for him individual emancipation as a citizen of his newly acquired fatherland. A complementary philo-Semitic attitude lends support to the Zionist aspirations for collective emancipation, and the restoration of the Jewish people in their old country, as heirs to the ancient nation of Israel.

The philo-Semitic trend in the days of Emancipation, as exemplified by the American and French revolutions, introduced the novel concept of equal rights for Jews and Christians before the law. These revolutions destroyed absolutism and feudalism, abolished the privileges of clergy and aristocracy, separated Church and State, and thus created the conditions necessary for Jewish civic equality. The very logic of modern society demanded that the principle of equality should be applied to all the inhabitants of the land regardless of religion and origin. "We hold these truths to be self-evident, that all men are created equal; that they are endowed by their Creator with certain inalienable rights; that among these are life, liberty and pursuit of happiness."[162] It is "a natural right of mankind that religious opinions shall never offset civil capacities, and that no man can be compelled to support any religious worship."[163]

Beginning with the French Revolution, which overthrew Bourbon absolutism, and ending with the Russian Revolution in March 1917, which brought an end to Tzarist despotism, the attitude of individuals and political groupings towards Jewish equality became the yardstick of reaction and backwardness on the one hand, liberalism and progress on the other. The forces which waged the relentless battle for the democratic social order also fought courageously for the complete equality of Jewish citizens. Similarly, the camp which defended the old order, was adamant in its struggle against any attempt to improve the civil position of Jews. It is important to note that the complete emancipation of the Jews was preceded by enlightened absolutism which was responsible for the ideas of religious tolerance and was instrumental in removing those restrictions which hampered the economic activities and cultural development of the Jews in the upper mercantile class. As early as 1665 the British authorities in Surinam granted extensive and hitherto unparalleled rights to the Jews because "they have found that the Hebrew nation, already resident here, have with their persons and property proved themselves useful and beneficial to this colony." And so they desired to encourage them to continue their residence and trade there.[164] Other Christian authorities were moved by a spirit of tolerance, granting the Jews certain limited rights they did not possess hitherto in order "to make the Jewish nation useful and serviceable to the State mainly through better education and enlightenment of its youth, as well as by directing them to the sciences, arts and crafts."[165]

The philo-Semitic trends of toleration in the pre-emancipation era constitute a stage between the Christian philo-Semitism, based on the religious mystery of Jewish existence, and the liberal sympathy for the individual Jew as fellow man. The main motive was the consideration that the Jews are useful and serviceable to the common weal, that their religion is an integral part of their collective existence, to be tolerated and respected, and that the Jewish community should be enabled to enjoy religious freedom and to pursue their trade without harm. Ultimately the principle of full equal rights and duties, as befitting the modern age, was included in the constitutions of the Western world, with full freedom of faith and liberty of conscience. It signified a victorious culmination of the struggle for complete emancipation of the Jews, a triumph for philo-Semitism.

Anti-Semitism was no longer a matter of State policy, but a trend, compounded of religious, racial and economic motives, with the aim of counteracting the official equalitarian policy in the Western world. The philo-Semitic trends in the modern era are either "Christian," in the noblest sense of the word, founded on the consciousness of the Judeo-Christian spiritual affinity, or anti-clerical, combating Christianity, even its Jewish roots, while at the same time championing the cause of the Jew as the victim of clerical abuse and religious fanaticism. The humanitarian tendencies regard Jews as human beings entitled to human rights; the socialist brand of philo-Semitism eliminates any distinction between the Jewish and Gentile working-man, while the Zionist philo-Semite wishes to integrate the resurrected Jewish people into the family of sovereign nations. However, some criticism with regard to Jewish life is not lacking in the philo-Semitic movements. They either attack the economic structure of Jewish life, or demand the abandonment of Jewish separate existence and the elimination of its national historic elements from Jewish life. "To the Jews as individuals everything," declared Clermont-Tonnerre, a convinced democrat and champion of Jewish emancipation, in the French Parliament in 1789, "to the Jews as a nation nothing." Some philo-Semites aim at the disappearance of the Jewish Community through assimilation, thus solving the problem of anti-Semitism; others believe that the immigration of sections of Jews into the ancient land of Israel or some other territory would offer a final solution to the problem of Jewish existence among the nations. The events of the Nazi era manifested the dangerous implications of any notion of a final solution for a "minority" problem; this latter theory is no longer advanced by philo-Semites.

The transition from the idea of mere toleration to full emancipation is exemplified in the famous letter of George Washington to the Hebrew Congregation of Newport (1790). "The citizens of the United States of America have the right to applaud themselves for having given to mankind examples of an enlarged and liberal policy worthy of imitation. All possess alike liberty of conscience and immunities of citizenship. It is now no more that toleration is spoken of, as if it were by the indulgence of one class of people that another enjoyed the exercise of their inherent natural rights, for happily the Government of the United States, which gives to bigotry no sanction, to persecution no assistance, requires only that they who live under its protection should demean themselves as good citizens in giving it on all occasions their effectual support."[166]

The spokesmen of Emancipation adduced a variety of motives to further their cause. Wilhelm von Humboldt, famous German statesman and author, a noble champion of Jewish Emancipation in Germany, affirmed that "Judaism and Christianity, if viewed under the right aspect, belonged to the same spiritual category, and the notion that Christianity is the opposite of Judaism must be universally discarded. Only an immediate concession of full and equal rights to the Jew is just, politic and consistent. We must abandon inhuman and prejudiced ways of thinking, by which a man is judged not by his actual characteristics, but by his origin or religion, and he is regarded not as an individual, but as a part of a race, whose attributes he necessarily possesses. The state is not an educational, but a political institution. No legislation system in favour of the Jew will achieve its end, if it uses the word 'Jewish,' otherwise than in its religious connotation. Loss of citizenship should be imposed on Jews only in cases where the same penalty would be imposed on Christians."[167]

The failings of the Jews are ascribed by philo-Semites to the unjust treatment they received — a cardinal point in philo-Semitic argumentation. In his famous treatise, *Political Emancipation of the Jews* (1787), Count Mirabeau asserted that "Holland and England have been enriched for several hundreds of years by the Jews who were driven from these two kingdoms (Spain and Portugal), and who brought with them not only their industry, but often considerable wealth. It is in those countries that the Jews have most nearly gained rights of human beings and of citizens, and it is also in those countries that they are the most loyal servants of the State. What conclusion can one reach, after taking into account the actual condition the Jews in Europe, other than that the better they are treated, the more valuable citizens they make."[168]

An early champion of emancipation was John Toland (1670-1722), British deist whose publication *Reasons for Naturalising the Jews in Great Britain and Ireland, on the same Foot with all other Nations,* bearing the sub-title "A defence of the Jews against all vulgar prejudices in all Countries," anticipated, by more than half a century, Moses Mendelssohn's effort for the emancipation of the Jews. The pamphlet, which is extremely rare, has recently been republished in a bilingual English-German edition. The republication was possibly prompted by the desire to rectify the distorted image of the Jews in Germany, still lingering on from the days of the Nazi era.

Reasons for Naturalising the Jews is a denunciation of the persecutions to which Anglo-Jewry had been subjected during the period between their admission in 1070 by William the Conqueror and their expulsion in 1290 under Edward I. Toland was primarily appealing to the idea of tolerance; but he went further and challenged all the arguments brought against the Jews in opposition to their readmission to Britain and their naturalization. Toland used the main arguments of the philo-Semites; Jews were not parasites but would make obedient and loyal citizens; if they were at the moment engaged in financial undertakings only, this was because all other occupations were closed to them. In the past, moreover, they had been farmers, seafarers and soldiers; they had no national characteristics; they did not seek power; they would favour freedom of conscience; an increase in population was beneficial to the coun-

130

try. There is no argument in Jewish defence of the eighteenth and nineteenth centuries that was not anticipated in Toland's pamphlet.

Toland appealed to the bishops and archbishops to consider the case of the Jews especially to mark their noble ancestry. "Your piety not only leads you to promote the good of all mankind; even of your very enemies, but to look with particular eyes of affection upon the Jewish Nation. . . . By them you are undeniably come to the knowledge of one God, from them you have received the holy Scriptures, of them is descended Moses and the Prophets, with Jesus and all the Apostles: nor is it from any other pattern or original, but their Hierarchy, that the distinguishing posts you now fill in the Church, can be illustrated or defended; and the same holds as true of Liturgies, Tythes, Vestments, and Ceremonies. Your learning convinces You, that this people deserves not that contempt under which they so generally labour at present; since no other Nation can produce more authentic monuments of its rise and antiquity, of its religious and political State, nay, or of its military and heroic exploits . . . all of us proud to bear the proper Names of the very people, we no less inhumanly, than inconsistently hate and despise . . . I may not doubt, My Lords, but that, as you are the advocates of the Jews at the Throne of Heaven, so you will be their friends and protectors in the British Parliament."[168a]

Toland's pamphlet is of great value as a document of Jewish history; it helped to create a climate of philo-Semitic opinion that made a vital contribution to the movement for emancipation of the Jews. Toland may be counted among the most prominent philo-Semitic thinkers of the pre-emancipation era. His thought was based on the philosophy demanding separation of Church and State, espousing the idea of tolerance and furthering sympathetic Christian interest in Judaism, its teachings, and in those who professed it.

Toland also adduced the philo-Semitic argument concerning the benefits which the economic activity of the Jews brings to

131

the country. He ascribed the decline of Spain to its expulsion of the Jews and considered Holland's tolerance towards the Jews as one of the reasons for its prosperity.

In his essay on "The Civil Disabilities of the Jews," T.B. Macaulay, celebrated English historian, essayist, statesman and champion of Jewish Emancipation, based his plea on the assertion that government is in no way connected with the private views and habits of the individual citizen. Its object is to secure property, keep the peace and to compel citizens to settle their disputes by arbitration instead of settling them by blows. People who are not interested in fulfilling these tasks should have no share in the powers which exist for the purpose of securing property and maintaining order. "But why a man would be less fit to exercise those powers because he wears a beard, because he does not eat ham, because he goes to the synagogue on Saturdays instead of going to the church on Sundays, we cannot conceive. The points of difference between Christianity and Judaism have very much to do with man's fitness to be a bishop or a rabbi. But they have no more to do with his fitness to be a magistrate, a legislator, or a minister of finance, or to be a cobbler."

As to the shortcomings of the Jews, Macaulay asserted in a memorable passage, that the Jew is what we made him. "Foreign attachments are the fruit of domestic misrule. It has always been the trick of bigots to make their subjects miserable at home, and then to complain that they look for relief abroad; to divide society, and to wonder that it is not united; to govern as if a section of the state were the whole, and to censure the other sections of the state for their want of patriotic spirit. If the Jews have not felt towards England like children, it is because she has treated them like a stepmother. There is no feeling which more certainly develops itself in the minds of men living under tolerably good government than the feeling of patriotism. Since the beginning of the world, there never was any nation, or any large portion of any nation, not cruelly oppressed, which was wholly destitute of that feeling. To make it, therefore, ground of accusation against a class of men, that

132

they are not patriotic, is the most vulgar legerdemain of sophistry. It is the logic which the wolf employs against the lamb. It is to accuse the mouth of the stream of poisoning the source . . . The English Jews are, as far as we can see, precisely what our government has made them. They are precisely what any sect, what any class of men, treated as they have been treated, would have been."[169]

The mood of the enlightened attitude to the Jews can be gauged from the determination to abolish shameful anti-Jewish restriction, considered an insult to the dignity of man and a disgraceful sign of inhumanity. Characteristic is the proclamation dated August 1797, abolishing the ghetto of Padua after occupation by the French and renaming it Via Libera. The Central Government of the Paduan Delta Districts decreed: "First, that the Hebrews are at liberty to live in any street they please; secondly, that the barbarous and meaningless name of Ghetto, which designates the street which they have been inhabiting hitherto, shall be substituted by that of Via Libera; a copy of these present decisions shall be sent to all the district municipalities so that they may be executed by the respective police departments in the most convenient manner. Padua, Fruttidor II, year V of the French Republic and year I of Italian liberty."[170]

PHILO-SEMITES AND
CHRISTIAN ZIONISTS

The "black" memory of the Jewish people is, as a rule, much better than the "white" one. They remember tenaciously their enemies for thousands of years; their numerous friends, admirers and well-wishers do not fare so well in their collective record. To recall the role of some of them in shaping their fortunes in the modern era is to discharge a debt of honour.

Pierre van Paassen, a Dutch-Canadian journalist (1895-1968), was one of the staunchest Christian believers in the urgent need for a Jewish State in whose interest he wrote several best sellers, including *The Forgotten Ally*. He was national chairman of the Jabotinsky-sponsored Committee for a Jewish Army during World War II. In 1927 he insisted that the Jews should be evacuated from Poland and from all Eastern Europe at no matter what cost. They should be directed to Palestine, in their millions if possible. "Save their lives! There is no time to lose. If left in Eastern Europe, masses of Jews are doomed to die if not of hunger then by persecution." He uttered that ghastly prophecy after an extensive trip to Poland as a journalist, and in the same vein, time after time. Emigration of Jews from Eastern Europe was demanded not only by anti-Semites and Zionist leaders, but also by honest philo-Semites who sensed the danger inherent in unprotected Jewish existence in areas of Jewish mass-settlement. But American and European Jewish leaders refused to believe in what he prophesied, and less than twenty years later practically all the Jews of Eastern Europe had been killed by the Nazis, aided by local Jew-haters. Van Paassen was able to issue this solemn warning not only because he was one of the most remarkable Christian philo-Semites of our time, but because he knew and loved Judaism while remaining a dedicated Protestant minister, and also because he did not confine his Jewish contacts to the "leaders" but had a way of getting close to the masses of the people. "I always took the Jewish people seriously," he wrote in *The Forgotten Ally*. "Though prone to renounce all distinctions of race, nationality, and religion from my youth onward, I nevertheless identified myself voluntarily and steadily with Jewish people's national cause to an extent not seen, as far as I know, in the case of any other contemporary gentile. I do not claim any merit in this matter. My deeper acquaintance with Judaism and the Jewish people proved a greater blessing to me in a quite personal sense than any honors, recognition, or reward could have furnished. Without it, I am sure the course of my intellectual development would have been sensibly different."[171]

One of the most steadfast friends of Zionism was *Jan Christian Smuts,* South African statesman, soldier and philosopher. As a member of the Imperial War Cabinet, Smuts was one of the architects of the Balfour Declaration and, through good days and bad, remained unswerving in his faith in the Jewish National Home. His allegiance to the Zionist ideals was permanent and he remained a lifelong, devoted champion of Jewish rights and the Zionist cause. His concern with the fate of the Jewish people, his veneration for the wisdom and beauty of the Hebrew Bible, made him one of the most illustrious Gentile representatives of philo-Semitic and pro-Zionist thinking in our days. The settlement of Kfar Jochanan (Jan Smuts) in Israel will remain a living monument to the special place which the memory of Jan Smuts ever holds in Jewish hearts.

Smuts consistently upheld the historical significance of the Balfour Declaration, the most decisive event in Jewish history since Cyrus' Proclamation of Return in 538 B.C.E. This Declaration, Smuts wrote in the foreword to a Commemoration Brochure, published by the South African Zionist Federation on the tenth anniversary of the Balfour Declaration, is one of the notable events of history, and its true importance will be realised more and more in the decades to come, when much else in the history of the great war will have become but a dim memory. It is based on historic justice. It constitutes a great act of historic reparation and renews once more a promise which is basic to Jewish history. "The Balfour Declaration was the renewal and fulfilment of the promise; it showed historic justice triumphant at last across the long stretch of centuries, it was a great act of fulfilment after almost two thousand years of doubt and denial! In its great setting of history it is one of the most wonderful confirmations of the moral and spiritual principle of human affairs."

Throughout many political vicissitudes, General Smuts remained faithful to the pledge he had helped to formulate. Together with Lord Balfour and Mr. Lloyd George, he signed a letter of protest to *The Times* when Lord Passfield's notorious White Paper curtailing Jewish immigration to Palestine and prohibiting further acquisition of land was issued in 1930. The letter urged that steps should be taken to make it clear that "Britain has not weakened in a task to which her honour is pledged." Smuts intervened with an indignant protest to the British Prime Minister, Ramsay Macdonald, declaring that, as one of those responsible for the Balfour Declaration, he felt bound to warn the British Government against defaulting on "a debt of honour."

In a memorandum submitted in 1946 to the Anglo-American Committee, then inquiring into the situation in Palestine, he told the Committee that, "as one who took an active part in the framing of the Declaration," he looked upon it as a solemn and sacrosanct document giving assurances to the Jewish people which "should not be abridged or tampered with more than is absolutely necessary under all the circumstances of the case."

When, finally, a Jewish State was proclaimed in Israel in May 1948, Smuts wrote to Ben Gurion, "I, as one who took part in the original formulation of the policy of the Jewish National Home, rejoice that even more has been achieved than the most optimistic thought possible." Among the first governments to announce recognition of the State of Israel was General Smuts's — it was the first government in the British Commonwealth to do so.

Dr. Chaim Weizmann, writing in his book *Trial and Error* about his own pro-Declaration efforts, has this to say of Smuts: "I had gone into his office with a letter of introduction. Utterly unknown to him, I was received in the friendliest fashion and given a most sympathetic hearing" — in contrast the cool reception from some influential Jewish figures that Dr. Weizmann mentions. "A sort of warmth of understanding radiated from him, and he assured me heartily that something would be done in connection with Palestine and the Jewish people. He treated the problem with eager thought, and one might say with affection." Recalling those critical times, during a speech in Cape Town in 1926, General Smuts said: "I remember the travail and the labour that was required to secure the formula of the National Home. I remember when, in the War Cabinet, it was discussed many a week, many a month, and there was a great struggle of ideas centering round this principle — a struggle in which opposition of the National Home and the formula came from two sides. One side was the people who argued: 'Why should we declare in favour of a National Home; why should we go against the Arabs? . . .' Then we had the opposition from some of the Jews themselves. It is always like that . . . you are always wounded in the house of your friend."

Smuts's sympathy for the cause of the Jews may be traced to several powerful motives. As a member of a small nation, he had profound understanding for the aspirations of the Jewish people, scattered and dispersed across the face of the earth, to have a homeland of their own. The Boer, fighting for independence and survival, felt deep sympathy for the Jews' endeavour to retain their identity and achieve national sovereignty. "As for me," he said, at the Weizmann Forest dinner in 1949 in

London, "a Boer with vivid memories of the recent past, the Jewish case appealed with peculiar force." Smuts also saw a distinct parallel between the strivings of his own people and that of ancient Israel. "The history of South Africa," he uttered in the course of an address on Dingaan's Day at Roodebank, Transvaal, in December 1924, is like a chapter out of the Bible. "When thinking of the providence of God, it was not enough to read of the wanderings of the children of Israel in the wilderness. They (the Afrikaners) had their own history. In the last hundred years they had witnessed great things in South Africa. They had seen great miracles. Their children, when they grew up, would know that the country had been bitterly fought for, and was a country with a great history behind it."

Smuts's pro-Zionism was inspired by a profound veneration of the Hebrew Bible and the creative quality of the Jewish mind, exemplified in thinkers like Maimonides and Spinoza. As a lover of Scripture, he felt spiritual kinship with the people of the Book. "The older I get the more of a Hebraist I become. They knew God those Jews. They understood the need of the soul. There is no literature like the great psalms. Then comes Isaiah; I put the Bible above Shakespeare, who has, to me, the deficiency of being without religion. I need not remind you that the white people of South Africa, and especially the older Dutch population, has been brought up almost entirely on Jewish tradition. The Old Testament has been the very marrow of Dutch culture here in South Africa. In my own case I may say that whenever I see anything great or anything really moving, my mind always passes into the language of the Old Testament, which is the greatest language ever spoken by the tongue of man."

Smuts was a passionate believer in historic justice. In his world-view of "wholeness" (Holism) the triumph of righteousness in the affairs of man plays a fundamental part. In words that will ring down the ages, Smuts, in one of his last great speeches, delivered in 1949 in London at the Weizmann Memorial Forest dinner, proclaimed his fervent belief in historic justice: Something was due from the Christians to the Jews, not only as compensation for unspeakable persecutions, but as the people who produced the divine leader to whom we Christians owe the highest allegiance. Moral and religious motives thus reinforced the political consideration. "No finer effort of recovery and restoration has been made anywhere in the world in post-war times. It is blessed work, blessed of heaven, whatever hostile critics may say about it."

Smuts had an almost mystical regard for the powers inherent in the Jewish people, particularly for their spiritual quality, their religious devotion, their intellectual genius; he felt happy at the thought that the agony of the people of the Book was coming to an end. In a memorable address delivered in November 1919, he declared: "I look forward to the Spinozas and the Maimonides of the future. There is no reason why Israel should not hold aloft once more the banner of the spirit among the other peoples of the earth. That was your mission in the past; I hope that will be your mission in the future. I mean the universal language of the human heart . . . the language of the Psalms and the Prophets is the basis of our culture in South Africa, and therefore we are standing together on a common platform, the greatest spiritual platform the world has ever seen. On that platform I want us to build the future South Africa. It is our ambition to see in South Africa a country of men and women, where the poor man is as great as the rich man, where the great ideals which you find expressed in the prophets of the Old Testament will find their realisation, where it will be recognised that the greatest thing on earth is the human soul."

Smuts upheld the belief that the Jews would integrate into South African life while retaining their own spiritual traditions to their own advantage, and to the benefit of South Africa. "The Jews came to South Africa with great traditions, fine ideals and a tenacity of purpose which no one can wrest from them. So long as the Jewish community respect their own past, they will make good citizens."

Smuts frequently expressed horror about the Nazi persecutions and the apathy which had overtaken Europe in the face of

139

unprecedented happenings. "Humanity is disgraced as never before in the records of civilization. The Jews are once more the heart, the crux, the spearpoint of the whole human issue." Against those British leaders who tried to minimize the significance of the Balfour Declaration, Smuts proclaimed that the case for the Balfour Declaration had thus become overwhelmingly stronger. "Instead of the horror of new ghettos in the twentieth century, let us carry out our promise and open up the National Home . . . We dare not fold our hands without insulting the human spirit itself. The Balfour Declaration is not dead. It still stands on rock foundations, and the structure that will arise from it will be greater than the Declaration itself."

It was the mystical element in Smuts's personality, mingled with his realistic insight, that endowed him with a special spiritual quality, the hidden source of his power and influence. In his comprehensive work *The Balfour Declaration* (London, 1961) Leonard Stein discusses the problem why in the postwar years Smuts went out of his way to identify himself personally with the unpopular Balfour Declaration, and to use all his energy to persuade the British authorities to honour it in full. Stein holds that Smuts's consistent and enthusiastic support for the Zionist cause is partly due to a visit which Smuts paid to Palestine in 1918 at the request of the War Cabinet. He saw the Holy Land with the eyes of one belonging to a people steeped in Hebrew scripture. "I could feel how that apparently deserted country, so forbidding and grand, gave birth to the greatest religion on earth, the loftiest religious spirit in history. It required something rugged, something terrible to have bred and to have created that literature and that spirit which has been, perhaps, the most powerful influence in the history of the human race. Palestine is a forbidding country, just as the Karroo is a forbidding country, but with my African heart that wild country appeals to every fibre in my being, the air and the spirit of Palestine penetrated me. Your little people has had a civilising mission on the world, second, perhaps, to none among

140

the nations of the earth . . . and I do not see why they should not once more play a great part in the history of the world."

Men of goodwill, both Jews and Gentiles, remember Smuts, a great South African and a noble Christian, for his broad humanitarian vision, his devotion to the cause of justice, his love of Zion and his distinguished role in restoring Israel to its Land of Promise. His prophetic words have come true in our days: "The structure that will arise from it, will be greater than the Declaration itself."[172]

One of the most illustrious philo-Semites in the field of statesmanship was *Thomas G. Masaryk,* Czech scholar and patriot, founder and first president of Czechoslovakia. Masaryk related how he was originally affected by anti-Semitic feelings, like all the other students in his class in a small town in Moravia, where children were admonished by their mothers not to go near the house of Jews, because Jews were using the blood of Christian children. In high school, there was a single Jewish fellow student who was ill treated by his fellow students in an "unchristian" manner. It was sympathy for this student that drew him away from anti-Semitic ideas. It happened once, during an excursion, that this Jewish student disappeared from the table at sunset, and when his fellows went to look for him, they found him praying. "All at once I forgot to tease him and to poke fun at him. While we were enjoying ourselves, Leopold did not forget his praying. From that moment on my anti-Semitism suffered a shock, even though it was not fully overcome as yet. My parents then moved to Goding, and I had occasion to study the ghetto of that town and a number of Jews living there. My acquaintances with the Jews brought about a feeling of friendship — a friendship both faithful and full of beauty. In Brunn and Vienna the circle of my Jewish friends became larger and larger, so that prejudice vanished into the thin air, even though my childhood days would claim their toll from time to time. Past experience is mighty and dreadful. By becoming acquainted with each other, by living together, by economic mutual relations, blood will be forgotten. A new generation brought up in a public school cannot conceive of anti-Semitism in the form in which we had conceived it, when they had their Jewish ghetto and we Christians had ours . . . Would that I may unmake all that anti-Semitism caused me to do in my childhood days."

Masaryk became famous for his courageous defence of Leopold Hilsner, a Jew from Polna, Bohemia, accused of ritual murder in 1899. The case was fought with a virulence which almost equalled the bitterness that surged about the Dreyfus affair. The enemies of the Jews became the enemies of Masaryk.

Masaryk's philo-Semitism is expressed in a saying which characterizes the sentiments of a man who cannot overlook the connection between the Jewish community which he knows, and his belief in the Saviour of Christendom who originated among the Jews. "I am convinced that he who has Jesus for his guide cannot be an anti-Semite. That is clear to me because Jesus was a Jew, because the apostles were Jews, because ancient Christianity, especially Catholicism, has much in itself that is essentially Jewish. No. If I accept Jesus, I cannot be an anti-Semite. I can be only one or the other, Christian or anti-Semite."

Masaryk had a positive attitude not only towards Judaism as an abstract concept, but towards the Jews as a living community. "The Jews do not care for alcohol, therefore suicide is less frequent among them. Their joy of life, clinging to the religion of their forebears, practical optimism and spirituality make them strong."

Masaryk regarded Zionism primarily from a moral standpoint; as the fulfilment of a noble dream, "I see in Zionism a drop of oil of the Prophets." He did not think that all the Jews should go to Palestine, but maintained that every individual has the right to make his own decision. When visiting the Czech colony in Palestine (1927), he said: "I hope that the Jewish people in Palestine will lead a life of freedom, and that God will bless this work of reconstruction." His son Jan Masaryk, Foreign Minister of the Czechoslovak Government in exile, gave frequent expressions of philo-Semitic ideas in the spirit of his father. Speaking at the session of the National Conference for Palestine (New York City, 1939), he said: "The Jews are a small minority everywhere, and without tolerance and decent treatment of minorities, democracy cannot survive. . . . One of the most important pillars of hope in these dark hours is the idea of the national home; a homeland for defenceless people who for centuries were never masters of their own destiny." At a mass rally (1941), he said: "I remember the Jews of my mother country, locked in a ghetto, with the same sorrow as I remember my own mother"[173] To him, the Jewish problem was one aspect of the general struggle of humanity for freedom. There can be no profounder and more deeply-felt pro-Jewish sentiment than is expressed in this comparison between a man's affection for his mother and the loving memory of the persecuted Jews of his country.

The name of the Masaryks shines brightly in the firmament of philo-Semitism throughout the ages. It will remain evergreen in the memory of the people whom Thomas Masaryk esteemed as the nation of his Saviour and Jan revered as a son reveres his mother.

Dr. Paul Tillich (1886-1965), an illustrious friend of Jews and Judaism and a staunch opponent of Nazi doctrines, was one of the most distinguished theologians and philosophers of our age and a founder of Christian existential philosophy within the field of Protestant thought. He served as Professor of Theology at German universities until 1933, when he lost his position at the University of Frankfurt because of his opposition to Nazism. On his arrival in America he declared that he had the great honour to be the first "Aryan" professor dismissed from a German university by the Nazi authorities.

The famous American theologian Reinhold Niebuhr invited him to a chair at the renowned Union Theological Seminary in Manhattan. As teacher and lecturer, Tillich proved to be one of the most creative thinkers of our age and exercised a profound influence on contemporary religious thought. The influence of Tillich has grown during the past years, extending far beyond the circle of the religiously interested. He always found the face-to-face encounter, involved in lecturing and teaching, a source of greatest anxiety and greatest happiness. "I have always," he writes, "walked up to a desk or pulpit with fear and trembling, but the contact with the audience gives me a pervasive sense of joy, the joy of a creative union, of giving and taking, even if the audience is not vocal. But when it becomes vocal in periods of questions and discussions, this exchange is for me the most inspiring part of the occasion. Question and answer, yes and no, in an actual disputation, this original form, of all the dialectics, is the most adequate form of my own thinking."[173a]

Tillich's work is of vital interest to those concerned with relevant theological thinking. The scarcity of Jewish theological thought is a characteristic defect of contemporary Judaism. Rare are the books of Jewish interest which provide guidance for the genuine seeker after God and which give a lead for meaningful Jewish religious existence. Thinking Jews realize the crisis of faith which besets this modern age, and feel the need for a re-statement and re-affirmation of Judaism in contemporary terms. Thoughtful and intelligent men cannot be permanently content with an exposition of their religion that is no longer adequate for modern needs. They will want a compelling system of religious thought to justify religious practice; they will demand a theology that is not antiquated and unscientific, but seeks to face the modern advances of knowledge and discoveries of truth. There is in the world of Jewish religious thought no elaborate system of theology, comparable with the massive works of Barth, Brunner, Niebuhr or Tillich. But there is today a stirring in the ranks of Jewish thinkers who set themselves against superficial liberalism and atheistic humanism which emptied Judaism of its profounder contents. Where crisis theology takes a despairing view of human life, it runs counter to Jewish religious tradition, but where, as in the case of Tillich among the Christians, and Rosenzweig and Buber among the Jews, it seeks deeper levels of truth, a more genuine communion with the living God and a closer relation between religion and life, it leads to sanctification of life on the highest level. Tillich articulated a new concern for man's practical problems in a dangerous age. The fruitful insight of his work will remain a permanent heritage of all men who grapple with the problem of religious existence in this modern era.

Profound utterances on Jewish history, the Jewish fate, Jewish life in every age and particularly on the holocaust, are to be found in an interview with Paul Tillich granted shortly before his death. In this interview, Tillich expressed noble thoughts representing the highest reaches of philo-Semitism, deep understanding for the unique fate and fortune of the Jewish people, for the cosmic quality of their history, the meaning of their suffering for their own and mankind's betterment. Suffering uncovers that depth of our being which enables us to challenge evil and to overcome suffering, to work for the fulfilment of the ultimate goal, which is the goal of history. You see, said Paul Tillich, you cannot just ask: why did it happen to us? It happens to all, and it is still taking place. We do have particular questions about the nature of the world in which we live. "Now, there is the revelation in Judaism that gives you an answer; and there is the revelation in Christianity that helps me in understanding what happened. But we each have to reach our own answers; and while they will agree, your students must discover the answer of Judaism. Nevertheless, there are some answers that I can give, and that I have given before. They deal with the fact that Hitler represented everything to which Judaism was opposed, that it simply had to be the opponent of the false nationalism which we find in National Socialism."

Space and time, Tillich teaches, fight against one another in the world. But pagans make space the ultimate value; their gods are tied to space which they defend against other gods. They do not believe in one God, because they cannot believe in a unique God. And belief in space leads to belief in blood and race and nation. It also leads to war; nations who believe in themselves live next to other nations — and space wants to expand. While it is good to believe in one's self and land, if that

145

becomes the most important belief, it leads to a tragic existence that always remains imprisoned in space. Then came the Jews and announced the victory of time over space. The command to Abraham to leave the land of his fathers and his father's home meant giving up the gods of blood and soil, of tribe and nation. For Judaism did not teach that its God was more powerful, that he ruled over all gods. It taught that God was unique; that there are no other gods; that God is not bound to any place in the world and space, but that He rules time. The temple could be destroyed, Palestine could cease to be a Jewish State — God was not affected by this, and His people were not destroyed by it. And the God of time is the God of history, who has given history a goal and a purpose, and who has given a task to Israel; to fight the belief in the gods of space. For Judaism teaches ethical monotheism; and ethical monotheism means universal justice — one justice, one God, one humanity.

The Jewish people, Tillich affirmed, is uniquely the people of time. It represents the eternal fight between time and space. It stayed alive even when living space was constantly taken from it by the other nations of the world. Seen just as a people in space, it has had a tragic history; but seen as the people of time, it stands beyond tragedy, for it is an eternal people. "It will always be persecuted (this applies also to the true Christian in the Church who fights the battle of time over space), because its mere existence challenges those pagan gods found within might, imperialism, injustice, demonic ecstasy — personified by the Nazis and similar groups. There will always be those who hate and fear the one God and those who follow Him. And there will always be the need for Israel to be the witness of one God. All Jews and Christians who believe in the One God and in universal justice have to confront this evil in the world. Church and synagogue must be united here in fighting for the realisation of God's justice, I mean this in the Hebrew sense; the word tz'dakah must be understood as creative justice. And part of Jewish suffering, and part of Jewish greatness, is that the Jew has historically aligned himself with universal justice, and has been the great opponent of evil. Jewish students

146

should read the prophets: let them read Second Isaiah and Jeremiah .... We cannot fully judge what happened in the camps .... We were not inside the camps. And so I cannot support some scholars' indictment of Jewish leaders. Of course there were some who faltered. But when I think of the greatness that was revealed there ...."

For Paul Tillich, great theologian of Christianity, the fate of the Jews was not just a matter that concerned the Jewish community; he saw it as a challenge to all humanity. Tillich once stated that he had not at first approved of the Zionist movement. He had thought it a good thing that a group — the Jews — should survive in the modern world to represent a religious faith independent of patriotism, whose kingdom — since they had no country — could not be of this world. But it was then pointed out to him by a Jewish friend that he was being quite unfair to "the petty bourgeois Cohens and Levis" in expecting them to be Moseses and Isaiahs, and in restricting them to the status of aliens in countries in which they were still not accepted on quite the same basis as other natives and in which they were liable to anti-Semitic panics. Dr. Tillich was so struck by the justice of this that he at once joined a Zionist organization.[174]

The most prominent gentile Zionists of the modern period — Lloyd George, A.J. Balfour and Winston Churchill — were inspired by the Bible to believe that Britain was the right country to liberate Palestine and that the Jews, descendants of Biblical Israel, should be reinstated in the land of their fathers. There were of course other motives, such as British Imperial interest, the desire to gain all-Jewish support and the wish to remove the cause of anti-Semitism by creating a Jewish State, which prompted British politicians to champion Jewish claims to Palestine. *Winston Churchill's* deep and inner relationship to the Bible is reflected in the moving words which he spoke on Mount Scopus in Jerusalem in 1921, on receiving a Scroll of the Law from the Late Chief Rabbi in Mandatory Palestine, Abraham Isaac Kook. He turned to the thousands of Jews assembled and, holding the Torah, said: "This sacred book which contains

147

truth accepted by Jews and Christians alike is very dear to me, and your gift will remain in my family as an imperishable souvenir." It is through a deep insight into the eternal religious values that he came to the conclusion that "we owe to the Jews in the Christian revelation a system of ethics which, even if it were entirely separated from the supernatural, would be the most precious possession of mankind, worth, in fact, the fruits of all other wisdom and learning together." Stressing thus the importance of Christian ethics in the contemporary world and its roots in the system of ethics and the faith of the Jews, Churchill crowns his argument with the affirmation: "On that system and by that faith there has been built out of the wreck of the Roman Empire the whole of our existing civilization."[175] "I am in full sympathy with the historical aspirations of the Jews," wrote Winston Churchill in 1908. "The restoration to them of a centre of racial and political integrity would be a tremendous event in the history of the world. No two cities have counted more with mankind than Athens and Jerusalem. Their messages in religion, philosophy and art have been the main guiding lights of modern faith and culture," he asserted in his War Memoirs. In his message to the Hebrew University in Jerusalem on its twenty-fifth anniversary, Winston Churchill expressed his hope and belief that the University "as it stands aloft on Mount Scopus, will cast a mellow, shining light around it, and proclaim to a distracted generation true progress, not only in literature, scholarship and science, but in those tolerant, comprehending humanities, without which all the rest is only mockery to human beings."

What attracted Churchill to the ideal of a Jewish renaissance in Palestine and to the rebirth of the Jewish nation? It was his profound sense of history, his vivid historical imagination. "The coming into being of a Jewish State, in Palestine," he declared in the House of Commons early in 1949, "is an event in world history to be viewed in the perspective not over a generation or a century, but in the perspective of a thousand, two thousand or even three thousand years. This is an event in world history."

Churchill was the first great statesman to grasp the grand Herzlian Zionist conception. He constantly and openly voiced his horror of anti-Semitism, insisting in World War II that retribution for the Nazi crimes against the Jews must be a primary war aim.

Winston Churchill ranks amongst the greatest friends the Jewish people had in their long history of suffering and achievement. His philo-Semitic sentiments were imbued with profound sympathy for the people of the Bible, with deep devotion to the cause of Zion Redeemed — one of the most worthy political causes of the modern era.

PHILO-SEMITIC TRENDS IN LITERATURE AND THOUGHT

The image of the Jew in the literature of the Christian world is complex and contradictory. The good and the bad Jew, hero and villain, prophet and infidel, Judas Maccabeus, zealous fighter for a holy cause, Judas Iscariot, traitor who sells his master for money, exist side by side in Christian consciousness. The deeds of the Maccabees fired the imagination of poets who glorified heroic martyrdom. Calderon, Longfellow, Otto Ludwig found in the Maccabean exploits themes for poetry and drama, while Judas Iscariot figures as a favourite type in the Christian Passion play until today. Western literature embraces the dark figure of Shylock, the usurer, and the shining image of Nathan the Wise, Lessing's hero of humanitarianism. The Jew is loathed for the crime of deicide and, in a different context, revered as the recipient of the first revelation, the son of the people of Christ, the agent of ultimate salvation for all mankind. The Jew as Christ-killer and usurer, as patriarch and prophet, existed side-by-side in Christian literature. The "Wandering Jew," popularized by Eugene Sue's novel, is condemned to eternal restlessness for the crucifixion of Christ, yet is ultimately saved, because the "gifts and calling of God are without repentance." The Economic Jew, the wealthy Jewish merchant and money-lender, is depicted in those works of Chaucer, Marlowe and Shakespeare which reflect current anti-Semitic bias. There is the poor Jew, the old clothes pedlar, the "smous" of South African literature; the romantic Jew of Puritan imagination, Byron's Biblical hero, sitting by the rivers of Babylon, weeping for Zion, hanging his harp on the willows and remembering Jerusalem as his chief joy. The patriarchal Jew, such as Isaac in Scott's *Ivanhoe,* a venerable figure, father of a beautiful daughter, Rebecca, personifying the traditional image of the romantic Jewess. There is the Jew of the Emancipation era, sharing the duties and privileges of his newly-won fatherland with his Christian fellow citizen, a full member of his new nation, distinguished from his compatriots only by his Jewish persuasion, but no longer separated by civic discrimination and voluntary self-segregation. There is the heroic Jew of two types: the patriotic Jew who fights for his new fatherland and lays down his life in defence of the common home which he shares with his Christian fellows. Another type, the harbinger of Israel reborn, such as Disraeli's David Alroy, and George Eliot's Daniel Deronda, wishes by his personal valour to give his people a new status among the nations of the world.

All these types of Jews comprise the composite image which the Western world has formed of the sons of the ancient people of Israel who resided in their midst. These types partly reflected, partly moulded, the attitude adopted towards the Jew in the Christian world, an attitude frequently anti-Semitic, at times philo-Semitic. The anti-Semitic tendencies reflected two theories: the anti-Semitism of the Church, depicting the Jews as cursed for the guilt of Christ's passion and hating the Christians, Shakespeare's Shylock and Marlowe's Barabas, presenting a hostile image of the Jew in literature; the racial anti-Semitism of European nationalism, considering the Jew as a permanent alien, unassimilable to the general body politic of the nation, such as the notorious Veitl Itzik in Gustav Freytag's *Soll und Haben.* On the other hand, two distinct philo-Semitic trends arose in literature resulting from the personal contact with the Jew, made possible through the political, cultural and economic emancipation of the inhabitants of

151

the ghetto: The Jew is now seen as the persecuted, homeless victim of fanaticism and intolerance yet faithful bearer of his noble ideals, such as Lessing's Nathan. From this flows the second philo-Semitic idea: the need to restore the homeless wanderer to his ancestral soil — the romantic Zionist dream — George Eliot's Daniel Deronda.

The most illustrious name among the representatives of romantic philo-Semitism in the realm of poetry is that of Lord Byron. Lord Byron, a lover of freedom, distinguished himself by the personal sacrifice he made for the cause of Greek liberty. The devoted philo-Hellen was also a convinced philo-Semite. At the request of his friend Douglas, he wrote his *Hebrew Melodies* as the text for a musical composition by Isaac Nathan. As a romantic poet, Byron appreciated the inspirational values of Jewish life; as a champion of liberty, he desired freedom for the Jews and the re-establishment of Israel in the cradle of its nationhood. His sentimental sympathy for Jewish return and resurrection is echoed in his wonderful Hebraic poems, some of them reaching lofty heights of emotional sympathy for persecuted Israel.

> Oh, weep for those that wept by Babel's stream,
> Whose shrines are desolate, whose land a dream;
> Weep for the harp of Judah's broken shell;
> Mourn — where their God hath dwelt the godless dwell!
>
> And where shall Israel lave her bleeding feet?
> And when shall Zion's songs again seem sweet?
> And Judah's melody once more rejoice
> The hearts that leap'd before its heavenly voice?
>
> Tribes of the wandering foot and weary breast,
> How shall ye flee away and be at rest!
> The wild-dove hath her nest, the fox his cave!
> Mankind their country — Israel but the grave.

Among the Victorians, Robert Browning occupies a special role. In his poems "Holy Cross Day" or "Rabbi Ben Ezra,"

152

Browning passionately protested against religious bigotry and he exalted genuine goodness, irrespective of race and creed. "Holy Cross Day" depicts Jews in Rome once a year forced to attend a particular Church and to hear a special sermon. The narrator relates how the Jews were herded into the Church and imagines what they may have thought on this occasion. They ridicule the proceedings, bewail the lost glory of Israel and sing hopefully of its future grandeur. The poem, a moving testimony to philo-Semitism in the Victorian era, reflects the intense humanitarian faith of the Victorian poet.

> The Lord will have mercy on Jacob yet,
> And again in his border see Israel set.
> When Judah beholds Jerusalem,
> The stranger shall be joined to them;
> To Jacob's House shall the Gentiles cleave,
> So the Prophet saith and his sons believe.
> By the torture, prolonged from age to age,
> By the infamy, Israel's heritage,
> By the Ghetto's plague, by the garb's disgrace,
> By the badge of shame, by the felon's place,
> By the branding tool, the bloody whip
> And the summons to Christian fellowship.

Commenting on Browning's Hebraic sympathies, a Jewish critic observed in 1891 that it might be held a blessing that one of England's greatest poets had shown such sympathetic intelligent comprehension of the claims of the Jewish people. The value of the Hebrew element in Browning's poems is that it does much to remove prejudice, and to place the philosophy of the Jew in its true place among the world's Credos. A Ben Ezra and a Jochanan may supplant a Shylock and a Fagin in public estimation. This is an effect much to be desired.[176]

Similar friendly attitudes were exhibited by other English poets of this period. Tribute to Hebrew culture and learning was paid by Matthew Arnold in his essay on Heine: No account of Heine is complete which does not notice the Jewish element of him. His race he treated with the same freedom with which he treated everything else, but he derived a great force from it and no one knew this better than he himself. He has excellently pointed out how in the sixteenth century there was a double renaissance — a Hellenic renaissance and a Hebrew renaissance — and how both have been great powers ever since. He himself had in him both the spirit of Greece and the spirit of Judaea; both these spirits reach the infinite, which is the true goal of all poetry and all art — the Greek spirit of beauty, the Hebrew spirit of sublimity. By his perfection of literary form, by his love of clearness, by his love of beauty, Heine is Greek; by his intensity, by his untamableness, by his "longing which cannot be uttered," he is Hebrew.[177]

In a poem entitled "On the Russian Persecution of the Jews," Algernon Charles Swinburne expressed deep sympathy for the Jewish victims of the Russian persecution of the Jews in 1882, and uttered passionate words of contempt for so-called "Christians" who by their evil deeds betray their Lord.

> O son of man, by lying tongues adored,
> By slaughterous hands of slaves with feet red-shod
> In carnage deep as ever Christian trod
> Profaned with prayer and sacrifice abhorred
> And incense from the trembling tyrant's horde,
> Brute worshippers or wielders of the rod,
> Most murderous even of all that call thee God,
> Most treacherous even that ever called thee Lord;
> Face loved of little children long ago,
> Head hated of the priests and rulers then,
> If thou see this, or hear these hounds of thine
> Run ravening as the Gadarean swine,
> Say, was not this thy Passion, to foreknow
> In death's worst hour the works of Christian men?

From the thought that Israel has "but the grave" (Byron) flows sympathy for the Jewish people's desire to be restored to independence and a new life. From compassion for the "tribe of the wandering foot and weary breast" follows the ardent longing to bring about Israel's renaissance on its ancestral soil — the Zionist vision. A new phase in philo-Semitic thought and action was the Zionist trend in literature.

The most powerful motive in English philo-Semitism was the romantic sympathy with a Jewish return to Zion. "England, awake! awake! awake! Jerusalem thy sister calls ..." sang William Blake. When one considers the love the British people possessed for the Old Testament, it is not surprising that they should have turned their attention to the idea of Israel's return to the Holy Land. The jewish Historical Society in England published a pamphlet by Henry Jessey, a Baptist minister and a Christian correspondent of Menasse Ben Israel, the Dutch rabbi who paved the way for the resettlement of Jews in England as far back as the year 1655. Here we are told concerning the Jews of Jerusalem, that their brethren abroad among the nations have been willing to uphold them there, that the place should not be left destitute of some considerable number of their nation so as to keep it, as it were, in possession, or at least a footing in it, and to show their hopes till a full restitution comes. The traditional theological approach to the question of Zion is well illustrated by the following paragraph. "Although God will have them to be cast down, yet he will not suffer them to be destroyed; although He will have them perplexed, yet he will not suffer them to despair."[178]

The return of the Jews to the Holy Land was a continuous theme of nineteenth century English literature; some of the writers were true lovers of Zion, others, again, religious visionaries, yet others, missionary propagandists.

The most celebrated representative of philo-Semitism, expressed in passionate Zionist sentiment, was the English novelist George Eliot (1819-1880). Her novel *Daniel Deronda* (1876) has done much to influence British public opinion to sponsor the rehabilitation of the Holy Land by the Jews. The Balfour Declaration was, not without justification, called a "footnote to Daniel Deronda." In her youth George Eliot entertained the common prejudices against the Jews, but later grew into a profound student and admirer of the Jewish genius; she became one of the spiritual forerunners of modern Zionism and one of the most illustrious representatives of philo-Semitism in the modern era. In *Daniel Deronda* and in her essay "The Modern Hep Hep" she voiced her reverence for Jewish tradition and her espousal of the right and duty of every Jew to remain loyal to his historic faith and destiny.

"The soul of Judaism is not dead. Revive the organic centre. Let the unity of Israel be an outward reality. Looking towards the land and polity, our dispersed people in all the ends of the earth may share the dignity of a national life which has a voice among the peoples of the east and the west ... then our race will have an organic centre, heart and brains to watch and guide and execute. The outraged Jew shall have a defence in the court of nations as the outraged Englishmen. And the world will gain as Israel gains."

George Eliot attempted, as she herself expressed it, to contribute something towards the ennobling of Judaism in the conceptions of the Christian community and in the consciousness of the Jewish community. As propaganda for Zionism *Daniel Deronda* is still eloquent, even moving. However remote it may have seemed in 1876, today a Jewish State exists.

Occasionally we find aversion to Jews turning into love and admiration. A striking example is George Eliot, who changed her attitude in the course of her life. In a letter, she attacked Disraeli's staunch Jewish loyalties and spoke with disdain about Judaism, declaring that everything specifically Jewish is of a low grade.

"My gentile nature kicks most resolutely against any assumption of superiority in the Jews, and is almost ready to echo Voltaire's vituperation. I bow to the supremacy of Hebrew poetry, but much of their early mythology, and almost all their history, is utterly revolting. Their stock has produced a Moses and a Jesus; but Moses was impregnated with Egyptian philosophy, and Jesus is venerated and adored by us only for that wherein he transcended or resisted Judaism. The very exaltation of their idea of a national deity into a spiritual monotheism seems to have been borrowed from the other oriental tribes."

Later George Eliot travelled a long way from these sentiments and, through her Zionist classic, *Daniel Deronda*, became the spiritual mover of Zionist thought.[179] George Eliot's philo-Semitism finds expression in a passionate defence of the Jews in her outspoken essay "The Modern Hep Hep" where she claims that the affinity of Englishman and Jew is only the more apparent when the elements of their peculiarity are discerned. The essay is characterized by a passionate appreciation of the Hebrew character — a striking antithesis to the equally vehement condemnation found in anti-Semitic literature. It delineates the image of the "Jew-Saint" as opposed to the figure of the "Jew-Villain." "One of the most remarkable phenomena in the history of this scattered people (the Jews) made for ages 'a scorn and a hissing,' . . . is that they have come out of it (in any estimate which allows for numerical proportion) rivalling the nations of all European countries in healthiness and beauty of physique, in practical ability, in scientific and artistic aptitude, and in some forms of ethical value."

The foremost champions of philo-Semitism in German literature were G.E Lessing and Thomas Mann. Lessing (1729-1781) was the illustrious representative of the humanistic type of philo-Semitism, literary fighter for enlightenment and religious tolerance, intrepid champion of the cause of liberty and powerful preacher from his stage-pulpit. In his youth, at the age of 12, Lessing wrote in a vein which contained already the germ of his later views. "It is a sign of barbarism to distinguish between the nations, all of which have been created by the Lord and endowed with reason by Him. Especially it behoves the Christian to love his neighbour; and, according to the word of Christ, our neighbour is he who needs our help. Now we all need the help of others, therefore we are all neighbours, the one of the other. So let us not condemn the Jews, although they condemned Christ. For God himself says: Judge not, lest ye be judged. We will not condemn the Mohammedans; there are

157

upright men also among these. In fine, nobody is a barbarian, unless he has been inhuman and cruel." In 1749 he published a one-act comedy entitled *The Jews*. The play portrayed Jews who are courteous, frank and magnanimous — an image contrary to the customary concept of the "Jew." His final plea for tolerance is contained in his great drama, *Nathan the Wise*, 1779, the "Song of Songs of Toleration." *Nathan the Wise* is a didactic poem, a powerful weapon in Lessing's battle against religious intolerance and a confession of his own beliefs in the love for one's fellow men. His own view on the meaning of the poem, Lessing clearly states in his preface. "There are people," he declares, "who do not believe in revealed religion and yet are known to be estimable persons. If anybody thinks that there are no such noble characters among Jews and Moslems as portrayed in the play (Sultan Saladin and Nathan the Wise), let him know that the Jews and Moslems were the only learned men at that time; that the detriment which revealed religions must bring to mankind must have been at no time more striking to a rational being than at the period of the crusades."

Nathan the Wise proclaimed a gospel of brotherly love in the spirit of the enlightenment; it had a powerful influence on all philo-Semitic trends in later German thought and literature. Boccaccio's tale of the *Three Rings* is utilized by Lessing to proclaim that every good man who loves his neighbour and proves his love by his life and his deeds may consider himself to be the owner of the true ring — the true religion. Lessing proclaimed the message that love alone is the kernel and touchstone of true piety and he preached this exalted gospel in a world that was not ripe for it. Lessing's plea for Jewish equality and Jewish emancipation was motivated by purest humanity; he demands an attitude to life that rises above the divisions of nationality and barriers of revealed religions. Lessing considered his drama as a lay sermon, his stage as a pulpit. His Nathan became one of the most powerful factors in the cause of Jewish emancipation, and has served in the German-speaking world as a symbol of tolerance and humanity. It has been the most valid, dramatic contribution to the immortal ideas of the eighteenth century, the ideals of enlightenment and humanism. There can be no doubt that Lessings attitude to the Jews was influenced by the personal nobility of his illustrious friend Moses Mendelssohn, the celebrated Jewish philosopher, just as a century later George Eliot's Zionist convictions were formed by the impact of a personal contact with Albert E.W. Goldsmid, an ardent Anglo-Jewish Zionist whom Herzl called "My Brother." Yet the basic motives of Lessing's attitude were the ideas of tolerance, which superseded the clerical exclusiveness of the Church and embraced Jews as brothers within the world-wide community of man.

In 1945, in the hour of total German defeat, Lessing's *Nathan* was the first play to return to the German stage. German theatres opened their post-Hitler repertory with Lessing's drama, as a token of atonement for Germany's guilt, a peace offering to a civilized world, as if Germans were begging forgiveness for having departed from the message of Lessing, once the glory of German humane civilization. The performance of *Nathan the Wise* on the German and Austrian stages served as a symbol for the return of humanitarian thought into that German literature which gave to human civilization men of the stature of Goethe and Kant. Lessing's Nathan stimulated Goethe, in whose thought early anti-Semitism was superseded by profound understanding of the Jewish genius, to make this famous observation; "May the well-known story of Nathan the Wise, auspiciously related, forever remind the German people that it is called upon not only to view but also to listen and understand. May this absolutely divine idea of tolerance and forebearance ever remain holy and dear to the nation." Lessing's work and personality have remained one of the most potent sources of philo-Semitic stimulation in German life and letters and, hopefully, outlived the barbarism of the Nazi era.

The idea of tolerance is movingly expressed in the sublime prayer composed by the Austrian Emperor Joseph II whose Edict of Toleration, 1781, forms a landmark in the history of Jewish emancipation. "Eternal, incomprehensible Being! Thou art perfect toleration and love. Thy sun shines for the Christian as well as for the atheist. Thy rain fructifies the field of the erring as that of the orthodox; and the germ of every virtue lies in the hearts of both heathen and heretic. Thou teachest me thus, Eternal Being! toleration and love — teachest me that diverse views do not deter Thee from being a beneficent Father to all people. And shall I, Thy creature, be less tolerant, not conceding that everyone of my subjects may worship Thee in his own manner? Shall I persecute those who think differently from me, and convert the erring by the sword? No, Omnipotent! with Thy love, all-embracing Being, I shall be far from doing so. I will resemble Thee as far as a creature can resemble Thee — will be tolerant as Thou art! Henceforth be all intolerance in my country removed. Where is a religion that doth not teach the love of virtue and the abhorrence of vice? Everybody shall, therefore, be tolerated by me. Let everyone worship Thee, incomprehensible Being! in the manner which seemeth to him best. Do errors of mind deserve banishment from society? Is severity, indeed, the means of winning the people? of converting the erring? Broken shall henceforth be the infamous fetters of intolerance! Instead of it, may the sweet bond of toleration and brotherly love unite forever!"[180]

German philo-Semitic thinking was influenced by J.G. Herder's (1744-1803) theory that diversity of culture rather than cosmopolitan levelling of differences is the aim of historical evolution. Herder's glorification of ancient Hebrew poetry[181] was in line with the view that the true aim of culture is the harmonization of various cultural units. His eloquent proclamation that the older a people, the more distinctive its individuality, appealed not only to young Jews, but stamped Jewish existence with renewed value in the eyes of the Christian world. His saying that the history of the Jews is the greatest poem of all times[182] is an eloquent expression of the admiration which the leaders of enlightenment felt for the heroic persistence of the Jews in the face of severe trials.

The most important bearer of philo-Semitic sentiments in modern German literature was Thomas Mann (1875-1955). There is in present-day Germany much interest in Jewish history, contemporary Jewish life and the State of Israel. Young Germans do not grasp the tragedy of the holocaust and look for an explanation in works on the Jews and on Israel. Books by Jewish writers, banned by the Nazis, are being printed, friendly proclamations of great Germans on the Jewish question find publishers and a large reading public. This notable interest in the written word concerning Jews and Judaism is a manifestation of the desire to atone, which is also the main motive of Germany's pro-Israel attitude today. Thomas Mann, the most universal German writer since Goethe, was one of the greatest novelists the modern era has produced, encompassing both the masterly naturalism of his *Buddenbrooks* and the rich symbolism of his great *Joseph Saga,* "Joseph and his brothers." His name is held in special affection by the contemporary German champions of the Jewish cause. He was not only the creator of a superb literature, rich in spirit and enduring in influence, the unequalled modern interpreter of the Bible, but also a courageous leader in the eternal fight for justice, morality and humanity. Thomas Mann publicly opposed Nazism, and from 1933, remained outside Germany to become a voluntary emigrant. Originally he believed that his books, imbued with a humanitarian spirit, might still exert some influence in Germany; but in 1936 he proclaimed his abhorrence of the barbarism prevalent in the Third Reich, condemned Nazism as the arch-enemy of Western civilization and of the Jewish-Christian tradition of religion and morality. The human interest in this great man of letters thus far exceeds the purely literary aspect of Mann's genius. Throughout his life, Thomas Mann was a devoted humanitarian, a bold champion of truth and right, who, like a prophet, dared to combat darkness and reaction in his own fatherland. He was an implacable foe of Nazism, an unfaltering friend of the Jewish people and a passionate fighter for liberty and *Humanität.*

Even before the Nazis came to power, Mann described the anti-Semitic atmosphere in Germany as a regression from the liberal ideas of the nineteenth century. "It is humiliating and revolting," he wrote,[183] "to look upon anti-Jewish conduct; it is a source of deep depression not only for Jews, but also for every person who looks with reverence and sympathy upon the significant and characteristic contribution which the evolution of the human mind owes to this so highly gifted, peculiar, unusual Jewish people which has so varied and fruitful a destiny."

Thomas Mann's *Seven Manifestos on the Jewish Question* (Sieben Manifeste zur Judischen Frage) published by his wife, Katja, (1966) reveals how Mann's deeply-felt rejection of anti-Semitic arrogance grew into abhorrence of those base instincts "which formerly were confined by the corrective pressure of good customs, but had since 1933 gained the upper hand through barbaric propaganda and gruesome deeds."

Mann's ringing manifestos are a testimony to his moral courage and his devotion to the cause of humanity. His striking utterances are not to be considered as a mere apologia of Judaism against anti-Semitism. Mann's attitude to "Jewish Spirituality" is motivated by sentiments of human solidarity. The hatred which breaks out from time to time against the Jews is not, he declared, aimed at them alone; it is aimed against Europe and all that is higher in its culture. It expresses the attempt to eliminate from the Western educational system an element which is considered as being sombre and foreign, but in reality it is the very element which enlightens and humanizes. Without these elements the culture produced in Germany would be not much more than savage primitivism.

Thomas Mann held a firm belief in the power of the Jewish people to survive suffering, even that peculiar Nazi anti-Semitism which ended in the most horrible crime of European history. Always, he believed, when anti-Semitism breaks out, it is a sign that the people feel ill at ease, hampered in their evil desires, that they are doing wrong, playing "hookey" from school, are up to bloody tricks and are eager to engage in warlike massacres, instead of doing such things as are right, sensible and necessary. Then the Jews have to suffer. But they will suffer and survive. And we may all be certain that their strong sense of this world, their devotion to the cause of social justice, will play an important part in the upbuilding of a new society struggling slowly out of its crisis. "Why should the Jewish people not despair?" Mann was asked in November 1936 by the editor of a paper which appeared in Mukacevo in Czecho-slovakia. Anti-Semitism, he replied — aptly called the "socialism of the fools,"[184] the racial myth of the rabble, is revolting and hateful. "It is the aristocracy of the vulgar who say: I must admit that I am nothing, but at least I am not a Jew. So he believed he is something. Anyone, however, who is anything at all, does not need so negative an advantage to prop himself up."

Thomas Mann was not motivated by a liberalistic all-world shallow philanthropy, nor by a purely emotional sympathy for the Jews based on facile generalizations concerning "the Jews." Fundamental religious feeling prevented him from ever making the slightest concession to the anti-Jewish mischief (Unwesen). All men are made of the same material and filled with the same spirit. It is a sin against God to refuse a section of humanity which has contributed so much to the fundaments of civilisation the right to live. As to the power of survival — with that, Mann believed, the Jews are splendidly equipped. The energy of the Jews will play an important part in the shaping of a new and better order of society. They still preserve their intelligence, their spirituality, endurance, "their experience of suffering" (Leidenserfahrenheit). They cannot be destroyed, Mann proclaimed. They have outlived many a storm and will doubtless overcome the vicissitudes of the present moment. Mann quoted Goethe: "They are the most enduring people on earth; they were, they are, they will be in order that they may glorify the name of God through all ages." The cultured German, Mann proclaimed, educated in the spirit of Goethe, for whom according to the words of his master, "the only problems of importance are those of culture against barbarism" — cannot be an anti-Semite and must deny to himself any part in this cheap folk-amusement; for he senses with accuracy that the very foundations of his own world are here assailed. In his Goethe novel, "Lotte in Weimar," Mann depicted the greatest German poet as the champion of a world which Hitler has set out to destroy.

On September 27, 1942, Thomas Mann reached his German countrymen through the radio. In one of his monthly, deeply moving eight-minute speeches to his fellow nationals, he informed the German people of the unspeakable atrocities on millions of innocent people: "And you Germans," he exclaimed, "are amazed, even indignant, when the civilized world considers what methods of education will be required to humanize generations of Germans, whose brains were deformed by Nazism, who had become depraved killers." On July 9, 1943, Thomas Mann addressed a Jewish mass meeting in San Francisco in which he emphasized the vast Jewish contribution to European civilization and, pointing to examples of kindness shown to Jews by individual Germans, pleading that accusations of German collective guilt should not be made. He also stressed the isolation of Germany from the outside world. If the Germans in their isolated country were permitted to know the truth about events such as the tragic perishing of the Jews in the Warsaw Ghetto and the preceding epic struggle, they would shudder before their rulers and before themselves. Things would change, Mann firmly believed, and Israel would survive as it always had survived. But what it suffers today cries to Heaven, and nations, who boast that they are fighting for humanity and human dignity against barbarism, must ask themselves whether they at least do all in their power to allay the indescribable suffering which debases all of humanity. Perhaps it is too cheap to declare, "One cannot do more than wage war against the Nazis." Only little can be done because much was neglected before the war, while there were still great possibilities to act. "We retain shameful memories of those bygone days. I only want to recall that phantom ship with Jewish refugees, which sailed the seas in the year 1939 without finding a port of admission, until finally the emigrants were received by Holland and Belgium, small countries both. The world, in the inertia of its heart, permitted Hitler to deride it. He challenged it: If you are so humane, why don't you accept the Jews?"

On the occasion of the seventieth birthday of Chaim Weizmann, Thomas Mann contributed a remarkable essay to a Jubilee volume. "I know," he writes, "of no better way of expressing my veneration for Weizmann, the wise and powerful leader of the Jewish people, whom these pages are meant to celebrate, than to yield myself wholly to those feelings of horror and boundless revulsion which fill me when I ponder the indescribable sufferings of European Jewry — those bestial persecutions of an ancient, highly gifted, and indispensable people throughout the whole territory under Nazi rule — I rose to awaken the protest of the civilised world against these contemptible crimes. In so doing, I have never forgotten the claim that the other oppressed and violated peoples of Europe have upon our sympathy."

A profound understanding for the essence of Zionist success is displayed by Thomas Mann in various contexts. Out of the agony of the Jewish people, he affirms, is bound to rise a renewed nation in its own homeland; Jews will ascend from the depth of sorrow to the height of rejoicing, from lowest degradation to triumphant statehood. "Now, persecutions and sufferings strengthen one's feeling for one's own being and one's own worth; they add new strength, too, to the sentiment of solidarity. It is no wonder, it is but right and just, that the national consciousness of the Jewish people has been immeasurably intensified by the events of recent years and that the Zionist idea proves to possess a steadily growing persuasiveness and power. The idea of a national concentration of the Jews in a place other than that of the Dispersion, that is to say, the Zionist idea, is no longer a controversial one today. It is a spiritual fact which must be respected, and it will overcome every resistance that opposes its realisation."

In 1945 Thomas Mann sent a message to a Jewish meeting in New York, held on the seventh anniversary of the burning of the Synagogues in Germany; it was the first commemoration of

165

the tragic event after the defeat of the Nazis. In his powerful address, *Save the Jews of Europe,* Mann declares that the hope of a true peace which must be based on justice and human dignity cannot be separated from the salvation of the Jewish people which is a testing-stone for the rightness of our civilization and its desire for the good. One should hope that after the collapse of Fascism, anti-Semitism is being detested by the whole world and has become impossible as a way of thinking. But this also is by no means the case. Hitler's poisonous seed has sunk deeply into confused minds everywhere. In 1948, Mann, in an address, *"Gespenster von 1938," Ghosts of 1938,* with reference to the Munich surrender, raised a sharp protest against the decision of the United States to refuse assent to the creation of a Jewish State in Palestine. The small Jewish state in Palestine will be a democracy of industrious and culture-loving people which should earn the whole and natural sympathy of a country with democratic traditions, such as the United States of America. Why, he asked, should the Americans be considered in the whole world as retrogressive supporters of odious causes, such as the feudalism of the Arab Oil Magnates, and destroy democracy by pretending to defend it?

Thomas Mann was not only a friend of the Jewish people, but also the foremost modern expounder of the Biblical heritage in a European language. His chosen hero was Joseph, a man "blessed with blessing from the heavens above and from the depth beneath," a blessing pronounced by his father Jacob. "As for me," Mann wrote, "that was the most telling formulation of my idea of humanity. Wherever in the realm of mind and personality I find that ideal manifested, as the union of darkness and light, feeling and mind, the primitive and the civilised, in short as the humanised mystery we call man, there lies my profound allegiance, there my heart finds its home."

In the choice of the Joseph theme and in the interpretation of its mythical and historical dimensions, Mann has shown attachment to the Jewish-Christian tradition and the categories of its thought and exposition.

In his acceptance of the Honorary Degree of Doctor of Hebrew Letters from the Hebrew Union College, Cincinnati, in 1946, Mann expressed his belief that it was his Biblical work which had brought him this honour. "I look back to my orientalistic studies and particularly the intensive Midrash (rabbinic exegesis) studies I undertook in preparation for my work. I conceived the plan for this work at a time when in my native country these dark tendencies began to gather which, while I was writing it, came to such terrible outbreaks against a people to which occidental civilisation owes so much, and that has always been a pillar of the spirit: the Jewish people. The sinister powers that brought such shame upon Germany and such immeasurable suffering upon the whole world are crushed to the ground; but we all knew that, unfortunately, the base and perfidious ideas which these corrupted people have worked, and with which they tried to undermine liberty and humanity all over the world, have not disappeared with them, but that they continue to exist everywhere, and that it takes indefatigable vigilance and the co-operation of all God-fearing people who believe in right and tolerance to make the masses of the people immune against this poison."

Jews and Judaism concerned Mann not only in the context of his literary work, but also within the framework of his views on political and social questions. As early as 1907 he contributed an article to a symposium on the Jewish question in which he called himself a "convinced and undoubting philo-Semite." (Ein uberzeugter und sweifelloser Philosemit). The Jewish question, he asserted, was a question of social status and culture; in Russia the problem posed a more horrible appearance than in the Western countries, "because Russia was still much nearer to barbarism than the Western half of Europe." Twenty-five years later, the barbarism of the West revealed its gruesome face.

Not only the Jews, but all men of goodwill are heirs to Mann's humanitarian legacy and owe him gratitude for not secluding himself in an artistic ivory tower, but fulfilling the demands of the day, using the power of his words as a weapon in the battle against tyranny.

In 1945 Mann published a work, *Nobility of the Spirit,* essays on the problem of *Humanität.* It contains discourses on Lessing, Chamisso, Kleist, Goethe, Tolstoy, Schopenhauer, Wagner, Storm, Freud and Cervantes. Mann himself belonged to these aristocrats of the spirit; his moral courage in the service of mankind was a fundamental element of his noble spirit.

The memory of Thomas Mann's genuine affection for Jews and Judaism may assist in recreating a spirit of harmony between the German nation and world Jewry, including the State of Israel, which would be of importance not only to these two peoples, but to humanity at large. [185]

In Russian letters the overwhelming tendency concerning the Jews, their economic and political role in society, their life and thought, was anti-Semitic. The Jew was considered an alien in the Slavic world, an infidel in the Russian Orthodox Church, a parasite in the economic sphere, a disruptive, dangerous force in social life. For most of the Slavophiles the world outlook of the Jews, their way of life, their religion and their social occupations were repulsive and foreign. Moreover they considered the Jews dangerous to the inviolability of the Russian patriarchal system of life into which they were bringing discontent and decay.

Among Russian religious philosophers, one finds an ambivalent attitude towards Jews and to Judaism; some glorify the Biblical past of the people of Israel, yet oppose the contemporary Jews in the Pale of Settlement; others manifest a philo-Semitic attitude towards Russia's Jewish inhabitants, endeavouring to understand their plight and to sympathize with their unfortunate situation in the alien Slav world. The Russian theologian Alexei Khomyakov (1804-1860) could readily compose stately odes celebrating Biblical Jewry, but had no sympathy for the contemporary Jew who, he considered, had initiated the seduction of the patriarchal Russian peasant into capitalist heterodoxy. It is important to note, however, that when anti-Semitic rioting called forth protest from Russian writers, Khomyakov was among those who signed the proclamation.[186]

Vladimir Soloviev (1853-1900), one of the profoundest Russian religious thinkers, may be considered one of the noblest representatives of philo-Semitic thought. His approach to the Jewish question was determined by his position as a sincere and devout Christian and by his sense of justice. Some Jewish traits displeased him and called for severe censure, but he never considered them as enduring characteristics of the Jews but attributed them to historical conditions. His Christian attitudes to the Jewish problem excluded the very possibility of any kind of anti-Semitism. The Jewish problem was for him, simultaneously, a Russian problem, the problem of Russian conscience and justice, of Christian understanding and attitude. The perspective of thousands of years showed him Judaism as a religion of revelation which proclaimed to the whole world a new message without which Christianity could not have arisen. He denied that he was either an anti-Semite or sentimental Judeophile. It is difficult to find anything more noble and worthy of a Christian than these utterances from a Russian philosopher who blended religious mysticism with a passion for earthly justice. "A great number of people," he states, "extol me as a Judeophile; others reproach me for blind partiality towards Jewry. Thank God, they don't suspect me of bribery with Jewish gold! But how does my Judeophilism show itself? Or my partiality to Jewry? Is it perhaps that I haven't recognised the weak points of the Jews, or that I excuse them? Have I ever displayed the slightest tendency to idealise Jewry? Actually I am just as far from Judeophobia as I am from Judeophilia. But I cannot close my eyes to the obvious facts just to satisfy poor taste and bad ethics. I will not and cannot act against my conscience and follow the example of the anti-Semites who make certain Jews responsible for all the troubles and misfortunes besetting us. I do not conceal the fact that I am intensely interested in the fate of the Jewish people, but this is because their fate is extremely interesting and remarkably instructive. Do I sometimes intercede on behalf of the Jews? Yes, but unfortunately not as often as I would like to and should do as a Slav and a Christian. As a Christian, I acknowl-

169

edge that I am deeply indebted to Judaism. Was not my Saviour after the flesh a Jew, the prophets and the apostles were also Jews, and the corner stone of the universal church was taken from the houses of Israel. As a Slav, I feel a great guilt in the presence of the Jews and would like to redeem it as much as I can. The Jewish question is essentially a question of truth and justice. Justice is trampled underfoot in the face of the Jews because there is not even the slightest excuse for the persecutions to which they have been subjected. The accusations levelled against them by the anti-Semites fail to hold up even under the most lenient criticism — they are, for the most part, wicked lies.

Soloviev endeavours to define the peculiar characteristics of the Jews and immerses himself in reading books on Jewish history and on ideology. He notes that the Jew reveals, above all, a unique combination of cosmopolitan and national elements. This very combination of two contradictory elements explained why the Jews are simultaneously accused of both narrow nationalism and wide cosmopolitanism. Soloviev correctly observes that while the Jewish ethical religious concept was a solely Jewish national creation, it had at the same time proclaimed and achieved universal significance.

Soloviev distinguishes three basic qualities in the Jewish national character: an ardent and living faith in God; a supreme conviction in their personal and national individuality; and an insatiable yearning that their faith be completely realized and materialized. It was these three qualities, Soloviev says, in this order of importance, that gave Israel its great advantage and glory and made them God's chosen people. Soloviev repeatedly points out that Judaism, in direct contrast to Christianity, was able to combine the idea of holy souls with that of holy bodies, to create, as Soloviev puts it, the concept of "holy corporeity." Soloviev speaks of the great majestic role played by Jews in history and how Christianity was nurtured in the bosom of Jewry. At the same time, however, he emphatically states that the Jewish people strayed from their historic path; they did not understand their historic vocation, and

170

without recognizing Him, they turned away from the real Messiah who had been sent down to them in the person of Jesus.

There exists a notable philo-Semitic tendency in Russian thought and letters which has been overshadowed, even submerged, by the more powerful manifestations of anti-Semitism in the Tsarist era and lately by the unrelenting pressure of Bolshevik rule. There is a quality in the spiritual life of the Russian people that can be gauged neither from Tsarist oppression nor from Soviet persecution. It may reside in the profound identification with human suffering, which suffuses the works of Maxim Gorki and finds expression in Yevgeny Yevtushenko's celebrated poem *Babi Yar* (1960).

. . . . It seems to me that I am as old
As the Jewish people itself.
It seems to me that I am a Jew.
I am tramping through ancient Egypt
I am dying, crucified on the cross
And till this time I have traces of the nails.
It seems to me that I am Dreyfus . . .
It seems to me that I am a youngster in Bialystok.
Whose blood is running over the floors
The victim of the hooliganism of the leaders from the
    saloons . . .
It seems to me that I am Anne Frank . . .
Over Babi-Yar there is the hum of thick grass
The trees look powerful, like judges
Everything screams silently here, and, removing my hat,
I feel that I am growing grey slowly
And that I am myself a totally soundless shriek
Over the thousands of thousands who are buried.
I am each old man that was slaughtered here
I am each child that was slaughtered here.
Nothing in me can forget this.
Let the "Internationale" sound out joyously
When the last anti-Semite on earth will be buried . . . .

Some Russian writers such as Vladimir Korolenko and Leonid Andreyev showed compassion towards the Jews, and sympathized with the sad state of their political and economic position; they opposed the anti-Jewish propaganda of Church and secular authorities, and came out in defence of Russia's much-maligned millions of Jewish inhabitants. Korolenko demanded complete equality for Jews in Russia and opposed the government's incitements to *pogroms*. In his novels he stressed the brightest aspects of Jewish character and also headed the Russian Association for the Victims of Pogroms. His main work, *The Blind Musician,* was translated into Hebrew.

The most outstanding Russian men of letters, who valiantly championed the cause of the Jews, were Leo Tolstoy and Maxim Gorki. Gorki constantly defended the Jews of Tsarist Russia against vilification and violence. He blamed the Kishenev pogrom (1903), not upon the mobs, but upon the anti-Semitic journals which were misleading them. In an article for the *Shield,* a collection of essays, stories and poems by non-Jewish Russian writers, defending the Jews of Russia against the anti-Semitism of the government, edited by Leonard Andreyev, Gorki stated that, as a Russian, he was troubled by the Jewish question since hatred for the Jews, as indeed for any people, was degrading to the haters; the self-respect of Russians, as well as reason, justice, and gratitude, required that the Jews of Russia should have equal rights. The hatred of the Jews, declared Gorki, is a bestial zoological phenomenon and has to be fought in an active way . . . we must see the Jews as our friends and have to be grateful to them; they created and are still creating many values which were followed by the best sons of the Russian people. He recalls the philosophy, the morality the deep thinking of the people of Israel and mentions especially the wisdom of Hillel in his saying, "If I am not for myself then who am I and if I am only for myself what am I." Gorki testified that the wisdom of Hillel fortified his own spirit in the days of his youth, and helped him to overcome many difficulties in life. He praised Jewish wisdom for the love it manifests to man and for its deep humanity.

It strengthened, in his heart, the belief that the "holy of holies" is man. In this spirit, Gorki continued to write and speak about the Jewish people after the revolution until his death in 1936. Gorki is one of the staunchest representatives of dedicated philo-Semitism in Russian literature. His thoughts have outlived Tsarist Judeo-phobia and will be remembered after the present anti-Jewish trend in the Soviet Union has passed into oblivion.

A statement issued in favour of the Jews persecuted during the First World War in 1915 was signed by many Russian notables, among them Andreyev, Bunin, Gorki, Mereshkovski, Kerenski, Rimski-Korsakov, A.N. Tolstoy and others. The signatories deplored the fact that the long-suffering Jewish people, which had given the world so many precious gifts in the field of religion, philosophy and poetry, which had ever contributed toward the development of the common Russian life and which had demonstrated, more than once, its love for Russia and its devotion to the cause of Russia, in spite of the degrading and unjust treatment accorded to it, was again being subjected to new trials, hardships and humiliations. The cessation of Jew-baiting in all its forms, the complete emancipation of the Jews and the recognition of their civic rights, constitute the fundamental conditions of a truly salutary imperial policy.[187]

Leo Tolstoy (1828-1910), the great Russian novelist and reformer, artist and thinker, story-teller and preacher, was one of the most illustrious representatives of philo-Semitism in modern literature. If there was any man in the nineteenth century who endeavoured to bring a message of peace and salvation to mankind, it was the Saint and Sage of Yasnaya Polyana. In the latter part of his life he arrived at intellectual conclusions which involved non-resistance to evil, the abolition of governments and nationalisms, of churches and dogmas, but stressed the belief in the love of God and the love of man. The influence of this Russian genius spread far beyond his homeland and made him the prototype of a modern prophet and saint to many choice spirits in the West and in the East. His teachings made a profound impression on Mahatma Ghandi, who endeavoured to carry out resistance to evil by non-violent methods, such as non co-operation with the oppressing government and civil disobedience. A short while before his death Tolstoy wrote a letter to Ghandi which is considered Tolstoy's spiritual testament of non-violence. Ghandi acknowledged later on that it was Tolstoy who helped him to realise the infinite possibilities of universal love. Of all the utterances of modern ethical doctrine, it was Tolstoy's writings which most strongly confirmed Ghandi in his ideas of the positive power of non-resistance, and of the renunciation of all types of violence.

Tolstoy's message was a message of peace among men, among nations, among classes and creeds. After he had renounced his artistic vocation and had become converted to preach the gospel of pure morality, he exhorted his fellow men not to think primarily in terms of nationalism, but on a universal human basis. He withdrew from the state and from his church, declaring, "I cannot recognize states or nations, nor take part in quarrels between them, either by writing on the subject or by serving a single state. I can take no part in anything which rests on the difference between states, like custom houses, tax collections, the manufacture of explosives and arms, or any warlike preparations."

As an enemy of nationalism, Tolstoy could have little understanding for Jewish national aspirations, and as a disciple of the Christian Gospel he assigned to Judaism a place together with the patriarchal religions of the Romans, Chinese and Japanese. Yet as a great humanitarian he was, throughout his life, a friend of the Jewish people and an admirer of their religious and literary traditions. When, under the rule of Tsar Alexander III, a large part of the Russian public and the Russian press had succumbed to the prevailing anti-Semitic tendencies fostered by Plehve, the Russian Minister of the Interior, and the notorious Pobyedonostzev, the head of the Russian Orthodox Church, the progressive elements of the Russian intelligentsia were gradually aroused to a feeling of protest. In 1890 a Christian philosopher and friend of the Jewish people,

Vladimir Soloviev, mentioned above, published a protest against the *pogrom* atmosphere over the signatures of Leo Tolstoy, Vladimir Korolenko and other literary celebrities. Despite its mild tone, the protest was barred from publication by the Russian censorship. The following remarkable extracts from the public protest against anti-Semitism deserve to be quoted: "The movement against the Jews which is propagated by the Russian press represents an unprecedented violation of the most fundamental demands of righteousness and humanity. In all nationalities there are bad and ill-minded persons; but there is not, and cannot be, any bad and ill-minded nationality, for this would abrogate the moral responsibility of the individual. It is unjust to make the Jews responsible for those phenomena in their lives which are the result of thousands of years of persecution in Europe and of the abnormal conditions in which the people has been placed. The fact of belonging to a Semitic tribe and professing the Mosaic creed cannot serve as a basis for an exceptional civil position of the Jews. The increased endeavours to kindle national and religious hatred, which is so contradictory to the spirit of Christianity and suppresses the feelings of justice and humaneness, is bound to demoralise society at its very root and bring about a state of moral anarchy."

The news of the Kishinev *pogrom* (1903) horrified the entire civilized world. The liberal Russian press voiced its indignation against the atrocities perpetrated in Kishinev and the most prominent writers expressed their sympathy with the victims. Tolstoy expressed his indignation in very sharp terms. A declaration he had composed was given to the governor of Kishinev.

"Profoundly shocked by the atrocities committed at Kishinev, we extend our heartfelt sympathy to the innocent victims of mob savagery and express our horror at the acts of cruelty perpetrated by Russians, our scorn and disgust with all who have driven the people to such a pass and have allowed this dreadful crime to be committed."[187a]

Leo Tolstoy voiced his sentiments in a letter which reveals

Tolstoy's profound insight into the causes of the Kishinev barbarities. Tolstoy especially blamed the perverted notions concerning Christianity which had prompted the massacre: "My opinion concerning the Kishinev crime is the result also of my religious convictions. Upon the receipt of the first news I fully realised the horror of what had taken place, and experienced simultaneously a burning feeling of pity for the innocent victims of the cruelty of the populace, amazement at the bestiality of all these so-called Christians, revulsion at all these so-called cultured people who instigated the mob and sympathised with its actions. But I felt a particular horror for the principal culprit, our Government, with its clergy which fosters in the people bestial sentiments, and fanaticism, with its horde of murderous officials. The crime committed at Kishinev (1903) is nothing but a direct consequence of that propaganda of falsehood and violence which is conducted by the Russian Government with such energy."[188]

Of special interest is a chapter in Tolstoy's work *What I Believe* (1884) in which he discussed the doctrine of nonresistance. Tolstoy was reading the fifth chapter of the Gospel of Matthew with his Hebrew teacher, Rabbi Solomon Minor, a native of Vilna, who in 1869 was called to Moscow to lead the recently formed Jewish congregation and who became the first rabbi in Russia to preach in the Russian language. At almost every sentence of the Gospel the rabbi said, "That is in the Jewish Canon, that is the Talmud," and he pointed to sayings in the Old Testament and in the Talmud similar to those of the Sermon of the Mount. But when Tolstoy and the rabbi reached the verse of non-resistance to evil, the rabbi did not say "and that is the Talmud"[189], but asked ironically, "Do the Christians fulfil that? Do they turn the other cheek?" "I had no reply to this," said Tolstoy, "especially as I knew that at that very time Christians were not turning the other cheek, but were striking cheeks the Jews had turned." Tolstoy was interested to know whether there was anything similar in the Old Testament or in the Talmud and asked the rabbi about this. The rabbi answered in the negative, but asked Tolstoy whether the

Christians fulfil this law of non-resistance. "By this question he showed me that the presence of this rule in the Christian law, which not only is not performed by anyone, but which Christians themselves admit to be impracticable, is an admission of the irrationality and superfluity of this Christian law. And I had no reply to give him."

Tolstoy spent many years in an attempt to harmonize the great wisdom of the East and West, an undertaking which he considered as the most significant of his life. "All my artistic works are unimportant and will be forgotten, but this one — what I believe — will last, because it serves the good of all mankind," he wrote. In 1904 Tolstoy was engaged in compiling the thoughts of various writers, sages and philosophers on the meaning and truth of life. The book was called *The Road to Life* and contained sayings of wisdom and ethics from ancient religions down to modern writers, for the purpose of formulating the religious unity of the history of nations and leaving them as a veritable spiritual testament for the direction of future generations. This great work was arranged in the form of selected readings for each day of the year and constitutes, in the words of Tolstoy's son, an exact mirror of the Tolstoyan doctrine. *The Road to Life*[190] contains no less than seventy quotations from the Talmud, some of them recognizable, others obviously transcribed and formulated from an unknown source, probably Rabbi Solomon Minor's oral teaching.

Tolstoy's most prominent disciple in the world of Jewish thought was A.D. Gordon, the spiritual father of the second and third *aliyah* and the prophet of the Religion of Labour. Under the influence of Tolstoy, Gordon preached a return to nature, fought against the artificial character of modern life; he condemned the degradation of modern society, which is motivated by the urge of material profit, and demanded a revolutionary renewal of the individual, based on inner responsibility and dedicated labour.

One of Tolstoy's Jewish admirers was the great historian Simon Dubnow who published, in the Hebrew Journal *Hashiloach,*[191] an essay under the title "Tolstoy and Judaism" in which he endeavours to discover the Jewish element in Tolstoy's thought: The greatest of Europe's writers, an heir to the aesthetic wealth of Hellenism, interrupted his artistic work, stood at the cross road and asked: "Which is the best way a man shall choose?" and an echo from ancient Judaism answered: "See I put before you life and good, death and evil. Who is a hero? Who subdues his evil inclination? I command thee today to love the Lord and walk in his ways; as He is merciful, so be thou merciful." And then the great man turned from his trodden path and created a new theory on the basis of the replies which came to him out of the depth of ancient Judaism. He denied the value of European culture, based on the rule of force, and put in its place the rule of morality. If Tolstoy would have only emphasized this one point, we would be permitted to register a new victory of the teaching of Judaism in its eternal battle with Hellenism.

Tolstoy was one of those rare spirits who battled for justice on earth not only with the power of the word, but with the moral example of his personality. The miracle of his soul was its capacity to seek the light and strive toward fraternal love and faith. Tolstoy was one of the "Righteous among the Nations" whose message and memory will endure as an everlasting blessing.

The famous Russian philosopher Nicholas Berdyaev,[192] already mentioned, may be considered as an advocate of philo-Semitic thinking arising from amazement at Jewish persistence in the face of untold hardship and the mystery of Jewish survival through the ages. Jewish destiny, he wrote, is too imbued with the metaphysical to be explained either in material or positive terms. The materialistic interpretation of history, which may be verified by applying it to the destinies of peoples, breaks down in the case of the Jews, where destiny seemed absolutely inexplicable from the materialistic standpoint. And indeed according to the materialistic and positive criterion, this people ought long ago to have perished. Its survival, Berdyaev declared, is a mysterious and wonderful phenomenon demonstrating that the life of the people is governed by a special determination transcending the processes of adaptation expounded by the materialistic interpretation of history. "The survival of the Jews, their resistance to destruction, their endurance under absolutely peculiar conditions and the fateful role played by them in history, all these point to the particular and mysterious foundations of their destiny . . . A comparison between the Jewish religion and that of other pre-Christian pagan peoples confirms the contention that Jewish history represented the revelation of God in the historical destiny of humanity, while that of other pagan peoples represented the revelation of God in Nature. This distinction between the foundations of the Jewish and the pagan Aryan religions helps us to establish the historical character of the Jewish people . . ."

Jewish religion, Berdyaev holds, is permeated with the Messianic idea which is indeed its pivot. Israel lived in expectation of the day of judgement when it would abandon the sorrowful historical destiny which was the lot of its people, to enter upon a sort of all-illuminating world era. The Messianic idea is the determining factor in the historical drama of the Jewish people. The expectations of the future Messiah and the passionate longing for his coming gave rise to that dualism in the Jewish religious consciousness which bound the destiny of the Jewish people to that of mankind. The Jewish people, Berdyaev affirmed, were obsessed by the passionate idea of justice and its terrestrial fulfilment. The other specific idea of the Jewish people, the demand for justice to be realized on earth together with their aspiration toward the future, predetermined the whole complexity of Jewish historical destiny. "Socialism is not a phenomenon peculiar to our time, although it has in our day acquired an extraordinary force and unprecedented influence over the entire field. It is one of the universal historical principles. These latter however have roots in the remotest ages and, like all ancient principles, are constantly active and in conflict with their opponents. I believe that Socialism is based upon a Jewish religious principle . . . Hatred of the Jews is a non-Christian feeling; within Christian history itself there is a constant interaction of the Hebrew and Hellenic principles which together make up the main sources of our culture."

Berdyaev stressed the idea that socialist longing for a better society, the passionate demand for the fulfilment of the millenary kingdom of God on earth, when an end will come to injustice and suffering, has its source in the moral idealism of the Hebrew prophets. Philo-Semites cherish the thought that the humanitarian aspirations of ideal socialism are rooted in the thoughts of the Hebrew Bible, particularly in the prophetic striving for absolute justice.

Jewish historians today reject the one-sided view concerning anti-Semitic action and thought, and stress the need of emphasizing the philo-Semitic attitude of liberals concerning the Jews in Tzarist Russia. Revealing, for instance, is Professor S. Zeitlin's review of Maurice Samuel's book on the Strange History of the Beilis Case. Zeitlin rightly disposes of the impression gained from some studies of the theme that the Beilis case — notorious ritual murder accusation against Mendel Beilis in 1911 — was simply a matter of all Russia against the Jews. Many Russian liberals believed that the defence of Beilis should have been conducted not by Jews, but by Russians. They held that while the accusation against Beilis was a libel against the Jews, it was also an affront to the Russian people. The defence should have been handled by Russians to defend the honour of Russia. Zeitlin stressed that in his narration Mr. Samuel gave the names of those who were on the side of the persecution. It is surprising that he did not refer to the Russians who were on the side of the defence. The name of the internationally renowned scientist Pavlov is not mentioned. Professor Kokovtzof, the brilliant orientalist, is not referred to, though he vigourously testified at the trial against the blood accusation. He was one of the noble souls in Russia, a wholehearted friend of the Jews and sympathetic to Judaism. In his writings on Karaism and Judeo-Arabic literature he enriched and enlightened one of the dark chapters in Jewish history. He was one of the pious Christians who loved the Jews. "I had the privilege of knowing him," wrote Zeitlin, "while I was a student in St. Petersburg and recognized in him his devotion to truth. While I was in Russia in 1926 I visited him. He was a suffering old man and no longer a professor, but was still imbued with admiration of the Jews. I vividly recall our conversation about the Beilis trial. . . ." It is surprising that there is no mention in the book of the reaction of the Russian liberals, for example Maxim Gorki and Leonid Andreyev, who were active in the defence of the Jewish cause. Many liberal papers also came out in defence of the Jews. *Ruskie Vedomosti* in Moscow, one of the oldest and most venerable papers in Russia, opposed the ritual accusation.[193] There was also some light even in Tsarist Russia, not only darkness.

Poland's greatest poet, Adam Mickiewicz, (1798-1855), was an eminent protagonist of philo-Semitism in the Slav world. His pro-Jewish feeling had partly mystical motives. Inclined towards Messianic ideas, he believed in the mission of the Jewish people whose suffering would lead them to redemption, just as he allotted to the oppressed Polish nation a special task in the liberation of oppressed nations. To express his sympathy towards Judaism and particularly to the idea of "Zion Rebuilt," the poet attempted to organize a Jewish Legion, whose task it would be to liberate Palestine from the Turkish yoke. Mickiewicz advocated the restoration of Jewish morale by military service which would serve as a basis for the emancipation of the Jews as a people. Mickiewicz upheld Jewish rights to retain their national characteristics, called for participation in the liberation of Poland, and the co-existence of Jews and Poles in a liberated Poland. On Sabbath (Sept. 5, 1855), Mickiewicz and Armand Levy, his Jewish friend, attended the services at the Smyrna Synagogue. The poet was greatly impressed by the mood of the worshippers, just as he had been ten years earlier when he brought his circle of friends to the Tisha B'Av rites in the Paris Synagogue at 14 Rue Neuve St. Laurent. Following the services in Smyrna, Mickiewicz told Levy that "God will eventually harken to the prayers of this nation, whose sons know how to pray with such religious fervour and strong

181

faith." He also confided to Levy his thoughts about the future of the Jews in Poland: "I would not want the Jews to leave Poland because, just as the Union of Poland with Lithuania, differing by origin and religion, brought our Polish state to its greatness and happiness, so I am certain that the union of Poland and Israel will assure our spiritual and moral strength." Mickiewicz championed Jewish equality and may be considered as an advocate of the idea of national emancipation for the Jews. Mickiewicz created in his Pan Tadeusz the sympathetic figure of a Jewish patriot, Jankiel, the musician.

Mickiewicz's mystical attachment to Jews and Judaism, compounded of many motives, constitutes a fascinating chapter in the history of philo-Semitic thought. While manifestations of anti-Semitism in Poland are amply documented and frequently assumed tragic proportions, the pro-Semitic trend, exemplified in the writings and actions of Adam Mickiewicz, deserves to be stressed and understood as a major factor in the survival of the Jews on Polish soil for over a millennium. With its large numbers, great density, more complete cultural and linguistic separation than anywhere in the world, Polish Jewry has played a central role in Jewish history throughout the millennia of Jewish dispersion; the extinction of Polish Jewry was due to outside forces — the Nazi invasion. Through the centuries Judaism in Poland remained an inexhaustible spiritual and physical reservoir, large enough to fill the gaps caused by persecutions all over the world, or by the radical assimilation in the ranks and files of Jewish communities in the Western World. Mickiewicz and his circle have written a golden chapter in the history of philo-Semitic sentiments in Slav lands. Other Polish authors followed in the footsteps of Mickiewicz. The names of the novelists Eliza Orzeszko and Adam Szymanski should be recalled in this context.[194]

The literature of France portrays the Jew both as friend and as enemy. The return to the sources of Western civilization, including the Old Testament, in the days of the French Renaissance, culminated in Racine's Biblical dramas *Athalie* and *Esther*. A century before the era of emancipation, *Esther* contained a powerful plea for tolerance, revealing a link, however tenuous, between veneration for the Old Testament and concern for the people who descended from the heroes of the Hebrew Bible and lived in the Christian world in misery and subjugation.

French literature in the nineteenth century dealing with Jewish themes evinced two basic tendencies, anti-Semitic and philo-Semitic. The anti-Semitic trend presented the Jew in an adverse light; he was a lover of mammon, a greedy capitalist, who remained a foreign element in the midst of the French people. Balzac in *La Maison Nucingen,* Alfons Daudet in *Le Roi en Exil* portrayed the Jews as ruthless speculators, who could not be assimilated because of the irreconcilable differences between the Semitic element and the Gentile society. Opposed to that, there were numerous French playwrights and novelists in the nineteenth century who viewed the Jew with sympathetic understanding and even with a certain amount of admiration. Many nineteenth-century French authors pleaded that a Jew be accorded the tolerance which he fully deserved; they glorified the self-sacrificing patriotism shown by the Jew, whether he was a humble citizen or statesman. Some Jews see Utopian visions such as a cosmopolitan society or a restored Jewish nation but these Utopian visions testify to his idealism. The philo-Semitic writers portray the Jew as a noble figure, exalt his family life and sing the praises of Jewish womanhood.

The Dreyfus affair in the 1890s created a climate for anti-Semitic thought, yet, at the same time, inspired a number of French writers to defend Jews and Judaism. The great political struggle between the Right and the Left in which the Jews were actually no more than pawns also reflected in the literature of the time. The Dreyfus case is at the centre of Anatole Frances *L'Anneau d'Amethyste.* One of the heroes of the story, Bergeret, who sides with Dreyfus, has nothing but contempt for the misguided mob shouting Down with Zola — Death to the Jews. He respects the Jews for their intelligence, denies the theory of incompatibility between races: "Race does not make a country, for there is no people in Europe that is not made up of a host of different races." He cites Renan's wise saying: "What welds men into a people is the memory of the great things they have accomplished in the past and the will to accomplish more great things in the future."

Anatole France defends the cause of the Jews in his story *Le Procurateur de Judee*. Philo-Semitic writers, such as E.M. de Voguein in *Le Maitre de la Mer*, demand not mere tolerance which could be considered as a special privilege rather than as a right, but absolute and unlimited freedom. French literature in the nineteenth century also presents the nationalist Jew, who voices his longing for Zion. Alexander Dumas Fils portrays a modern-type Zionist in his drama *La Femme de Claude*. Daniel's heart is in Zion; he is imbued with love for Israel's ancient homeland. He is not content to know that Jews of many lands tend to identify with their brethren in other countries in times of trouble; his ideal is the physical ingathering of all the Jews in Palestine. Anatole deLeroy-Beaulieu, celebrated French publicist, fighter for political liberty and religious freedom, one of the strongest warriors against anti-Semitism in the nineteenth century and author of the classic philo-Semitic volume *Israel Among the Nations* (1896) and of *Anti-Semitism* (1897), described Dumas's Daniel as an idealized Jewish type, the progenitor of an entire generation; he seems to be the proto-type of Mordecai, the latter-day prophet in *Daniel Deronda*.

As a consequence of the Dreyfus affair, the Zionist movement had gained a foothold in France where it gave rise to the Zionist novel, such as *La Juive* by Enacryos (pseudonym for J.H. Boex). The heroine of the novel, Rachel, is an ardent Zionist who arouses admiration for the race to which she belongs. Her friend Picard pays a tribute to Jewish power of persistence with the following words: "The very survival of Judaism," Picard declares, "attests to the excellence of the race. While all the ancient civilisations have perished, the Jews have survived. Despite its close contacts with European civilisation, Judaism has succeeded in preserving its inconquerable unity. The struggle between ancient Greece and Persia and that between the Roman Empire and the rest of the Ancient World are only minor episodes compared to the unflagging strength and staying power of the ancient tribe of Jacob."

Up to the nineteenth century, Jewish characters in French literature represented mainly the commercial type of Jew, rising from the small pedlar to the big banker. In the post-emancipation era, philo-Semitic trends pervaded French literature and portrayed the Jew in a different light: the loyal citizen, even devoted patriot, a Socialist dreamer, a Zionist visionary. However, philo-Semitic tendencies in French literature did not produce a noble type of the stature of Lessing's Nathan the Wise.[195]

As a reaction against Jewish emancipation, an anti-Semitic trend entered into French literature. It was represented by writers like Ferdinand Celine, Charles Maurras, the brothers Tharaud, who presented an unfavourable image of both the individual Jew and the Jewish community. On the other hand, there existed a definite philo-Semitic tendency in French letters, represented by Jacques Maritain, Paul Claudel, Francois Mauriac, Jean-Paul Sartre, Romain Rolland, Andre Malraux, Antoine de Saint Exupery. The philo-Semitic motif in modern French literature may be traced back to a tradition established by Emile Zola. Zola was imbued with a genuine feeling of justice and sensed the grave wrong perpetrated in the Dreyfus case. As champion of Dreyfus he published his famous letter *J'Accuse,*[196] accusing the military caste and the clerical leaders of France of fomenting the sordid anti-Semitic libel against Dreyfus in order to divert the French people from the true causes of defeat in the Franco-Prussian War of 1870-71. In *J'Accuse* Zola proclaimed his fervent belief in the invincibility of truth: "If you shut up truth and bury it under the ground," he declares, "it will but grow and gather to itself such explosive power that the day it bursts through, it will blow up everything in its way . . . I know none of the people I accuse; I have never seen them. I bear them neither rancour nor hatred. They are no more to me than entities, spirits of social mischief. And the act

I am performing here is but a revolutionary means to hasten the rule of truth and justice. I have but one passion: the truth, in the name of humanity which has suffered so much and has a right to happiness. My flaming protest is but the cry of my heart. Then let them dare to force me into the assize court and hold the enquiry in broad daylight. I am waiting."

Zola was not a sentimental philo-Semite; his motives were humanitarian and anti-clerical. In his open *Lettre a la France* (6 January 1898) Zola expressed his opposition to Church Rule: "France, you are heading back to the church; you are returning to the past, to the intolerant and theocratic past which your most eminent sons have fought with their skill and their blood."[197]

When, at the height of his fame, he gallantly defended the Jewish minority, he did so because he was imbued with the same spirit of justice that earlier made him stand up in defence of the French working class. In his novels he condemned anti-Semitism and interceded for the Jew in a country where Edouard Drumont's *La France Juive (Jewish France,* 1886) with its violent anti-Semitic accusations had a wide circulation. Sustained by his genius and by the strength of his courage, Zola went forward in the battle for justice. Zola's attitude was inspired by the love of the common man: he believed that the masses were contaminated by their leaders. "The dear and humble people who persecute the Jews today, would tomorrow start a revolution to free Captain Dreyfus, if only some honest man instilled in them the sacred fire of justice." On many occasions Zola fiercely condemned the outrage of Jew hatred. "And now, anti-Semitism. There is the culprit. I have already noted how this barbaric campaign which throws us back a thousand years, arouses my need for fraternity, my passion for tolerance and human emancipation. To go back to the religious wars, to resort again to persecutions, to wish for races to exterminate one another, is so meaningless in our century of liberation, that such a proposition seems above all stupid. It could only have been born in the hazy, ill-balanced brain of a fanatic (Edouard Drumont), of the great vanity of a writer long unknown, wishing at all cost to play a part, even an odious one. And I cannot think that such a movement will have a decisive importance in France, this country of free-will, of brotherly generosity and clear sightedness."[198]

Zola referred to the hidden poison which made the masses delirious, otherwise how could they have taken part in such madness? That poison is the enraged hatred of the Jews, fed to the people every morning for years. "There is a band of professional poisoners, and the worst of it is that they do it in the name of morality, in the name of Christ, as avengers and judges. And who says that the atmosphere in which the court martial sat did not influence its decisions? A Jewish traitor selling his country, that goes over without debate. If no human reason can explain the crime — if he is rich, wise, hard working, steady, lives an impeccable life — is it not enough that he is a Jew?"

Throughout his utterances about the Jews, Zola was motivated by philo-Semitism based on humanitarian sentiments. The mystique of Christian pro-Semitism, based on veneration of scripture and promise to Israel, he disregarded. The Jews are neither better nor worse than others, they are people like all the other inhabitants of France. One of his figures, Madam Caroline, remarks, "To me the Jews are made like any others. If they are apart, it is because they have been put apart." (L'Argent.) This saying is the key to Zola's attitude and to the entire humanitarian trend in his philo-Semitic scheme of thought. Jews are people, like everybody else; if they have faults, the guilt is not theirs. Zola became a world-wide symbol of truth in his relentless struggle for justice in the Dreyfus affair. He became the conscience of mankind in his unfaltering exposure of the true situation in which the Dreyfus struggle took place.

At Zola's funeral, Anatole France, an illustrious philo-Semite, who also fought on behalf of Dreyfus's rehabilitation, said: "Zola has been an instance of a human conscience. He fought social evils wherever he met them. In his last books he showed plainly his fervent love of humanity. He tried to foresee

187

a better society. He has honoured his country and the world by his stupendous labour and great accomplishment. His destiny and his heart achieved for him the grandest of fates. For a moment he was the conscience of mankind."

It has been aptly remarked that one of the characteristic but frequently overlooked features of the Dreyfus affair was the existence of a dedicated group of Catholic Dreyfusards. Though they commanded only a small percentage of public opinion, some pulpits and pastoral visitations were open to them as many of them were priests. Official Catholicism was anti-Dreyfusard, but there were among them dedicated defenders of Dreyfus, in spite of official difficulties put in their way. The most influential of the group was one, Paul Villet, who turned from the anticlerical *Ligue des Droits de l'Homme* to found the *Comite Catholique pour la defense du Droit*. He and the Abbes Pichot, Fremont and Brugerette were the most eloquent exponents of their cause. Abbe Pichot wrote one particularly cogent open letter arguing that anti-Semitism was fundamentally un-Christian.[199]

Judaism has to a remarkable extent found understanding and sympathy in certain Roman Catholic circles, chiefly among French intellectuals, influenced by the eminent Catholic philosopher Jacques Maritain (1882-1972), one of the great minds of our time. In the view of Maritain and his spiritual associates, mostly disciples of Henri Bergson at the College de France, the Jews are tied to Christian believers by bonds of religious relationship which create close spiritual contact between Christian and Jew. In the history of God's dealing with mankind, the Jews have played an essential part as the bearers of divine revelation: Judaism represents a body of beliefs which Christ came not to destroy, but to fulfil. Christians, Maritain teaches, being themselves grafted on the olive tree of Israel, must look on the men involved in the Jewish tragedy with a brotherly eye and not without trembling for themselves; for ultimately any Jewish tragedy leads to destruction of Christian morality and civilization itself. Maritain assigned a sublime role to Israel's mission in the world. He affirmed that it was Israel's vocation to stimulate and move the events of history. Israel, he says, is like an activating ferment giving the world no peace; it bars slumber, it teaches the world to be discontented and restless as long as the world has no God; it stimulates the movement of history.

A notable pronouncement was Maritain's discussion of the evergreen problem of the crucifixion story and its possible anti-Semitic consequences. In a letter to Haim Greenberg, the noted Zionist thinker, he extolled the kinship between the Christian and Jewish spirit. Christ's condemnation and death, he declared, are a divine mystery, and cannot be conceived in terms of a lynching party; any Jew today is as innocent of the murder of Christ, as every Catholic of today is of the murder of Jeanne d'Arc or the imprisonment of Galileo. "Who killed Christ?" he asked. "The Jews? The Romans? I have killed him, I am killing him everyday through my sins. There is no other Christian answer."[200]

Maritain's teacher was Leon Bloy (1846-1917), mentioned above, a notable Catholic thinker and writer. Bloy, too, preached an exalted concept of Judaism, considering the people of Israel as a *corpus mysticum,* and the Jews as a source of human salvation.

Two great French Catholic poets, Charles Peguy and Paul Claudel, frequently expressed profound thoughts about the mystery and significance of Israel's existence. Peguy, (1873-1914), whose poetry ranks with the greatest and profoundest religious poetry of all times, shared a deep veneration for Judaism with his idealistic Jewish friend Bernard Lazare, the champion of Dreyfus. Peguy referred to Lazare as *un juif de la race prophetique;* Lazare's character evoked a noble eulogy from Peguy who exalted the Jews' "unshakeable fidelity to the mysticism of friendship." The whole world, he writes with compassion, are unhappy in this modern era; the Jews are more unhappy than the others.[201]

Charles Peguy sympathized with the difficult situation of the Jews, as exposed in the Dreyfus case. "It is not easy to be a Jew. When they remain insensible to the appeals of their brothers, to the cries of the persecuted, to the wails, to the lamentations of their bruised brothers throughout the world, one says: 'They are bad Jews.' And if they merely open an ear to the lamentations which arise from the Danube and the Dnieper, one says: 'They betray us: they are bad Frenchmen!'"[202]

Jews played an important role in Peguy's life. Two of them had a great impact on his thinking and writing, earlier Bernard Lazare, and later Henri Bergson, the philosopher. The Jewish question was one of his great concerns. Peguy had a deep love both for the Jews and for Judaism. "We have loved the people of Israel," he wrote in his great poem *Eve*. He spoke of Israel with a sincerity, rare in French literature. To him there was no God other than the God of the Bible: the God of Abraham, Isaac and Jacob, and it was this God Christianity was called to make known to the world. In fact, as he said, without Judaism, Christianity would not exist at all. Peguy never grudged his admiration for Judaism. Though equipped with a classical education, he had the highest and purest notion of the Hebrew culture which he placed on a level with the Greek, the Christian and the French traditions. He felt the psychology of Israel has been shaped by its vocation, its sufferings and historic experiences. The Dreyfus case had made this clear to him. "It is sad to be a Jew, because a Jew atones for all the sins of Israel." But it is also a blessing to be a Jew. Indeed Israel has been a blessing for the whole of mankind, through the Holy Books it gave to the world. Anti-Semites cannot understand or judge the Jews, Peguy thought, for it is not easy to be a Jew.[203]

The indebtedness of French literature to the Jewish element is another motif of philo-Semitism. It is poignantly expressed in the remark by the French literary critic Ferdinand Brunetiere that without Hebrew inspiration the French would not have Bossuet, Pascal, Hugo and "the poets of the obscure and the inaccessible . . . those who have given us the thrill of the infinite and finally those among us who have kept alive the sentiment and notion of the Divine."[204]

Paul Claudel (1868-1955) felt a mystic attachment to Israel and cherished a particularly deep love for the light and blessing flowing from Hebrew scripture. He published three letters in which he paid tribute to Israel. "The continuous study," he writes, "which I make of the Bible has imbued me with the exceptional importance of Israel from the point of view of God and of humanity. It is Israel, with its heroic courage and intellectual audacity, inexplicable without a vocation from above, who has always upheld against the seductions of Greece, the idea of a personal and transcendent God, superior to all the superstitions of paganism. I have now renounced all fictitious expressions, and live upon my knees in the brightness which comes to me in increasing measure from the Holy Books. It is a marvel, which does not cease to grow as I devote to it my interest, my heart and my mind. *Quelle gloire pour Israel d'avoir ete choisi comme redacteur et depositaire d'un tel message.* What glory for Israel to have been chosen as the editor and repository of such a message?"[205]

Jules Michelet, (1798-1874), the famous French historian, represented sincere philo-Semitism based on his belief in the creative power of the "collective people" which he found exemplified in Jewish history. It was Jewish loyalty and unflagging perseverence which moved him to a deep admiration of the faithful people, expressed in moving words. In a true humanitarian spirit, he believed that the faults of the Jews are due to the maltreatment at the hands of Christians — a frequent argument against anti-Semitic accusations. "I love the Jews. I have not let slip any occasion to recall to mind their martyrdoms, their family virtues, the admirable abilities which they have displayed in our time. How could a man remain unconcerned about the destiny of this people, authors of the Christian world, and so much persecuted and maltreated by the Christians. As soon as one wishes to be severe toward them, he regrets it and says: 'The vices of the Jewish people are those which we have produced in them; their virtues are their own.' Let us then respect the patient people, whom, for so many centuries, the world has smitten so hard and who, in our days, have suffered so much in Russia . . . . Let us respect the lively energy, from which the Oriental stock has raised up so many unforeseen talents, so many savants and proficient in every art."[206]

The sentiments displayed in the works of noble-hearted Frenchmen, such as the thinkers, poets and scholars quoted above, were translated into deeds during the Nazi occupation of France. The clergy of France played a role second to none in their opposition to the anti-Jewish decrees and in their rescue activities on behalf of the persecuted. The highest dignitaries of the Catholic Church in France condemned the Nazi war against the Jews.

Not only Catholic dignitaries but also leaders of French Protestantism showed compassion with the persecuted Jews. The French Protestants recalled the sufferings they had had to endure in former days. That both religious communities (Huguenots and Jews) had retained their consciousness of persecution until the present day was expressed in an admirably clear and strong manner in the courageous letter which the French pastor Marc Boegner, President of the French Reformed Church, addressed to the Grand Rabbin de France, at the time when the Nazi persecution of Jews in occupied France began: "Our Church, which once experienced all the sufferings of persecution, feels burning sympathy with your communities whose freedom of worship is already threatened in certain localities and whose faithful have been exposed so suddenly and unexpectedly to misfortune . . . ."[206a] The magnificent, self-sacrificing stand of the French Episcopat (1940-1944) earned it the title, *Defensor Judaeorum*.[207]

One of the most eminent representatives of French culture in our day is Jean-Paul Sartre (born 1905), existentialist philosopher, novelist, dramatist, literary critic and a controversial political essayist. He has gained international reputation as a provocative spokesman of French left-wing intellectuals. In 1964 he was awarded the Nobel prize for literature, but refused to accept it, thus asserting his spiritual freedom and protesting against literary formalities. Sartre's *Reflexions*

sur la Question Juive[208], published in Paris in 1946 and re-printed in several French and English editions, has permanent relevance for the Jewish situation. He shows an intuitive knowledge of the Jewish position in the Western world and also deep understanding of the causes of the Jewish-Gentile tensions. Sartre's work is one of the most profound modern statements on the problem of anti-Semitism, an issue which he regards as of central importance for modern civilization. Sartre is no arm-chair philosopher. He knows the conditions under which human beings live and understands the ultimate causes of their despair. His involvement with the Jewish problem may have arisen through an encounter with dejected Jews who were forced to wear the yellow badge during the Nazi occupation of Paris. "We have been indignant and rightly," he writes, "over the obscene 'yellow star' that the German government forced upon the Jews. What seemed intolerable about this was that it called attention to the Jew, that it obliged him to feel himself perpetually Jewish in the eyes of others. There were some who tried by all possible means to indicate their sympathy for the unfortunates so marked. But when well-intentioned people undertook to raise their hats to Jews whom they encountered, the Jews themselves felt that these salutes were extremely painful. Under the looks of support and compassion, they felt themselves becoming objects: objects of commiseration, of pity, of what you will — but objects. They provided these virtuous liberals with an occasion for making a general gesture, for uttering a manifesto. They were only an occasion. The liberal, when he met a Jew was free to shake his hand or spit in his face; but the Jew was not free to be a Jew."

In these words Sartre alludes to his main existential concepts, the freedom of man, the human situation, subject and object, concrete relations between people. In the course of his *Reflexions* he analyses the psychology of the anti-Semite, seeking to clarify the subconscious impulses which lead the anti-Semite to project his own hostilities and frustrations upon that mythical figure of the Jew. The anti-Semite, he affirms, is afraid not of the Jews, but of himself, his conscience, his instincts; he dreads solitude, society, the whole world. The Jew is only a pretext, and, at another time, a Negro, a Chinese, or, if the anti-Semite is a Frenchman, an Englishman might serve as well.

The liberal philo-Semite — the "democrat" — is, in Sartre's view, a sorry champion of the Jewish cause. Though the democrat maintains that all men are equal in the eyes of the law, he has no eyes for the historic differences among human beings. He does not recognize the Jew, the Arab or the Negro, but man alone. The democratic philo-Semite does not acknowledge the Jew's collective consciousness; in his defence of the Jew, he rescues the Jew as a man, but annihilates him as a Jew, regarding collective Jewish awareness as a danger. He wishes to separate the Jew from his religion, his family and his ethnic group, in order to plunge him into the democratic crucible, out of which he will emerge single and naked, an individual "in solitary particle, just like all the other particles."

Sartre's pro-Jewish sympathies conform with the twentieth-century national aspirations of the Jewish people. He affirms that in relation to the Jew, who is conscious and proud of being a Jew, who insists on the fact that he belongs to the Jewish community without at the same time ignoring the ties which bind him to a national collectivity, there is no difference between the anti-Semite and the democrat. The former wants to destroy him as a man; the latter wants to destroy him as a Jew. The democrat is afraid that persecution may help to give the Jew a sharpened awareness of himself. While the anti-Semite blames the Jew for being a Jew, the democrat is inclined to blame him for considering himself a Jew. And between the two, his enemy and his defender, the Jew seems to be caught in a dilemma. Is the Jew primarily a Jew or primarily a man?

The origin of European anti-Semitism Sartre ascribes to the teaching that the Jew is the murderer of Christ. He stresses the intolerable situation of the Jews, condemned to live in the heart of society "which adores the God whom they have killed." And though this fact does not constitute an explanation of modern anti-Semitism, yet if the modern anti-Semite has chosen the Jew as the object of his hatred, it is because of the religious horror the latter has always inspired. This horror led to economic discrimination and to the image of the Jew as following non-productive trades. Modern societies have seized upon the unfavourable memory of the Jew as money-lender and usurer and made it the pretext for their anti-Semitism.

While the Jew values the sympathy shown to him, this can never prevent him from regarding anti-Semitism, as a permanent element of the community in which he lives. While his enemies are impassioned, his defenders are lukewarm; Sartre, as a friend of the Jews, emphasizes the great Jewish contribution to culture which Jews have made since emancipation. The names of Spinoza, Proust, Kafka, Darius Milhaud, Chagall, Einstein are weighty enough to show what the Jews might have given the world had they been emancipated sooner.

Sartre's attitude is expressed in existentialist terms. A Jew is launched upon his path of Jewishness, whatever he does. He can choose to be brave and cowardly, but he cannot choose not to be a Jew. To be a Jew is to be flung into and abandoned in the Jewish situation, and at the same time to be responsible through one's own person for the destiny and the very nature of the Jewish people.

The authenticity of the Jew comes from living fully his condition of a Jew, his inauthenticity stems from denying it or attempting to evade it. The authentic Jewish mind has a "Protestant quality." The Jew, Sartre affirms, mistrusts totalitarian blocs; it is in this sense that the word "destructive" may be used concerning the Jews. The Jew upholds the rational outlook in life, is prepared to construct a human order founded on the universality of human nature; he opposes the irrational values, distrusts intuition, because it cannot be questioned and in consequence, drives man apart.

Sartre's philo-Semitism impels him to offer exaggerated generalizations concerning the virtues of the Jewish people. The Jews are the gentlest of men. They are passionately opposed to violence. And this unfailing gentleness, which they preserve in the midst of the most atrocious persecutions, this sense of justice and reason which they set up as their sole defence against a hostile, brutal and unjust society, is perhaps the best of the message they have to give us, and the true mark of their greatness.

While the anti-Semite considers the Jew as a permanent danger to national values because of his rational quality and his opposition to irrational romantic nationalism, Sartre sees the Jewish community as a valuable instrument of self-criticism, a kind of national conscience. By upholding the spirit of free criticism in society, the Jew makes his inability to become completely assimilated a valuable asset to national life. The authentic Jew claims his place as a Jew within the community in which he lives; but he may also, by free choice, demand for the Jewish nation land and autonomy. Jewish authenticity may require that the Jew be supported by a Jewish nation in Zion. It is possible to conceive that these two choices complement each other as two manifestations of Jewish reality. Sartre touches here on the vexing problem of "dual loyalty," though he does not use this expression. He delcares that Jews absorbed into the French collectivity could preserve their links with Tel Aviv; Palestine would represent in their eyes a sort of ideal value and symbol; the existence of an autonomous Jewish community would be definitely less dangerous for the integrity of French society than that of an ultra-montane clergy which France tolerates with perfect ease.

Every Gentile, Sartre believes, is bound by his conscience to act in the case of the Jews, not in the sense of a condescending liberalism, but as an expiation of the guilt of anti-Semitism in which all Gentiles share. "There is not one of us," he declares, "who is not totally guilty of martyrdom of the Jews. The Jewish blood shed by the Nazis is upon the head of all of us . . . The fate of the Jew is the fate of every man. No Frenchman will be free as long as the Jews could not enjoy the fullness of their rights. No Frenchman will be secure as long as the Jew not only in France, but in the world at large, need go in fear of his life."

Sartre describes Drumont's anti-Semitic *"La France Juive"*

as a "collection of base and obscene stories." Because the anti-Semite takes a perverse pleasure in evil, he is able to repeat to the point of obsession the recital of obscene and criminal acts which stimulate and satisfy his own perverse inclinations, but he attributes them to the infamous Jews whom he attacks and despises. In this manner he gratifies his urges without compromising his own good name.

Sartre castigates those who turn away from the fact of the Jewish question and refuse to acknowledge its urgency and significance. His compassionate words, written in 1944, retain their validity even today. "Today those Jews whom the Germans did not deport or murder are coming back to their homes. Many were among the first members of the Resistance . . . Now all France rejoices and fraternizes in the streets; the newspapers devote whole columns to stories of prisoners of war and deportees. Do we say anything about the Jews? Do we give a thought to those who died in the gas chambers at Lublin? Not a line in the newspapers. That is because we must not irritate the anti-Semites; more than ever, we need unity, well-meaning journalists will tell you. In the interests of the Jews themselves, it would not do to talk too much about them just now. For four years French society has lived without them; it is just as well not to emphasize too vigorously the fact that they have reappeared."

Contempt for those who stood by and never interfered while victims and executioners enacted their tragic roles is also expressed in his play *Les Sequestree d'Altona* (Paris 1956). In this drama Sartre accuses not only the Nazi leaders and the German people, but an entire generation whose cowardice and abject submission to brutality made them guilty of complicity with the Nazi horrors, though, in a formal sense, their hands were clean.

A dispassionate evaluation of philo-Semitism in the modern era cannot agree with Sartre's condemnation of the liberal-democratic motive in its approach to the Jewish problem. The humanitarian evaluation of the Jew as individual, as citizen of the nation in which he lives, the severance of the association between the new Jewish citizen and the image of the wandering Jew, the Christ killer, the perpetual alien, formed the basis of Jewish emancipation and led ultimately to Jewish national restitution. The liberal philo-Semite occupies his rightful place of honour in the history of Jewish-Gentile relations, and deserves better than to be termed a "sorry champion." His liberal attitude stems from the spiritual atmosphere of the French Revolution, its clarion call to liberty, equality and fraternity, its noble concept of the "Rights of Man."

The philo-Semitism of Jean-Paul Sartre is a reaction to the French anti-Semitism of the post-emancipation era, particularly to the shattering experience of Nazi persecution, the vileness of Nazi collaborators among Western nations and the moral decay of the French nation in the days of surrender to Nazism. He has neither knowledge nor understanding for the essence of Judaism, the spiritual values which sustained Jewish existence throughout the ages. As an atheist, he is impervious to the religious quality of Jewish perseverance and loyalty. He is aware of the Jew as a product of anti-Semitism; he proclaims the need for an authentic response on the part of the Jew who is exhorted to commit himself freely and proudly to his identity as a member of the Jewish people. Sartre's views have left their mark on contemporary French Jewry. Albert Memmi, the Tunisian-Jewish novelist, dedicates his book *Portrait of a Jew* (1963) to the "comrades of my youth, today Chalutzim, to Jean-Paul Sartre, a free man."

In March 1967 Sartre paid a much-publicized visit to Israel. This confrontation with the new Jew, particularly the *chalutz,* strengthened his conviction of the central place of a Jewish State of the preservation and strengthening of authentic Jewish existence. He was impressed by the universal values of the *kibbutz,* by the feeling that the Israeli Jew has been freed of the complexes of anti-Semitism, and by the strong ties of history and tradition. It was for him something of a liberation — not only evidence of Jewish liberation, but a liberation for the non-Jew himself ". . . who meets Jewish people, a kind of person with full rights who is as good as anyone anywhere, and often better, and who is called an Israeli, that is to say, a Jew who has chosen Israel as his homeland. Israel is the only country where one can say of someone that he is a Jew, without being an anti-Semite."[209]

Sartre desires to transcend the guilt complex which he shares with his fellow Gentiles by a determined pro-Jewish attitude and action. Together with the theologically motivated philo-Semitism in French-Catholic circles, Sartre's valuation of Jewish existence in the Diaspora and in Zion constitutes one of the most powerful factors in the philo-Semitic and pro-Zionist sentiment of the modern era.

Philo-Semitism in the literature of small nations is frequently based on a feeling of solidarity between weak peoples and the passionate desire to survive which knits them together in sympathy. A good example for this motive in philo-Semitism is offered by the contemporary Greek writer Nikos Kazantzakis (1883-1957), a Cretan, author of the masterpieces *Zorba, the Greek* and *Report to Greco*.

Nikos Kazantzakis claims spiritual affinity between the Jewish people and the Greeks, particularly his countrymen, the Cretans. The love of freedom, man's national and social freedom, the freedom of all peoples, could really be understood only by Jews and Cretans, Kazantzakis declares; For thousands of years, despite innumerable invasions of the island of Crete, its people's love of liberty and dignity had never been stifled. These same character traits, said the writer, can also be found in the history of the Jewish people.

In his novels Jewish figures appeared in a sympathetic light. Jewish girls appear throughout Kazantsakis's works, fighting for justice on the national or universal level. The work of this Greek writer contains Chassidic motifs. In *Report to Greco* he writes. "My old Rebbe Nachman taught me to understand when to open my mouth and speak, when to take up the pen and write. Rebbe Nachman was simple, vivacious and saintly. He always gave his disciples advice . . . One day, they came to him and reproachingly asked him, 'Why don't you speak like a real Tzaddik?' Rebbe Nachman smiled and said: 'Once upon a time, the nettles asked a rose, "Rose, oh rose, teach us your secret. How do you become a rose?" And the rose replied: "Throughout the winter, patiently, lovingly and with faith, I work with one thought in my heart: the rose. The rain whips me, the wind tears my leaves off, the snow strangles me, but I have one thought in my heart: the rose.""'"

In many of his works such as *Ascece*, Kazantzakis deals with basic ideals of Judaism and pays homage to the eternal power of the Hebrew prophetic spirit. With the publication of Helen Kazantzakis's biography of her husband (1968), the author's thoughts relating to the Jewish people and Judaism are clearly documented. He dealt with Judaism as if it were a secret and powerful myth, just as he dealt with other civilizations whose history he analysed with eagerness. His works contain many references to Jewish faith and fate, all in a passionate philo-Semitic vein. In a letter to a friend he wrote: "I still hope to see you again one day — not in Paris, that accursed, seductive Babylon, but in Jerusalem, Tel Aviv, in the Promised Land, which I love so much! There's a very large drop of Hebrew blood in my veins and this drop produces an effervescence and commotion in all my Hellenic and Cretan blood. I am obsessed and possessed by the Hebraic destiny. When I was ten years old, I begged my father to let me go to the home of the Rabbi of Canea to learn Hebrew. I went three times, and took three lessons. But my uncles, and more especially my aunts, were afraid and revolted against it. They were fearful that the Jews might drink my blood, and my father withdrew me from the rabbinical school."

Kazantzakis's philo-Semitism is expressed in his passionate desire for the rule of justice and his admiration for the Zionist effort and achievement. "Your eyes wander over the desert of Judea and you feel doubtlessly that no other people but yours would overcome its barrenness." (1951) He also wrote: "With the Jews I love to be inflamed against injustice which prevails without restraint."[210]

Kazantzakis revered the figure of the pioneer of modern Hebrew, Eliezer ben Yehuda (1857-1922). He seemed to him to symbolize the irresistible power of national revival and cultural Renaissance which also moved the Greek nation after hundreds of years of subjugation. In his book *The Fratricides* a chapter is devoted to Ben Yehuda the redeemer of living Hebrew and the love he inspired in his people and in the Bible-loving world to resuscitate the dead Hebrew language, the language of the Bible and to make it alive in the mouth of the Jews of the whole world. The chapter also includes motives of the Ben Yehuda legend, such as the story of his son who was born dumb and suddenly burst out in speech — in the holy tongue of the Tanach (Hebrew Bible). Kazantzakis's approach to the Hebrew renaissance is imbued with a love of Zion, love of the Hebrew bible and admiration of the Jewish people — genuine philo-Semitism.

There is a strong tendency of philo-Semitic sentiments in Afrikaans literature reflecting the respect in which the Boers held the people of the Bible. Abraham Jonker has given expression to the pro-Semitic feeling of a large section of Afrikanerdom. He deals in a sympathetic and comprehensive way with the history of the Jewish people, their contributions to South Africa, the causes and manifestations of anti-Semitism. Jonker believes that the root causes of anti-Semitism are to be found not in the Jew who is hated, but in the Gentile who hates. Jew-baiting, he asserts, debases the nation which resorts to it without helping to solve any problems. Many factors, religious, historical, economic and psychological, have caused the Jew to be singled out for this role of scapegoat, but perhaps the most decisive has been the teaching that the Jews killed Christ. Jonker believes that the only complete solution for the problem lies in an all-embracing Zionism which must be the ultimate objective of the Jewish people.[211]

Another illustrious South African philo-Semite was Olive Schreiner, renowned novelist (1885-1920). In her celebrated *Letter to the Jew* written in 1906 she gives expression to noble pro-Jewish feelings. One of her thoughts, expressing an idealistic version of Israel's survival, has become the spiritual possession of enlightened humanity: "The study of the history of Europe during the past centuries," she writes, "teaches us one uniform lesson: That the nations which have received and in any way dealt fairly and mercifully with the Jew have prospered: and that the nations that have tortured and oppressed him have written out their own curse." "When I remember, that all the religious and ethical teaching which has dominated and shaped the European peoples since they emerged from barbarism, has been that given them by the Jews: that it is the national record of the Jew, rich with his marvellous history, enriched by the songs and the psalms of his poets, mighty with the spiritual weight of the teachings of his prophets and seers, which has embedded itself in the very substance of our spiritual life — so that today some are even found to cry 'Take the Bible from our schools and religion and morality are dead! . . .' And When I turn to consider the noblest of those Jewish men and women whom I have personally known, I find that the quality most distinguishing them has been a large idealism; the power of grasping great impersonal conceptions, of tenaciously clinging to them, and living for their practical realisation. It is these qualities which have made the Jews in all ages the ethical leaders of the race; and which today find their expression in the fields of social and political reform. Among that small body of men and women found in every age, who devote great intellectual gifts, not to their own service but to the service of great ideals and the benefit of the whole race, the Jew holds today, as he has always held, his place in the front rank. . . . Because the Jew has maintained his domestic relations healthful and pure, because his womanhood has as a whole remained loyal to its duties, much enduring and strong, the Jewish race has been able to survive the awful centuries of oppression which have passed over its head; therefore, its very poorest members can enter a community without very largely increasing the percentage of crime and misery; therefore, with opportunity given it is always able to rise. . . . Therefore, I would welcome the exiled Russian Jew to South Africa, not merely with pity, but with a feeling of pride that any member of that great, much-suffering people, to whom the world owes so great a debt, should find a refuge and a home among us."[212]

The Jew very seldom appears as a character in Afrikaans literature. He is rarely portrayed as a full human being, frequently he represents the stereotype which has become fixed in the mind of people in the Christian world. Occasionally the Jew in the Afrikaans-speaking countryside is a typical shopkeeper who is treated sympathetically and shown kindliness and generosity when need arises. As examples may be adduced the Jewish shopkeeper Rabinowitz in Holmer Johanssen's novel *Die onterfdes* and Jack Rensky in Elise Muller's *Ek, 'n Samaritaanse Vrou*; types which are drawn with sympathy, even affection. Professor V.B. Gemser's translation of modern Hebrew literature, which includes tales from Peretz, Bialik and Sholem Asch, *Nieu-Hebreeuse Kortverhale,* is manifestly prompted by philo-Semitic motives. One may say that Afrikaans writings represent both tendencies — the stereotyped, strange, unsympathetic Jew, and the friendly, generous Jewish fellow man.

The freedom, opportunity and sympathy which Jews from distant Eastern Europe enjoyed among the Boer population, remote in civilization, yet near through the veneration of the Hebrew truth, leave no doubt as to the strength of philo-Semitic attitudes and actions within Afrikanerdom.[213] The friendly, even cordial, relations between the Jews and the Boers are reflected in letters by Jewish correspondents of Jews who travelled in South Africa and sent reports to their fellows in Europe; special emphasis is given to the bond of the Bible which united the early Jewish immigrants and the Boers. The devotion of the Boer to the Old Testament predisposed him to friendliness towards the people of the Book. While the political opinion of the Boers was not free from critical attitude towards the Jews on various grounds, especially after the relations between the Boers and the Uitlander population became strained, the general attitude of the Boer towards the Jew was a wholesome and friendly one, and the Jews appreciated the freedom which they enjoyed; the Kruger regime was free of anti-Semitism in any gross form.

Recognition of the Boers' generous attitude to the Jews is voiced in the address by the Reverend David Wasserzug, a

Jewish Minister from England, who had spent some years in the Transvaal (1897-1901) and remained at his post during most of the Boer War. After returning to England he wrote to the *Jewish Chronicle* of 16 August 1901, when the defeat of the Boers was already certain:[214] "Whatever offences are to be laid to the Boers' door, that of anti-Semitism must surely be excluded. Max Nordau stated recently that there was no country in the world where it was not a disadvantage to be a Jew. In speaking of Jewish relations with the Boers the reverse of Max Nordau's statement is near the truth: that in the Transvaal it was a greater advantage to be a Jew than a non-Jew. Among the grim and dour children of the veldt, the Bible and the people whose history is inextricably interwoven therewith are held in the deepest reverence. To 'Oom Paul' and his burghers, the Jew was the sacred vessel in whom the oracles of God were imperishably enshrined. Hence their singularly friendly attitude towards the People of the Book.

"Their persistent refusal to remove Jewish disabilities was the fruit of their narrow and sombre creed, which taught them to believe that the granting of political power to a Jew was an act of flat blasphemy to their God, and in no wise conflicts with the theory of their sincere personal regard for our people. Moreover the grave political problems with which they were wrestling at the time must also be taken into account in adjudging the motives which influenced their rejection of the petition for Jewish emancipation. Their day of rule is now past ... but the common dictates of gratitude should make a Jew pause before he unites his voice with the vilifiers of this ill-fated people."

The pro-Zionist sentiments of national Afrikanerdom find characteristic expression in a tribute paid to the State of Israel by the late Prime Minister, Dr. D.F. Malan, on his return from a visit in 1953. Israel, he said, had a great past. The way in which it grappled with the problems and difficulties of the present evoked universal wonder and admiration. He believed also that Israel had a great future and that as such it will again have a message for the world. The way in which the wasted face of the Promised Land had already been turned again into a land flowing with milk and honey filled every visitor with wonder and admiration.[215]

It is clear from numerous testimonies that the Afrikaans-speaking people have a powerful philo-Semitic tradition, far outweighing the manifestations of anti-Semitism which came particularly to the fore after the Nazi access to power in 1933. Philo-Semitism has been the dominant force in the attitude of the Boer people to the Jewish minority of the Republic. This fact deserves not only recognition, but constant emphasis so as to serve as a basic motive in the Gentile-Jewish group situation in South Africa.

BETWEEN PHILO-SEMITISM
AND ANTI-SEMITISM

In the consciousness of the Gentile world, anti-Semitism and philo-Semitism existed frequently side by side. Both attitudes are sometimes found in the same personality, posing an interesting problem about the polarity of human perceptions and the ambivalence of group instincts, residing in man. Sometimes people change from one attitude to the other, holding either view with great conviction. Their psychological metamorphosis is of great interest for the study of Gentile-Jewish relations.

The Jews were a separate entity, a group apart, largely unknown, condemned and ill-treated for their alleged vices, occasionally glorified for their imagined virtues. Every type of assertion has been made to abuse or to praise them; they have been perceived by Gentiles as being all things to all men.

The motives of anti-Semitism and philo-Semitism in one personality are often difficult to unravel. Under certain circumstances individuals express love and admiration for the Jewish people, its faith and tradition; on different occasions, this sympathy turns into aversion. On the other hand, we find that enemies of Jews and Judaism acquire, under the personal influence of Jewish individuals, or through study of Jewish sources, sympathy and understanding for the Jewish community and the beliefs it holds dear. The phenomenon of emotional and intellectual change in regard to the Jews may be illustrated by the following examples.

Martin Luther, quoted above, evinced in his youth great admiration for the Jews. "They are," he wrote in his work *That Jesus Christ was a Born Jew* (1523), "the children of the covenant and in comparison with them, Christians are the guests, the strangers, the dogs that eat the crumbs which fall from their master's table." Had he been a Jew, he would never have accepted Christianity as it is presented by bishops and monks. "They are blood-relations of our Lord; therefore if one were to boast of blood, the Jews belong to Christ more than we." He appealed to Christians to deal kindly with the Jews. It seems that Luther expected a general conversion of the Jews to the Reformed Church; he hoped that he might induce them to become Protestants and prove to the world the superiority of Protestantism over Catholicism. Being disappointed at their obstinate refusal to become converted, he changed his attitude and spoke of the Jews with bitterness and coarseness. In the writings of his last years, for example *Concerning the Jews and Their Lies* (1543), he urges the burning of synagogues, the prohibition of Jewish worship, the avoidance of the slightest intercourse with Jews, even violence and expulsion of the "devilish burden — the Jews."

Luther's friendly sentiments towards the Jews, though later superseded by venomous hatred, testify to a significant break with the traditional attitude of churchmen towards Jews. True, this change of heart had an ulterior purpose — the winning of Jews to Christianity, and it was a short-lived experience. Nevertheless, to formulate such an openly sympathetic statement on the Jewish plight and to put a finger of responsibility where it belonged was a shattering precedent. With all the inherent limitations of Luther's proposals to improve the material conditions of Jewish life, their very appearance in print justified a more humane approach to relations of Christians with Jews.

A contemporary Lutheran scholar has characterized the ambivalent role which Luther played in the attitudes of Protes-

207

tants to Jews, as follows: "Luther has been one of the key figures in Christian-Jewish encounters. He played on the one hand a fatal role in the tragic history of Jews in western Christianity. His authority in the Protestant world and his utterances, especially from his writings of the 1540's, were amply used in the anti-Semitic propaganda of the Third Reich. His Reformation approach, on the other hand, has paved the way for a new era in Christian-Jewish encounters."[216]

A Jewish scholar writes perceptively, "We know, that he expressed himself about the Pope, his archenemy, even more vehemently and obscenely than about the Jews. Such invectives, temptations, and outbursts of aggression certainly seem to combine quite naturally with the hatred of the chosen people. But Luther's character is too rich and complex, and the imprint he left on the history of his country and of our whole civilisation is too profound, for us to be content with an oversimplified, unidimensional interpretation, limited to the level of individual psychology . . . Luther was not always the enemy of the Jews. At the zenith of his activity, during the heroic period when this rebellious monk, sustained and justified by his faith, defied pope and emperor and for some time attained the dizzy peaks of total freedom, he had a very different attitude toward the Jews."[217]

The peculiar relationship between the Church and Israel is susceptible of two opposing interpretations. The mystery of Israel can be understood as a superhuman power, bringing together Israel and the Christian world in sympathy and charitable understanding, as in the works of Solovyev, Berdyaev and Maritain. On the other hand, Israel, rejecting Christ, is the "enemy" of everything that is Christian. This negative judgement is conspicuous in Luther's later writing, and in the words of anti-Jewish theologians such as Father G. Fessard who wrote, "Judaism, to the very extent that it rejects Christ, cannot help but be the enemy of all that is specifically Christian, of all that is human."[218] The mystery of Israel is both a source of anti- and of philo-Jewish sentiments and trends; both played an important part in the survival of Jewry in the Christian world. In Luther's thinking, both the friendly and the hostile judgement of Jewish life are represented.

Kant, the illustrious German philosopher, expressed to Moses Mendelssohn his great admiration for Mendelssohn's rational interpretation of the Jewish faith and even foresaw a salutary influence of Mendelssohn's views on the Christian Church. "You have succeeded," he writes to Mendelssohn, "in combining your nation with such a degree of freedom of conscience as was never imagined possible and of which no other faith can boast. You have, at the same time, so thoroughly and clearly demonstrated the necessity of unlimited liberty of conscience in every religion, that ultimately our Church will also be led to reflect how to remove from its midst everything that disturbs and oppresses conscience which will finally unite all men in their view of the essential points of religion."[219]

Yet at the same time, Kant shows himself not entirely free from anti-Semitic generalization, based apparently on an unpleasant personal experience. In a letter to K.L. Reinhold (28 January 1794) in Jena, Kant refers disparagingly to Solomon Maimon, the famous Jewish philosopher, rejecting Maimon's criticism of Kant's work. "The Jews," Kant writes, "frequently wish to reprove the works of others in order to enlarge their own honour at their expense."[220] "Die Juden!"

Goethe was far removed from popular anti-Semitism: ". . . I do not hate the Jews. The aversion which I felt against them in my early youth was more of a timidity before the mysterious, the ungraceful. The scorn which used to stir within me was more of a reflection of the Christian men and women around me. Only later, when I became acquainted with many talented and refined men of this race, respect was added to the admiration which I entertained for this people that created the Bible, and for the poet who sang the Song of Songs. It is despicable to pillory a nation which possesses such remarkable talents in art and science. As long as I am in charge of the theatre (in Weimar) this type of play (an anti-Semitic farce) will never be produced."[221] Goethe referred to Felix Mendelssohn as a "grandson of Nathan with the gift of Mozart." A memorable pronouncement! Yet, in a letter to the composer Karl Zelter, he opposed Old Testament subjects for the stage because, "if the Biblical heroes leave their respectable distance and appear on the stage, it occurs to us that they are Jews and we feel a contrast between the grandfathers and their descendants which confuses us."[222]

Herder glorified ancient Hebrew poetry out of his sincere conviction that diversity of culture rather than cosmopolitan levelling of differences is the aim of historical evolution. On the other hand, he predicted that the Jewish people would always remain an alien, Asiatic element in Western culture. Herder too represents the conflict which the men of the Enlightenment had to face: veneration for the ancient people of Israel and suspicion for the contemporary Jew.[223]

Ultimately, liberal views prevailed in the Western world. Their predominance enabled the Jews to survive, to derive spiritual strength from the sources of their own tradition, and to blend them with the values of Western civilization. Protected from without in the enlightened countries of the Western world, and fortified from within through the unhampered study and practice of their own faith, they could withstand the onslaught of anti-Semitism in East and West, outlive the agony of pogroms and the Nazi holocaust, and maintain their identity until the advent of the present era of individual liberty and collective equality in the Western world, and of national resurrection in the land of Israel.

The contrast between the Biblical Jewish figure which inspired philo-Semitic sentiments and the contemporary pedlar who aroused less sympathetic feeling was a source of constant tension between philo-Semitic and anti-Semitic attitudes. Samuel Taylor Coleridge gives this issue poignant expression. He notes: "The two images farthest removed from each other which can be comprehended under one term are, I think, Isaiah, — 'Hear O heavens and give ear, O earth!' and Levi of Holywell Street — 'Old clothes' — both of them Jews, you'll observe."[224]

It was the endeavour of philo-Semitic writers, thinkers and

politicians to prove that whatever unpleasant qualities "Old Clothes Levi" had, they were not inherited, and racially conditioned, but inflicted upon him by the Christian world. Every "Old Clothes Levi" was a descendant of the great figures of Scripture and bore in himself the potentiality to rise again to the greatness of his forefathers of ancient days.

Voltaire was led, through unfortunate experiences with individual Jews, to critical comments about the Jewish people as a whole. His attitude to Jews and Judaism was highly complicated and contradictory, motivated on the one hand by prejudices, on the other by enlightened views. Though a life-long fighter against cruelty and oppression, he was yet possessed of prejudice against Judaism and Jews. Generally, the Jews gained probably more from his commitment to the spread of enlightenment, than they lost through his hostility to them. His struggle against Church authority made him hostile to the religious element in the European tradition; Voltaire disliked the Old Testament, the matrix of the new dispensations; yet, as a humanitarian, he championed the cause of the under-privileged Jews, victims of clerical fanaticism which he detested. Memorable is his *Sermon du Rabin Akib,* expressing protest against the auto-da-fe of September 20, 1761, in Lisbon: "What was their crime? Only that they were born. They were born Israelites; they celebrated Pesach; that is the only reason that the Portuguese burnt them. Would you believe that while the flames were consuming these innocent victims, the inquisitors and the other savages were chanting our prayers? These pitiless monsters were invoking the God of mercy and kindness, the God of pardon, while committing the most atrocious and barbarous crime, while acting in a way which demons in their rage would not use against their brother demons. Your madness goes so far as to say that we are scattered because our fathers condemned to death him who you worship . . . No crucifixion was practised among us. Not a trace of that form of punishment is to be found. Cease, therefore, to punish a whole nation for an event for which it cannot be responsible. Would it be just to go and burn the Pope and all

211

the Monsignori at Rome today because the first Romans ravished the Sabines and pillaged the Samnites? O God, who has created us all, who desirest not the misfortune of Thy creatures, God, Father of all, God of mercy, accomplish Thou that there be no longer on this globe, on this least of all the worlds, either fanatics or persecutors."

The sentiments contained in this remarkable utterance are motivated by abhorrence of clerical fanaticism detested by the champions of the Jews in the days of Enlightenment. The rightlessness of the Jews furnished a glowing example for the intolerance of the Church. The philo-Semitism of the humanists, of Voltaire, Rousseau, Diderot, was limited. They were not particularly interested in gaining civic equality for the Jews, who also represented what, in the opinion of the philosophers, was a benighted faith. However, the champions of Enlightenment toppled the oppressive structure of the mediaeval Church and ushered in a new climate of opinion which was favourable to the granting of equality to all citizens, without regard to religious creed. The question of the Jews was the question of humanity, and the fate of the Jews was bound up with the fate of progress and civilization. This trend of thought was the decisive factor in the spread of philo-Semitic attitudes in the Western world. The emancipation of the individual Jew, the new citizen, prepared the way for Gentile philo-Zionism, the national auto-emancipation of the Jewish people, an old-new member in the family of nations.

Socialist thought is capable of both philo-Semitic and anti-Semitic tendencies. The anti-Semitic tendency in Socialism maintains that the Jews are champions of capitalism, prone to exploitation, and guilty of the social maladjustment and oppression dominant in the industrial society. This view was exemplified by Karl Marx, although Marxism, in spite of Marx's aversion to his own race, was not anti-Semitic. The philo-Semitic tendency, on the other hand, sees the Jews as objects of general prejudice and injustice, deprived of opportunities and used by the ruling class to divert the people from the ills of the social status in which they find themselves.

212

An ambivalence of feeling towards the Jews is to be found in the writings of Utopian socialists, like Saint-Simon and Fourier (1771-1837). The founder of French Socialism, Claude-Henri Saint-Simon (1760-1825), showed sympathy for the Jews in their social predicament. He knew that the Jews had always been persecuted in Europe and understood their reaction. "Degraded to the level of beasts," the Jew said to himself with imperturbability: "I am the man of God." Followers of Saint-Simon contradicted the Christian teaching that God had dispersed the Jews and declared that "God had sent out the Jews as apostles of peace and industry." Saint-Simon was a philo-Semite, while Pierre Josef Proudhon, George Sorel, Michael Bakunin, Charles Fourier ascribed all the ills of France to the emancipation of the Jews in the time of the French Revolution.

Saint-Simon quite explicitly linked his vision of the future to the Messianic hopes of Judaism. "The people of God," wrote Saint-Simon, "that people which received revelations before the coming of Christ, that people which is the most universally spread over the surface of the earth, has always perceived that the Christian doctrine founded by the Fathers of the Church was incomplete. It has always proclaimed that a grand epoch will come, which has been given the name of Messiah's Kingdom; an epoch in which religious doctrine shall be presented in all the generality of which it is susceptible and shall regulate alike the action of the temporal and of the spiritual power. All the human race will then have but one religion and one organization: The Golden Age was not behind us, it was before us."[224a]

Among the disciples of Fourier there were those who were open or camouflaged enemies of the Jews, while others openly advocated philo-Semitism, particularly the Pole, Jan Czynski (1801-1867), who worked to reconcile Jews and Poles with an ardour unprecedented for a Catholic. "Providence," he said, "which does not do anything without a reason, must have had a strong motive power in order to bring more than two million people of the Jewish race to the banks in the Vistula." That

213

motive power should be respected by the Poles, who would do well not to lose sight of the fact that the cause of Jewish emancipation is not a question of a party but a question of humanity.[225]

Jean Jaures, who was murdered in 1914, said anti-Semitism was a "capitalist swindle," nationalist fanaticism, and he praised the Jews who had produced such great men as Maimonides, Spinoza, Marx and Lassalle.

Unlike Karl Marx, who opposed both the Jewish and the Christian religions and regarded the Jews as a product of capitalist society, Friedrich Engels, his non-Jewish companion, represented philo-Semitic tendencies in socialist thought. Hatred of the Jews, he said, was "if not specifically Prussian, at any rate specifically East-Elbian." Anti-Semitism was "a sign of backward civilisation," and to be found in Prussia, Austria and Russia. "If you wanted to teach anti-Semitism in England or in America, you would simply be laughed at," he declared naively.

It has to be remembered that the Social Democrats of Germany and Austria stood in the forefront of the fight against German racialism and anti-Semitism and created an atmosphere in which Jews could prosper and Judaism could flourish.[226]

Friedrich Nietzsche, the famous German philosopher, (1844-1900) adopted an ambivalent attitude in Jewish matters. In as far as he considered Judaism as a precursor of Christianity, he opposed the Jewish creed as vehemently as its Christian successor. On the other hand, he frequently expressed admiration for the spirituality, virility and genial quality of Judaism and its importance for the future of Europe. In his book *Menschliches, Allzu Menschliches* he wrote that "every people and every nation has unpleasant, even dangerous qualities. It is cruel to demand that the Jews should form an exception." In his philo-Semitic mood, Nietzsche emphasized the Jewish contribution to civilization, and particularly the quality of mediaeval Jewish scholars and thinkers who acted as intermediaries between the ancient and the mediaeval cul-

214

tures. "The Jews," he writes, "are without any doubt the strongest, toughest and purest race which now lives in Europe; a thinker who is concerned with the future of Europe will have to take account of the Jews, as of the Russians." "In a general summing up, I should like to know how much must be excused in a nation which, not without blame on the part of all of us, has had the most mournful history of all nations and to which we owe the most loving of men (Christ), the most upright of sages (Spinoza), the mightiest Book and the most effective moral law in the world? Moreover, in the darkest times of the Middle Ages, when Asiatic clouds had gathered darkly over Europe, it was Jewish free-thinkers, scholars, and physicians who upheld the banner of enlightenment and of intellectual independence under the severest personal sufferings, and defended Europe and Asia; we owe it not least to their efforts that a more natural, more reasonable, at all events un-mythical, explanation of the world was finally able to get the upper hand once more, and that the link of culture which now unites us with the enlightenment of Greco-Roman antiquity has remained unbroken. If Christianity has done everything to orientalize the Occident, Judaism has assisted in occidentalizing it anew; which, in a certain sense, is equivalent to making Europe's mission and history a continuation of that of Greece."[226a]

Nietzsche's critique of European culture cannot be equated with shallow nationalism, or thoughtless anti-Semitism. Nietzsche's opposition to European detachment from nature and natural life found its echo in Hebrew literature, particularly in the works of writers such as Shaul Tschernichowsky, Micha Joseph Berdyczewski and Zalman Schneur, who represented the tendency of creative, heroic vitalism in Hebrew thought and who championed the national renaissance and transvaluation of traditional values and literature.[227] This tendency is in full harmony with the temper of contemporary Israel which has planned and accomplished a profound transformation of historic Jewish values. Under the impact of catastrophic circumstances, age-old Jewish spirituality had to be

215

harmonized with Spartan ideals of heroism. It is to be hoped that Yavne, symbol of traditional learning, blended with the spirit of both Sparta and Athens may find its rightful place in the shaping of the Third Commonwealth of Israel.

It is erroneous to connect Nietzsche with the ideologists of Nazism. On no account can Nietzsche be presented as an apostle of modern anti-Semitism. Nietzsche accused Judaism because it was the matrix of Christianity but, as far as its own quality was concerned, he exalted the grandeur of what he called "the world's historical mission and the moral masterfulness of Judaism." In *Beyond Good and Evil* Nietzsche tried to give a summation of "what Europe owes to the Jews." "Many things, good and bad, and above all, one thing combining the best and the worst: the grand style in morality, the fearful majesty of infinite demands, of infinite significations, all the romanticism and sublimity of the moral enigmas . . . . For this, we artists among the philosophers and contemplators must give thanks to the Jews."[228] Just as Nietzsche admired the Jews and unreservedly glorified them as the authors of the Old Testament, so he blamed them as being responsible for the creation of the New Testament. The Jews had Nietzsche's sympathy to the degree that they remained faithful to their Bible and national tradition. "In the Jewish Old Testament, the book of divine justice, there are men, things and sayings on such an immense scale that the Greek and Hindu literatures have nothing to compare with it. One pauses with fear and reverence before these stupendous remains of what man once was. . . . The taste for the Old Testament is a touchstone for recognising what is great and what is small . . . ."[229]

In another work, Nietzsche wrote, "The Old Testament — yes, that is something else again, all honour to the Old Testament! I find therein great men, a heroic landscape, and one of the rarest things in the world, the incomparable naivete of the strong of heart. And what is more, I find a people."[230]

If Nietzsche was of the opinion that these great Jewish values had been "adulterated" in the course of Israel's history by a process culminating in the New Testament, the philosopher asserted elsewhere that in Israel's classical epoch, particularly

216

in the time of the Jewish kings, the Jews "were in a just and natural relationship with all phenomena." Such is the position of Nietzsche in his *Anti-Christ,* which has been considered his most anti-Semitic book.

The author of *Will to Power* blamed those he called sacerdotal agitators for having transformed the exalted religion of the Jews into a decadent religion. But were not the Jews themselves decadent in Nietzsche's eyes, considering that it was they who had created the religion he called decadent? "But on the contrary!" declared the philosopher. "Psychologically speaking, the Jewish people possesses the most tenacious vital force . . . The Jews are just the opposite of decadents . . . ." And in his *Will to Power,* so often and so fraudulently quoted by Goebbels, Nietzsche wrote, "The Jews are the classical instance of a strong and successful race." Nietzsche was interested in the modern and the Biblical Jews. Of Heine he wrote, "It was Heinrich Heine who gave me the highest conception of what lyricism can be . . . I ransack in vain the kingdoms of antiquity and modern times for anything approaching his sweet and passionate music."[231] In Nietzsche's rich literary production, there are to be found critical remarks about Jews and Judaism, but he never subscribed to anti-Semitism — "in lying by principle, the anti-Semite does not become honest."

Nietzsche's main sentiment towards the Jews is his boundless admiration for their tenacity, resourcefulness and heroic demeanour in adversity. In Europe, he maintains, they have gone through a schooling of eighteen centuries such as no other nation has ever undergone, and the experiences of this dreadful time of probation have benefited not only the Jewish community but, to an even greater extent, the individual. As a consequence of this, the resourcefulness of the modern Jews, both in mind and soul, is most extraordinary.

Amongst all the inhabitants of Europe, he continues, it is the Jews who least of all try to escape from any deep distress by recourse to drink or to suicide, as other less gifted people are so prone to do. Every Jew can find, in the history of his own family and of his ancestors, a long record of instances of the greatest coolness and perseverance amid difficulties and dreadful situations, and an artful cunning in dealing with misfortune and chance. And above all, it is their bravery under the cloak of wretched submission that surpasses the virtues of all the saints.

It has been rightly recognized that Zionism, although rooted in religion and history and motivated by the dream of restored ancient glories, was a movement for secular national liberation; and that "some of its earlier prophets voiced distinctly Nietzschean accents, extolling *elan vital,* engaging in an almost pagan glorification of life, and resolutely condemning the ethics of the humble and weak. They would no longer bend their heads, but raise them high."[232]

Nietzsche's opposition to Judaism had a significant quality of its own. It was not based on the Jewish rejection of the New Testament; the Jews were to be blamed for creating the New Testament, and thus weakening the fibre of the Christianized nation. His philo-Semitism flows from the Jew's denial of the New Testament and the affirmation of the vital creative Old Testament values. His philo-Semitic motive was similar to that of the anti-clerical champions of the enlightenment who based their humanism on opposition to Christian dogma. That Nietzsche's concept of vitality has degenerated into Nazi ideology of German racial superiority is the fault of those who misunderstood and perverted his ideas. Strange indeed, and terrifying are the adventures of seminal thoughts. Romantic nationalism, proclaimed by noble German thinkers such as Herder, and salvationist Marxism, preached by Russian idealists like Bakunin, ultimately turned into degrading systems of universal tyranny — Nazism and Stalinism. The elemental fact of cultural uniqueness degenerated into vicious racialism, while the universal idea of a classless society yielded the bitter fruit of Communist oppression.[233]

In the works of the British novelist Maria Edgeworth (1767-1849), one finds the transition from the stereotype of the Jewish villain, such as is depicted in *Moral Tales and Belinda,* to the portrayal of the impeccable Jew in her novel *Harrington.* Maria Edgeworth felt remorse at the many evil types of Jews she had depicted in her books. Out of moral consciousness, and in a spirit of apology, she created saintly Jewish characters in order to atone.[234] Turning away from the wicked and avaricious Jewish types of her earlier works, she portrayed all the Jews of her later work as being morally perfect. Edgeworth followed the pattern of "self-conscious retraction of a novelist who feels that she has to make up for earlier slips of the pen!" Anti-Semitism had turned, under the influence of pangs of conscience, into outspoken philo-Semitism and had thus created a favourable climate in which to judge the veil stereotype of the Jew in a kindly light. The simple human consciousness of having done injustice to a much-maligned group of people led her to make amends in the form of what, sometimes, becomes exaggerated unrealistic philo-Semitism. The Jew villain turns into the Jew saint, invariably with a beautiful daughter.

In a preface to *Harrington,* the novelist's father, Richard Lovell Edgeworth, informed the reader that Maria Edgeworth had received a letter from a Jewish lady in America, Miss Rachel Mordecai of Richmond, Virginia, reproaching the novelist for her unpleasant representations of Jewish character, and begging her to write a romance with a good Jew in it. In response to this request, and as an "Apology" to the Jews, *Harrington* was written.

The philo-Jewish tendency of *Harrington* has to be understood against the background of the Jewish Naturalisation Bill of 1753. We are informed that one of the figures, a destitute Jewish pedlar named Jacob, was as unlike Shylock as it is possible to conceive. "Without one thought or look of malice or revenge, he stood before Us Thursday after Thursday, enduring all that our barbarity was pleased to inflict; he stood patient and long-suffering, and even of this patience and resignation we made a jest."

Sir Walter Scott speaks favorably of Edgeworth's *Harrington,* but declares that for him Jews would always be Jews. "One does not naturally and easily combine with their habits and pursuits any great liberality of principle, although certainly it may, and I believe does exist in many individual instances; they are money makers and money brokers by profession and it is trade which narrows the mind."

Shortly thereafter Scott himself produced a novel *Ivanhoe,* breathing admiration of Jewish "liberality of principle," and presenting to the world the character of Rebecca whose lovable, spiritual qualities helped to win civic rights, social courtesies, and a place in the heart of mankind for her people. Scott's *Ivanhoe* deserves special emphasis and discussion in this context. The author portrayed mediaevel Jewish life in England in a sympathetic vein, rare among writers who preceded him. In drawing a consistently favourable portrait of a young Jewess, and an understanding picture of Isaac, her father, Scott delivered a powerful blow to anti-Jewish prejudice. Although the Jew in English writing still appears as a shadowy figure, he is, in Scott's *Ivanhoe* already invested with the humanity of sympathy in the spirit of nineteenth-century liberal and humanitarian thought.

Isaac of York, modelled on the historical figure of Aaron of York, financial magnate of mediaeval English Jewry, is the historical ancestor of Shylock, the traditional stock figure of the implacable Jewish usurer. He is drawn after the pattern of the popular "Jew type," unprincipled, grasping and cowardly. However, on the whole, he is a milder Shylock, less petty, spiteful and materialistic than Shakespeare's Jew.

There is a vital distinction between Scott's portrayal of the typical Jew and that of the earlier anti-Semitic writers, Shakespeare and Marlowe. Scott, in the spirit of nineteenth-century humanitarian thought, tried to establish the historical facts which accounted for Isaac's avarice and to understand his motives, and thus to humanize him. He depicted the historical circumstances as they operated in 1194. He wrote: "There was no race existing on the earth, in the air, or the waters, who were the object of such an unintermitting, general and relentless persecution as the Jews of this period. Upon the slightest and most unreasonable pretences, as well as upon accusations the most absurd and groundless, their persons and property were exposed to every turn of popular fury; for Norman, Saxon,

Dane and Briton, however adverse these races were to each other, contended which should look with greatest detestation upon a people, whom it was accounted a point of religion to hate, to revile, to despise, to plunder, and to persecute. The kings of the Norman race, and the independent nobles who followed their example in all acts of tyranny, maintained against this devoted people a persecution of a more regular, calculated and self-interested kind . . . . In spite of every kind of discouragement, and even of the special court of taxations already mentioned, called 'The Jews' Exchequer,' erected for the very purpose of despoiling and distressing them, the Jews increased, multiplied, and accumulated huge sums, which they transferred from one hand to another by means of bills of exchange — an invention for which commerce is said to be indebted to them, and which enabled them to transfer their wealth from land to land, that when threatened with oppression in one country, their treasure might be secured in another."

Isaac, as portrayed by Scott, belongs to two worlds; on the one hand he retains all the features of the traditional Jewish miser; on the other, he is the pathetic victim of historical pressures. Scott tried to enlist the reader's sympathy for Isaac's intolerable position, to interpret his character, explain his conduct and stress his basic humanity.

He introduced the fifth chapter of *Ivanhoe* with Shylock's noble plea: "Hath not the Jew eyes? Hath not a Jew hands, organs, dimensions, senses, affections, passions? Fed with the same food, hurt with the same weapons, subject to the same diseases, healed by the same means, warmed and cooled by the same winter and summer, as a Christian is?" Occasionally his pro-Jewish sentiment adopts a religious character. "The Jews," he affirms, "are still 'the people Chosen of Heaven.'"

Isaac's conduct may justify the appellation of "Jew-Dog" and "Jew-Fox," but the tribe of Isaac deserves defence, even admiration. Isaac cannot enlist the reader's sympathy, but descriptions of the lamentable lot of the Jews must touch his heart. Scott here adopted the incontrovertible argument of the philo-Semites of all ages — the Jews are what the Christians made them.

The Jew stoops and bends before every attack, crouches in front of every enemy, but in his heart he nurses noble feelings of resistance. "Disinherited and wandering as we are, the worst evil that befalls our race is, that when we are wronged and plundered, all the world laughs, and we are compelled to suppress our sense of injury, and to smile tamely, when we would revenge bravely."

Like Shakespeare, Scott gave his Jewish usurer some excuse for his action. This, in effect, redeemed the Jew from villainy. Scott's picture of the Jewish money-lender, though painted after a mediaeval model, was coloured by the broad humanity of the nineteenth century. Scott was moved by his sympathy with an oppressed people and through his writings, he tried to arouse his readers' sympathy for the weaker party in the Jewish-Gentile encounter. The unrelenting persistence of the Jews in the face of unrelenting persecution aroused the admiration of high-minded Christians.

In prison Isaac of York had upon his side the unyielding obstinacy of his nation and that unbending resolution, with which Israelites have been frequently known to submit to the uttermost evils which power and violence can inflict upon them, rather than gratify their oppressors by granting their demands.

In *Ivanhoe,* Scott presented the character of Rebecca, Isaac's daughter, as an ideal figure of true Jewish womanhood, faithful in the defence of her people, her religion and her honour. Rebecca is the very paragon of virtue. She is one of the first Jewish characters in English literature to be portrayed as a generous, warm-hearted person. Isaac loved his daughter with the typical love of a Jewish parent for his children. In this love he demonstrated unlimited and utterly unselfish devotion.

When asked to pay ransom for his life, he stipulated, above all, the freedom of his daughter. "Take all that you have asked, Sir Knight — take ten times more — reduce me to ruin and beggary, if thou wilt — nay, pierce me with thy poniard, boil me in that furnace, but spare my daughter, deliver her in safety and honour. As thou art born of a woman, spare the honour of a helpless maiden — she is the image of my deceased Rachel. Will you deprive a widowed husband of his sole remaining comfort . . . . Think not so vilely of us, Jews though we may be . . . the hunted fox, the tortured wildcat loves the young — the despised and persecuted race of Abraham love their children. . . ."

Like her heroic ancestors of old, Rebecca resists any attempt at forcible conversion. In answer to a request to accept the counsel of "Holy Men," who will wean her from her "erring" law, she replies: "I may not change the faith of my fathers like a garment unsuited to the climate in which I seek to dwell . . . . There is true piety and charity among Jews as among Christians . . . among our people, since the time of Abraham downwards, have been women who have devoted their thoughts to Heaven, and their actions to works of kindness to men, tending the sick, feeding the hungry, and relieving the distressed. Among these will Rebecca be numbered."

Asserting her belief in "Him who made both Jews and Christians," Rebecca, in the spirit of her age, pronounced sentiments of tolerance and understanding for other religions and stressed the unifying quality of ethical conduct. It is the good deed that unites all believers. It cannot be displeasing "to the father of both our faiths to relieve the sick and wounded of another religion." Rebecca also voiced regret that there was no country which her people could call its own — foreshadowing George Eliot's Zionist sentiment. She would love to explain that "the peculiarities of my dress, language and manners are those of my people — I had well-nigh said of my country — but alas! we have no country." Longing for a sovereign homeland is also voiced in a sensitive speech in which Rebecca recalled the heroic heritage of Israel: "I am, indeed, sprung from a race whose courage was distinguished in the defence of their own land, but who warred not, even while yet a nation, save at the command of the Deity, or in defending their country from oppression. The sound of the trumpet wakes Judah no longer, and her despised children are now but the unresisting victims of hostile and military oppression . . . until the God of Jacob shall raise up for His chosen people a second Gideon, or a new Maccabeus, it ill beseemeth the Jewish damsel to speak of battle or of war."

Rebecca, embittered perhaps by the idea that Ivanhoe considered her as one not entitled to interfere in a case of honour, and incapable of entertaining or expressing sentiments of honour and generosity, concluded the argument in a tone of sorrow, which deeply expressed her sense of the degradation of her people. "How little he knows this bosom to imagine that cowardice or meanness of soul must needs be its guests, because I have censured the fantastic chivalry of the Nazarenes! (Christians). Would to heaven that the shedding of mine own blood, drop by drop, could redeem the captivity of Judah! Nay, would to God it could avail to set free my father, and this his benefactor, from the chains of the oppressor! The proud Christian should then see whether the daughter of God's chosen people dared not to die as bravely as the vainest Nazarene maiden, that boasts her descent from some petty chieftain of the rude and frozen north!"

Personifying beauty, magnanimity, nobility and pride, Rebecca represents a new and shining image of her people. Memorable is a devotional hymn, replete with lofty Biblical sentiments, which Scott puts in Rebecca's mouth:

When Israel, of the Lord beloved,
Out of the land of bondage came,
Her father's God before her moved,
An awful guide, in smoke and flame.
By day, along the astonish'd lands
The cloudy pillar glided slow;
By night, Arabia's crimson'd sands
Return'd the fiery column's glow.
There rose the choral hymn of praise,
And trump and timbrel answer'd keen,
And Zion's daughters pour'd their lays,
With priest's and warrior's voice between.

The Hebraic culture, as represented by Isaac and Rebecca, is a touchstone by which Normans and Saxons may be judged. The Jews are conventionally charged with avarice, but they are also the best representatives of the supposedly Christian virtues of love and sacrifice. Rebecca cares for Ivanhoe, even risks her life to nurse him with no hope that her affection can be reciprocated because the "prejudices of the age rendered such a union almost impossible" (Scott's Introduction to *Ivanhoe*). Her self-sacrifice and devotion represents the highest rung of feminine virtue.

Isaac rises to true heroism in his determination to endure any physical torture or financial sacrifice to save his daughter. The meeting of Ivanhoe and Rebecca typifies the encounter of the highest ideals of the traditions of chivalry with those of the Hebraic tradition. Ivanhoe champions chivalry which assigns to life a lower value than to "honour." Rebecca maintains that "domestic love, kindly affection, peace and happiness" are higher virtues than the love of honour and glory, that causes tears and bloodshed.

Hundreds of readers in England who had never read a line of Jewish history were introduced in *Ivanhoe* to the romantic aspects of the suffering of this ancient and oppressed, yet indomitable, people. In the pantheon of the great men of letters who devoted their genius to the breaking down of the wall of prejudice which divided Jews and Christians, Sir Walter Scott occupies a prominent place.

In the dual image of the Jew in literature, Dickens's vile Fagin and noble Riah, Maria Edgeworth's Solomon and her Harrington, the philo-Semitic tendency prevailed. Slowly the British "man in the street" connected David, son of Jesse, and Judas Maccabeus with his Jewish neighbour. He accepted his naturalization, elected him to Parliament, and ultimately sponsored his self-emancipation in the Holy Land. The good Jew prevailed over the bad amongst the Jewish stereotype in the literature of Western Europe.

These examples manifest the ambivalence of Gentile attitudes to the Jew from the days of the Reformation and even in the days of Enlightenment. Yet ultimately the philo-Semitic attitude asserted itself and led to the economic, political, cultural and occasionally even social emancipation of the Jews in the Western world, and enabled them to maintain their position as a distinct, but no longer separate group. From then on it became their problem, and their task, to adjust themselves to the new life of equality and to maintain a healthy balance between their striving for Jewish communal identity, their civic loyalty, and their devotion to the universal values of mankind. Reactions to the horrifying tragedy of Nazism generated strong philo-Semitic emotions, which found expression in support for Palestine (later Israel), in the Vatican Council Resolution of 1965, and in the bestowal of an outstanding literary award (the Nobel Prize for Literature) upon a contemporary Hebrew writer, S. J. Agnon, revealing appreciation for the much-maligned literary traditions of Israel. The various manifestations of philo-Semitism in contemporary Germany bear the mark of a powerful desire to atone for the Nazi misdeeds. Prominent Germans who influence public opinion emphasize Germany's duty to offer disinterested support for the State of Israel. They stress that the "unspeakable things" done in the name of Germany can never be undone or truly compensated; Germans should stand fast by Israel, which was established by the brothers and children of murdered Jews, without thought of demanding anything in return.[234a]

The defenders and friends of Israel were moved by a spirit of pity for the persecuted and under-privileged, by social ideologies founded on liberal, humanitarian thought, by hatred of religious fanaticism and by aversion to political demagogy. Occasionally philo-Semites were also prompted by a desire to make converts.

Philo-Semites manifested goodwill to individual Jews in times of persecution. Scholars, thinkers and writers exhibited sympathy and appreciation for the traditional values of Judaism. From these attitudes emerged a philo-Semitic sentiment towards the Jewish group as a whole, which leads to a recognition of Jewish claims for restoration of their nationhood in Palestine, and an acceptance of the individual Jew as enjoying full civic opportunity and legal protection, as well as his right to communal organization on religious and cultural lines.[235]

In the complexity of non-Jewish attitudes towards Jews, one finds anti-Semitic trends — well known and often described — and a number of philo-Semitic approaches. Some admired the ancient Jews, but held their contemporaries in the "Jew Street" or the "Jewish Quarter" in utter contempt. Some pitied the Jews and sought to convert them to the dominant faith; others held them up as heroic models for the times. There were still others who, in their wider interest in fighting bigotry and absolutism, became the defenders of the Jews. The majority of philo-Semites are moved by either feeling of mystic kinship with the people of Jesus, veneration for the biblical heritage, admiration for Jewish perseverance against immeasurable odds, or feeling of kinship with fellowmen of different faith and ethnic descent. Some philo-Semitic attitudes find expression on a personal level in social intercourse and friendship;[236] others demonstrate a positive attitude to the Jewish community in their efforts to secure complete equality within the law, based on tolerance for diverse cultures and religions. There were those who admired Judaism, considered its cultural creations pillars of Western civilization, displayed enthusiasm for the Jewish heritage. Genuine, complete, philo-Semitism is found in its purest form in the minds of true lovers of humanity, who transcend divisions of race and creed, and believe that above all nations is humanity: they hold with Francis of Sales that "love is the abridgment of all theology."

THE RIGHTEOUS OF THE NATIONS — PHILO-SEMITISM IN ACTION

"The Righteous of the Nations of the earth: theirs is a share in the world to come." This cherished rabbinic saying,[237] which also forms part of the Code of Maimonides, is an integral part of the Jewish faith and became the official doctrine of the Synagogue. In this generation it has especial significance and poignancy, for in many lands "the Righteous of the Nations," frequently at the sacrifice of their own lives or freedom, defied Nazi tyranny in order to save their Jewish neighbours from extinction.

A remarkable chapter in the history of philo-Semitism is the reaction of friends of the Jews in the days of Nazi persecution. In every country under the heel of the Nazis, there were Gentile heroes and heroines who helped the oppressed escape the Nazi terror. The motives of philo-Semitic thought and action in that era were manifold. The socialist section of the conquered peoples helped the Jews in the name of brotherhood, proclaimed by the idealists of the movement: "I am neither Jew nor Christian, I am a true Socialist" was one of the slogans of the socialist friends of the Jews.[238] Another source of philo-Jewish activity was the Christian consciousness of obligation to the people in whose midst the Christian Saviour was born.[239]

228

From innumerable pulpits pleas to protect the Jews from Nazi persecution, in the name of Christian love and out of a sense of duty to the people of the Covenant, were delivered. Another motive was the purely liberal concern with fellow men and the consequent need to practise justice and humanity without reference to the race or creed of the persecuted. "Where there are stronger ones, always side with the weak," was a motto of liberals and humanitarians. There was also a concern with the Jew as a fellow citizen and therefore as an aspect of the oppressed nation's resistance against the common enemy. The Danes rescued the Jews of Denmark because they considered them as fellow members of the Danish nation under the heel of the German conqueror. To help fellow nationals in distress was an imperative civic duty. All these motives, the socialist, the Christian, the humanitarian and the civic national, combined to create an impressive record of philo-Semitic thought and action which constitutes one of the most glorious chapters in the history of man's humanity to man.

Before the trial of Adolph Eichmann, little mention was made in Israel of these heroes and heroines. The loss of Jewish lives during the holocaust was so vast that isolated acts of rescue seemed insignificant. But the trial itself brought out many instances of Gentile friendship and acts of mercy. These are now receiving due recognition. Saplings, planted in their memory, are growing in the Avenue of the Righteous of the Nations in Jerusalem. The State of Israel bestows medals and certificates on individuals and invites various people to plant trees in the famous Avenue at the Yad Vashem Memorial Foundation. It is not the number of lives which the person saved, but the extent of the risk to which he exposed himself, that earns him the privilege of planting a tree and receiving public recognition in the State of Israel.

The Avenue, which is growing longer and longer, now (1979) numbers three thousand trees. Individuals from countries as far removed from one another as Japan and Portugal, have been honoured since the first sapling was planted in 1963. Not all of them, and they now include some quite ordinary people, are able to go to Israel to plant a tree, so they are presented with a medal or certificate at the Israeli Embassy in their own country, instead. Yad Vashem receives new applications all the time. Who applied? A person who has been rescued himself usually informs the authorities. However, it is realized that there are probably many unknown people all over the world who performed heroic deeds at the time of the holocaust. Sometimes honours are awarded posthumously.[240]

Were it not for the Righteous of the Nations, who found the moral strength to love and help their fellow men, the Nazi era would have gone down in history as totally devoid of human ideals and values. Jews have a long memory, they know too well how to remember the acts of hostility and persecution they have suffered during their long history and to recall the wrongs inflicted upon them. With no less fervour and intensity should they, therefore, respond to the rare good deeds, which, in some cases, were rendered with such great devotion to them by the sons and daughters of the nations of Europe.

In honouring those who risked their lives in order to save Jews from extermination by the Nazis, Jews renewed their faith in man, in the capacity of people to rise to the heights of heroism, and thereby provide the evidence that man is not hopelessly corrupt.

The most eloquent and authoritative Jewish testimony to philo-Semitic actions in the days of the Nazi tragedy was paid by the Attorney-General of the Government of Israel, Gideon Hausner, in his speech, before the Supreme Court of Israel on February 22, 1961, against Adolph Eichmann. After sketching the perversion and brutality of the Nazi creed and the horror of the persecution of the Jews, Hausner declared: "In order to complete the picture, we should point out that there were in Germany tens of thousands of scientists and ecclesiastics, statesmen and authors and ordinary people, who dared to help the Jews, to raise their heads in opposition to the iniquitous regime, and even to rebel against it, and among these were men whose names were famous in German science and culture. Thousands of opponents of the bloody regime were imprisoned and were later destined to suffer greatly in concentration camps before the Nazi monster was brought low. Thousands of these died without seeing the day of liberation. Hundreds of ecclesiastics were arrested and imprisoned. There were also examples of personal bravery — like that of the priest who was sent by Eichmann to a concentration camp for intervening openly on behalf of the Jews. There were Germans who hid Jews and shared their rations with them and who at the risk of their lives helped them to hide or obtain 'Aryan' papers, and there were others who maintained an anti-Hitler underground. During the war there were Germans who even protested to Hitler at the disgrace the Gestapo was bringing on the German people by acting like beasts of prey, as they described the extermination of the Jews. There were also soldiers who tried to frustrate the killings by direct intervention. But after all is said and done, these were a very small minority.[241]

The record of Nazi atrocities revealed the ineffable savagery of a depraved Nationalism, while the numerous trials against Nazi leaders and their underlings again focused attention upon the evil aspect of the human condition. But there is another element in the human character, the knowledge of which should not be suppressed but highlighted. There are, on record, acts of sacrifice on the part of Christians who risked their lives to defend and to protect the hunted and the persecuted. There is evidence of heroic compassion which restores the dignity of man. This evidence is found among all the peoples of Europe, enslaved by the Nazis; nor was it missing among the Germans. The late President of Israel, Yitzchak-Ben-Zvi, ruled that the version of the Jewish Memorial Prayer — El Molei Rachamim — which referred to those of the Jewish people "killed by the Germans and their assistants," be amended to read "killed by the Nazis and their assistants," a forceful protest against communal guilt.

Generalized condemnation of whole groups of human beings, Germans, Poles, Jews, Blacks, is not conducive to a comprehension of the complex realities of human life. Throughout Nazi Europe there were those sections of the population among

231

all conquered nations who became accomplices of Nazism; others who restricted themselves to mere expressions of sympathy with the persecuted and passed by on the other side; yet others who heroically and spontaneously offered aid to the victims of Nazi brutality, bravely facing the peril involved.

An illustrious representative of philo-Semitism in the Nazi era was Michael Cardinal Faulhaber, Archbishop of Munich, mentioned before. When the Nazi persecution of the Jews started, the Cardinal preached a series of sermons[242] under the title *Judaism, Christianity and Germany* in which he defended the values of the Old Testament against the new paganism of the Nazis and championed toleration against racial pride, humanity against nationalism.

"History teachers," he declared, "that God always punished the tormentors of the Jews. No Roman Catholic approved of the persecution of the Jews in Germany. When God made June 30 (1934) the Judgement Day for some of the tormentors of the Jews, their punishment was well deserved; racial hatred is a wild poisonous weed in our lives."

Conrad, Cardinal Count von Preysing of Berlin, in a pastoral letter, denounced the Nazi persecutions in the following words: "Every human has rights that cannot be denied him simply because he is not of our blood. We must realise that depriving him of those rights is a grave injustice, not only toward the stranger, but toward our own people."

These words, so vague in meaning, so mild in their rebuke, were considered treason in Germany in the year 1942.

Another towering example of philo-Jewish activity was set by the Bishop of Munster, Clemens August von Galen, who was a source of inspiration to the friends of Jews.

Today there exists an impressive record of Christians of all nationalities who translated philo-Semitic thought into action and, risking their lives, hid Jews or helped them to escape. The actual percentage of such heroes in comparison with those who either did not take any part in philo-Semitic actions or themselves actively supported the Nazis is of little concern in this context. Very few people have the stuff of martyrdom in their souls and very few would be willing to risk their lives, freedom, or property, for others. It is, however, an historic fact that it was philo-Semitism, a feature of Gentile-Jewish relations even in the Nazi era, which led to the rescue and survival of a number of Jews; it forged links of friendship between Jews and Gentiles and also created bonds of sympathy between the State of Israel and those individuals and groups which helped to create it.

Those Germans who, from the outset, were most conscious of the collective German guilt were also the ones who were most courageous in seeking to save whomsoever they could. A survivor once said to James Parkes, "Remember that for every one of us who escaped, ten Germans risked their lives."[243] The same fact applied in Poland. "Every one of us who has survived owes his or her life to some non-Jewish Pole who knew that we were Jews, hid us and enabled us, by his protection, to pass for non-Jewish Poles, at the risk of his own life. Many indeed paid with their lives for shielding Jews."[244]

While the names of the perpetrators of the extermination are widely known and recorded in mass trials, those who, in the spirit of self-sacrifice, defended and protected the hunted Jewish people — the priests and nuns, peasants, farmers and storekeepers — and who jeopardized their lives and the lives of their families to hide Jews in cellars and ovens, in bunkers, and haylofts, remain unknown and unsung! But their deeds add up to an impressive demonstration of goodness and heroism and counterbalance in no uncertain terms the impression that philo-Semitism held no place in the history of Jewish-Gentile group relations.

It was the philo-Semitic element in French thought which caused the German Security Police Commander from Northern France and Belgium to state, in a report which he submitted to his superiors in January 1941, "It is almost impossible to cultivate in Frenchmen anti-Jewish feelings, based on ideological grounds." In another report, the Chief of the Special Police of the Commission of Jewish Affairs reported in March 1942 that his henchmen met with incomprehension, even hostility, and that the French population considered anti-Jewish acts as something foreign imposed upon them by German authorities.

The large section of French "Aryans" continued to demonstrate sympathy with the Jews. Peasants, workmen, and professional people were parts of the great network created for the purpose of assisting and rescuing the Jews. Famous French writers created a philo-Semitic atmosphere which engendered feelings of sympathy and a desire to oppose actively the brutal plans of the Nazis. Among those who declared their sympathy for the persecuted Jews were Catholic writers Jacques Maritain, Paul Claudel; leftist writers Paul Elouard and Louis Aragon; the existentialist Jean-Paul Sartre; the eminent and venerable Romain Rolland; Andre Malraux, Antoine de Saint-Exupery; David Rousset, a survivor of Nazi concentration camps, and others. The clergy of France, Catholic and Protestant alike, played a decisive role in French resistance to the anti-Jewish decrees and in the rescue activities on behalf of the persecuted. Church dignitaries represented the best traditions of philo-Semitism. The Archbishop of Toulouse, later elevated to Cardinal Monseigneur Jules Gerard Saliege, stated in his famous letter of August 23, 1942: "There is a Christian morality . . . that confers rights and imposes duties. These duties and these rights come from God. One can violate them. But no mortal has the power to suppress them. Alas, it has been destined for us to witness the dreadful spectacle of children, women, and old men being treated like vile beasts; of families being torn apart and deported to unknown destinations. . . . In our diocese, frightful things take place in the camps Noe and Recebedou. The Jews are our brethren. They belong to mankind. No Christian dare forget that. France, my beloved land; France, which cherishes in the conscience of all its children the tradition of respect for the individual; France, the generous and chivalrous — France is not responsible for these horrors!"

The Bishop of Montauban, Monseigneur Pierre Marie Theas, instructed the priests in his diocese to read the following urgent message! "My dear brethren: Scenes of indescribable suffering and horror are abroad in our land. In Paris, by tens of thousands, Jews are being subjected to the most barbarous treatment. In our district we are witnessing wretched spectacles of families being uprooted, of man and women being treated like beasts and later deported to face the gravest perils. I indignantly protest in the name of Christian conscience and proclaim that all men are brothers, created by the same God. The current anti-Semitic measures are a violation of human dignity and the sacred rights of the individual and the family. May God comfort and strengthen those who are persecuted."

Bishop Theas was deported by the Nazis, but others rose to take his place. The philo-Semitic sentiments contained in pastoral letters and in public declarations, and the continued exhortations to the faithful, led to massive rescue operations by Frenchmen, from all sections of the population — Catholics, Protestants, Liberals and Leftists. Their efforts ultimately led to the survival of a large section of French Jewry. Philo-Semitism was a powerful factor in the history of Jewish-Gentile group relations within the French-speaking world, and has remained so until today. How effective the appeals of the clergy were may be gauged by the venomous attack on the Catholic Church published by a pro-Nazi journalist, Jacques Marcy. "Every Catholic family shelters a Jew,"[245] he said.

The Belgian priest Abbe Joseph Andre, who during the Nazi occupation of Belgium served the church of Namur, saved a large number of Jews. It is estimated that the number of Jews, mainly women and children, who owe their lives to Andre reached 3000, Andre influenced the inhabitants of the city and the small places in the surroundings to hide the Jews. He visited Israel under the auspices of the Israel-Belgium Friendship League, planted a tree in the Avenue of the Righteous Gentiles in Jerusalem, and visited many families whom he had rescued from the Nazi clutches.[246] He was vigorously supported in his shelter and rescue operations by the Bishop of Namur, Monseigneur Charue, and by the Jesuits and the Sisters of Charity, as well as by other religious groups. The municipal administration supplied him with forged documents, identification cards and food for his wards. One of the houses, where Father Andre hid the children, was less than a grenade's throw from Gestapo headquarters. Jacques Weinberg, a former guest in one of Father Andre's shelters, described a typical scene: "He (Father Andre) used to sit up all night, napping in his chair. He would not think of undressing and going to bed. There was the constant fear of a raid. If someone knocked on the door, Father Andre was on his feet. In a minute he had the children fleeing through a comouflaged exit to the neighbouring house, where a doctor lived. All the neighbours co-operated. Without their help Father Andre could not have accomplished so much. The butchers of Namur as well as the grocers and other merchants provided him with food and necessities for the children."

Father Andre took unprecedented action; he gave his foster children a sound Jewish education. Under no circumstances would he preach Christianity to them; he tried, instead, to teach them the ways of their parents. He took the trouble, and at no small risk, to celebrate a *seder* during Passover. In May 1944, Father Andre was warned of imminent arrest. He disappeared from Namur but continued his work from his hiding place.

Marie Syrkin recorded the help given Jewish Resistance Movements in Western Europe: In the Scandinavian countries, in France, in Belgium, in Holland, the Jewish underground received help from non-Jews. In Eastern Europe, too, there had been individuals who had risked danger and death for the sake of bringing aid to the martyred Jews in their midst, but these had been isolated instances whose exceptional nature only served to underscore the indifference or enmity of the majority. In Holland in particular, Jews found fellow-fighters among their Christian neighbours. The Dutch underground took an active part in protecting Jews of Holland. Some of its leading figures sacrificed themselves to save Jewish lives and human honour. The veteran Dutch Socialist leader, Professor Sam de Wolff, the old friend of Karl Kautsky and Rosa Luxemburg, rushed to the defence of the Jewish quarter when the Nazis began their attacks. The young members of Hechalutz Holland, whom he met at Dahlia and Chubeza, spoke of their Christian comrades, who had fought with them in Holland and who had helped them to reach Palestine, with a love and abiding gratitude which Marie Syrkin heard lavished on no other European country.[247]

In fairness and justice it has to be emphasized that the inter-group relations of the Jews in Western and Eastern Europe were totally different. In Western Europe the Jews were part of the nations amongst whom they lived, and the Nazi assault on the Jewish community was considered as an offence against the entire nation. In Eastern Europe, on the other hand, the overwhelming majority of Jews lived in isolation from the surrounding world, distinguished not only by religion as in the West, but by language, culture and way of life. They were completely separate entities. The nations amongst whom they dwelt were not conscious of the persecution of the Jews as being their concern to the same degree as the people of Western Europe. Rabbi J.B. Agus rightly observed that the acquiescence of the masses in Poland, Hungary, and Roumania was doubtless the consequence of the near-total absence of bonds of fraternity between the Jews and their neighbours. Thus, while 30,000 Dutch families received medals from their government, after the war, for sheltering Jewish refugees, and while thousands of Jews were saved in France, Belgium, Italy, and Denmark, there is no similar record in any province of Central or Eastern Europe. In the countries where Jews lived as "national minorities," they were effectively isolated from the general population, and marked for slaughter, with hardly a ripple, a protest, while in the Western countries, Holland, Belgium, France, Italy, Denmark and Norway, where Jews were distinguished by religion only, concerted efforts were made to save them from the insane fury of the Nazi murderers.[248]

The instances of help to the Jews in Eastern Europe and the tremendous risk involved in aiding the outlawed Jews, therefore, appear as specifically meritorious. It was not motivated, as in the West, by sentiments of national kinship with the persecuted section of the general community, but caused by feeling of simple human solidarity. In every case it was based on purely humanitarian feelings to the Jewish semi-stranger. The minorities who, risking the fury of Nazi revenge, imperilled their lives in aiding the Jews should become part of Jewish consciousness. They have rightly been termed "unsung heroes."[249] Those who believe in the humanistic doctrines of Judaism ought not to waste an opportunity to find empirical support for their belief in the divine image within man. Those who hold that the particularistic quality of Judaism is well compatible with its universalistic concern should seize every opportunity to witness the nobility in man. For a Jew, knowledge of non-Jewish heroism is a source of great inspiration and morale. For a non-Jew, it offers a model of behaviour and is the finest answer to the argument that there was no alternative to passive complicity in those areas where the Nazis held power.

Many of those who did justice to their consciences by saving Jews perished during the Nazi era or afterwards, in the wake of the upheavals that followed the Nazi defeat. But some were fortunate to be spared for the day when the Jewish people, having regained sovereignty in the land of Israel, decided to set up a permanent memorial to those who risked their lives in the defence of humanity. A large number had the rare privilege of experiencing poetic justice by planting trees in the Avenue of Righteous Gentiles which is devoted to those who risked their lives in defence of their Jewish fellowmen: others received "Medals of the Righteous" or special certificates. All are welcomed with joy and gratitude by those whom they had saved and who, in the meantime, had succeeded in re-establishing themselves in the free countries of the world. The Jewish people have decided to put on record, and keep sacred, the memory of those brave men and women who vindicated the light of humanity during the darkest era in man's passage through history. Some of these persons and events are recorded and known. The drama and danger, the hope and the suffering behind the dry lines, declaring that Mr. NN from Poland or Lithuania had saved a large number of Jews and was privilidged to plant a tree, cannot be described in mere words. Only those who themselves experienced the depth of horror engendered by the Nazi terror, can measure the spirit of sacrifice reflected in those lines.

Most of the Righteous Gentiles so far honoured have come

from Poland, the second longest number from Holland, Germans rank third or fourth.[250] An Israeli survivor of the holocaust recently inquired of a prominent rabbi whether he should recite the Kaddish — the traditional Jewish memorial prayer — for the soul of his Gentile saviour. He had just been apprised of the death in Poland of a Christian lady who had saved his life and that of many other Jews during the German occupation. She had hidden them, looked after their wants, eventually selling all her possessions in order to support all those dependent on her. The inquirer had come to regard her as a mother and ever since the end of the war had maintained contact with her and supported her. The rabbi declared that it was the inquirer's duty to perpetuate her memory and no way was more fitting than by reciting Kaddish which was in itself a sanctification of the Divine.[250a]

Few people are born martyrs, but those among the nations who dared and did, who risked their own lives to save those of others and who disdained ancient prejudices and new group affections, built bridges between the victims and the saviours. They created bonds which will remain firm and unbreakable links between sections of humanity, the Jews and their neighbours, Israel and the Gentiles, synagogue and church. The land of Israel and the Jewish people in all their habitations are inseparable parts of mankind and whatever facts and thoughts are liable to strengthen this feeling of unity, fortify the sentiments of humanity and solidarity with the world, will ultimately be of benefit to the existence of the State of Israel and the maintenance of a vigorous Jewry throughout the world. Hatred breeds hatred, sympathy creates sympathy.

It should never be forgotten that there was not only anti-Semitism in the world but that the sentiments of aversion were complemented by feelings of sympathy. There was, and there is, philo-Semitism in the world; the Jewish people have always had and will always have friends who esteem its qualities, venerate its past, value the Jewish traditions. They will remain their allies in the common fight for a more peaceful and sympathetic world.

Denmark has been honoured as the only "righteous nation" where 89 percent of Jewry was saved through the exertions of a valiant people. In October 1943 the Danish people wrote one of the most glorious chapters in the history of man's humanity to man, the ever-memorable rescue of almost the entire Jewish community of Denmark from the threat of deportation and extermination by the Nazis. The story of the valiant Danish resistance against German tyranny, their secret organization, illegal press, anti-Nazi sabotage, the sufferings of Danish patriots in German prisons and concentration camps, their martyrdom and heroism for the sake of freedom and humanity, is graphically depicted in the Danish Resistance Museum which constitutes a permanent monument to the dauntless bravery of a small yet unconquerable people. A special section is devoted to the suffering of the Danish Jews, and the efforts of the Danes on behalf of their Jewish fellow citizens, culminating in the glorious rescue of the Jewish community by the Danish people, who defied all the might of the Nazi Reich to carry out one of the most miraculous sea rescues in history.

When the Nazis proposed that the Jews wear the Star of David, King Christian X announced that he and the royal family would also wear this badge. "I am the King of all the Danes," he told the Nazi officials. The Nazis demanded the dismissal of Jews from public office; the King's answer was to put on his full dress uniform and, accompanied by Queen Alexandrine, the Crown Prince and the Crown Princess, attend services in the Copenhagen Synagogue. The Gestapo began its abominable hunt for Jews. The Danish clergy, under the leadership of the Bishop of Copenhagen, Foglsang-Dagmar, handed a pastoral letter, that was read in the churches, to the German officials. It proclaimed how much Christianity owed to the Jews and that the clergy would fight in order that "our Jewish brothers and sisters may be assured of the same liberty as ourselves." A joint statement of youth and professional associations, thirty in all, read, "In Denmark there is no antagonism toward the Jews, and action against them is regarded as action against the entire people."

When the order of deportation came in October 1943, fishing villages and resorts all along the coast of Zeeland — the island on which Copenhagen is situated — became the Danish Dunkirks. Danes and Swedes were outraged at the injustice aimed at the Jews. They decided to do something about it; the Danes to risk their lives, and the Swedes to throw open their doors. Every conceivable kind of vessel was pressed into service, boats of every description became rescue ships, ferrying Jews past watchful German patrols across the Sund, that stretch of sea which separates Denmark from Sweden, to hospitable Swedish shores. Practically everyone in Denmark, from king to fisherman, took part in these acts of human courage and kindness. About 300 Jews were captured *en route* and sent to an internment camp, but more than 8000 Jews, including 700 half-Jews, completed the exodus and reached safety in Sweden. Five hundred Jews, mostly aged and sick inmates of an old-aged home, were deported to the concentration camp of Theresienstadt. But they too received especially favourable treatment through the strenuous exertions of the Danish Foreign Office, and many of them returned in April 1945. After the liberation of Denmark, the Jews came back from Sweden, rededicated their beautiful Synagogue, on which the Nazis had not dared to lay their hands, and re-established their small but vigorous Jewish community.

There is another memorable aspect to the story. How did the Danish underground receive information about the impending deportation of Jews, so that they could swing into action? The news was passed on to them, at the risk of their own lives, by two high-ranking Germans, Count Helmut von Moltke and Captain Georg von Duckwitz. Von Moltke, who was later executed by the Gestapo as a member of the German anti-Nazi opposition, was privately informed of the shocking plan and passed it on to his friends in Denmark. Von Duckwitz, the shipping agent of the German Government in Denmark, had received a strictly confidential letter from his superiors ordering him to prepare four cargo ships, adequate in size, to transport all Danish Jews in one mass deportation. Disregarding the personal danger involved, Von Duckwitz advised two Danish leaders, Hans Hedtoft and H. C. Hansen, both of whom served as Prime Ministers after Denmark's liberation, of the grave menace to the Jews. The Danish leaders advised the heads of the Jewish community of the impending danger and alerted the Danish underground for rescue operations. Von Duckwitz returned to Denmark after the war as the West German Ambassador.

Jews and non-Jews remember the episode which ranks as one of the most remarkable events of the Second World War. "The Great Escape," which sheds a ray of light on the Nazi nightmare, testifies to the spirit of heroism and martyrdom on behalf of humanitarian ideals.[251] Jews and Gentiles recall Jewish martyrdom, Danish valour, Swedish hospitality. The decent Germans, too, should remain in grateful remembrance.[252]

It is easier to discuss the varieties of anti-Semitism than to pay attention to heroic resistance to hatred and persecution. Social scientists have found it scientific and natural to describe the hostile and aggressive features of human behaviour, but less natural to deal with altruistic conduct. It is a one-sided attitude which concentrates only upon a destructive aspect of human behaviour and does not sufficiently engage in any empirical study of the altruistic conscience.

There is a need to preserve the memory of those valorous men and women who, defying the invader and death itself, opened their hearts and their homes to a people marked for extinction. It is essential to focus attention upon the humane deeds of mercy which relieved the horror of the Nazi nightmare. It is of the highest importance not only to record the evidences of human degradation, but also to recount examples of human nobility. Let the deeds of love, as opposed to those of hatred, bear equal witness to unborn generations. Jews and Gentiles are called to unite in what is the glory of the genuinely Jewish, the truly Christian, the all-embracing humanitarian tradition — dedication to the loving service of humanity.

242

NOTES

1. R.H.S. Crossman, *Commentary,* June 1962, pp. 490 ff.
2. J.B. Agus, *The Meaning of Jewish History,* vol. II, p. 431.
3. Isaiah Berlin, Chaim Weizmann, p. 42.
4. J. Baron, Stars and Sands, p. 27.
5. See Chapter 2: A Balanced Concept of Jewish History.
6. See Chapter 4: Friendly Popes.
7. On the Torah Scroll Ceremony, see E.A. Synan, The Popes and the Jews in the Middle Ages, p. 79.

   A Torah scroll, magnificently executed, and veiled out of reverence, was at once their most characteristic and most precious possession as Jews. The Pope received the scroll from their hands with ceremony to symbolize the fact that the Jews have provided Christians with this essential part of their inheritance. Lest the real distinction between Judaism and Christianity be submerged in this proclamation of their continuity, the Pope recited a formula to express his acceptance of the Hebrew scriptures, but also his simultaneous rejection of the interpretation given them by normative Judaism. This ceremony, still performed in the nineteenth century, is one more reason for counting as "Middle Ages" for the Jews who lived in the patrimony of Saint Peter the period that ended with the loss of the Pope's temporal power.

7a. Solomon Ibn Verga, Shevet Yehudah; J.B. Agus, Meaning of Jewish History 2, 384.
8. M. Wiener, Contemporary Jewish Record, June 1944, pp. 261 ff.
9. N. Rotenstreich, The Recurring Pattern, pp. 39 f.
10. J.L. Talmon, The Nature of Jewish History, p. 13 ff.
11. AJR (Association of Jewish Refugees) Information. Nov. 1967, London.
12. M. Grunwald, Vienna, p. 355.
13. L. Bato, Die Juden im Alten Wien, p. 242.
13a. F. Landsberger, A History of Jewish Art, p. 271.

13b. Joys and Sorrows, p. 99 f.

14. London Jewish Chronicle, April 11, 1969.

15. Ch. Lewis, Jewish Affairs, Johannesburg, April 1969, p. 31 f.

16. A. Rogow, Introduction to The Jew in a Gentile world, p. XV.

17. Philip Friedman's Their Brothers Keepers may be considered a classic on the theme of active philo-Semitism. Other works on the theme are Stars and Sand, as well as Candles in the Night, edited by Joseph Baron. J.H. Schöps's Philo-Semitism in Barock deals mainly with Scandinavian writers.

18. The expression "lachrymose theory of Jewish history" was coined by Salo Baron in an essay "Ghetto and Emancipation." 1928 Menorah Journal, vol. XIV, p. 520.

19. The Chronicles of Ephraim of Bonn (12th century) in Hoexter-Jung, Source Book of Jewish History and Literature, p. 128 f.

20. Y.F. Baer, A History of the Jews in Christian Spain, vol. 1, pp. 182 f.

21. S. Baron, Proceedings of the American Academy of Jewish Research, vol. 12, p. 36 ff.

22. I.A. Agus, Jewish Quarterly Review, Jan. 1961, p. 251.

23. I.A. Agus, ib., p. 242 ff.

24. C. Roth, Hebrew Union College Annual, 1950-1951, part II, pp. 167 f.
    In the Preface to Personalities and Events in Jewish History Roth recalls that he initiated the wider reaction against the lachrymose concept interpreting Jewish history. He thinks that he was right at the time, but could not publish these articles after massacres a hundred times greater than any recorded in the past.

25. Judaism, Winter 1970, p. 122 ff.

26. I.A. Agus, The Heroic Age of Franco-German Jewry, p. 52 f.

26a. On the Radanites, L.I. Rabinowitz, Jewish Merchant Adventurers.

27. B. Weinryb, Jewish Quarterly Review, January 1959, p. 207.

27a. M. Mushkat in 1971 Annual of Israel and World Jewry, the Jewish Agency, Jerusalem.

27b. Reconstructionist, Jan. 1978, p. 4.

28. H. Hailperin's Preface to Jacob S. Raisin, Gentile Reaction to Jewish Ideals.

29. H. Sharf, Byzantine Jewry, p. 36. Jews in Byzantium in World History of Jewish People, ed. C. Roth.

30. S. Baron, A Social and Religious History of the Jews, Vol. 3, p. 172. J.R. Marcus, The Jew in the Medieval World, pp. 28 f. A. Rogow, ed., The Jew in the Gentile World, pp. 76 f.

31. J. Parkes, A History of the Jewish People, p. 50 f. p. 62.

32. L. Zunz, Synagogale Poesie 9.

33. M. Dimont, Jews, God and History, p. 250 f: "During these tranquil centuries, Jewish life flowed in an even tempo. There exists a popular misconception about this entire era, that the Jews were stuck away in

dark, dank, ghetto prisons for twelve hundred medieval years. Actually the medieval Jewish ghetto experience was a localized incident between 1500 and 1800, and prevalent only in northern Italy, the German-speaking countries, and a few Polish cities. The confusion stems from the indiscriminate use of the word 'ghetto,' as opposed to 'Jewish quarter.' There is a great difference between these two ways of life. The Jewish quarter was voluntary and self-imposed. The ghetto was involuntary and imposed from without. One spelled freedom; the other brought imprisonment."

Dimont's tendency to evalue correctly the positive aspects of Jewish existence throughout the ages is to be commended.

34. J. Parkes, A History of the Jewish People, p. 222 f.

The Visigothic Kings and the Canons of the Visigothic Councils were violently anti-Jewish. Their legislation ends with the supreme absurdity of ordering that all Jews are to spend all Jewish and Christian feast days in the presence of the local bishop, washed and in a suitable frame of mind, to ensure that they practise no Jewish observance and mock at no Christian one. However, Theodoric, the Ostrogoth King, rebuked the Roman Senate for levitas when they permitted a riot against Jews in Rome; in another case he defended Jews on the grounds of the need to preserve civilities; and it is Theodoric who, in reproving a Jewish attempt to claim more than the law allowed, ended by confirming their right to remain in their Jewish "incredulity" as long as they wished "since no one can be compelled to believe against his will."

Parkes rightly asserts that ordinary men and women in town and country, whether they were Jew or Christian, passed into the Dark Ages together, and experienced together the total insecurity of the times. This is the basic affirmation of the anti-lachrymose concept of Jewish history. The Jews shared in the darkness of the Dark Ages. . . . The bulk of them, like the bulk of Christians, lived out their lives in obscurity, and were happiest when left obscure. The specific Jewish situation deteriorated with the Crusades. The Jews had no rights except such as some Charter gave them. Even the horrifying massacres of the Crusades had a mitigating feature. It is significant that nowhere did their Christian neighbours turn upon the Jews. The burghers tried to hide them, the bishops or counts of the cities to protect them. But in almost every case the mob prevailed.

35. I.A. Agus, Judaism, Summer 1966, p. 360 f.

36. Jules Isaac has devoted a study, The Teaching of Contempt, to the Christian roots of anti-Semitism. The traditional Christian teachings of the dispersion as divine punishment for the Crucifixion, of the degenerate legalistic quality of the Jewish religion, of the crime of deicide, led to the emergence of the traditional anti-Jewish hostility, to acts of discrimination and persecution. Leaders of the Church today are en-

devouring to repent for this wrong against the Jewish people. It is however erroneous to suggest that anti-Jewish prejudice first arose as a result of the Christian doctrine. It goes back to the Greco-Roman times. Jews were resented because they did not conform — as all consistent non-conformists are resented. See W.W. Simpson in Facing Realities, aspects of Christian-Jewish understanding, p. 24 f.

37. Ben Halpern in Commentary, October 1964.
38. S. Baron — History and Jewish Historians, p. 88.
39. H. Hazaz, Ha-d'rasha The Sermon, English in "Israeli Stories," Shocken Books, 1962.
40. On anti-Semitism in the Greco-Roman world: I. Heinemann in Pauly-Wissowa, Realencyclopaedie des klassichen Altertums. Supplement V, A.
41. CLEARCHUS, 3rd century B.C. Th. Reinach, Textes D'Auteurs Grecs et Romains Relatifs au Judaisme 10 f; Josephus, Contra Apionem I, 22.
42. THEOPHRASTUS, 3rd century B.C. Reinach ib. 8.
43. PHILO: Proselytes spurn mythical inventions and embrace truth in its purity, or take up their abode with the honour of the one Being who is entitled to honour, abandoning the mythical inventions and multiplicity of sovereigns. H.A. Wolfson, Philo, I, 34. D. Bamberger, Proselytism in the Talmudic Period 24 f.
44. VARRO, 116 — 27 B.C.; fragment of Antiquities quoted by St. Augustin, De Civitate Dei, IV, 31.
45. STRABO, 64 B.C. — 21 A.D.; Geography XVI, fragments quoted by Josephus, Antiquities. E. Schürer, The Jewish People in the Time of Jesus Christ, vol. 2, 299.
46. HECATAEUS of Abdera, quoted in pseudo-Aristeas, Schürer, The Jewish People, vol. 2, 303. Josephus, Antt. XII, 2, 4: "And indeed this legislation is full of hidden wisdom and entirely blameless, as being the legislation of God: for which cause it is, as Hecateus of Abdera says, that the poets and historians make no mention of it, nor of those men who lead their lives according to it, since it is a holy law, and ought not to be published by profane mouths."
47. DIO CASSIUS, 2nd Century C.E. Reinach, p. 182.
48. B. Walker, The Annals of Tacitus, p. 244.
49. A. Marmorstein, Studies in Jewish Theology, p. 104.
50. Reinach, ib., p. 101.
51. JOSEPHUS, Contra Apionem, I, 22. Reinach pp. 39, 40, 159. The theory of Pythagoras' dependence on Jewish sources was later accepted by Jewish writers. Yehuda Halevi, Kusari II, 66.
52. Reinach, p. 154; Schürer, The Jewish People, vol. II, p. 323.
53. I. Heinemann in "Zion," Jerusalem, 1939, vol. iv. pp. 269 ff. and in Review of Religions, May 1940. p. 385-400.
54. London Jewish Chronicle, September 30, 1966. S. Baron in Proceedings of the American Academy for Jewish Research, vol. XII, p. 37 f.

55. J.R. Marcus, The Jew in the Mediaeval World, pp. 112 f. Gregory the Great writes to Januarius, Bishop of Cagliari in Sardinia, concerning a similar complaint by the Jews. Gregory protected the Jews against forced conversion. F.C. Burkitt, In Spirit and in Truth, p. 296 f.

56. J. Hoexter — M. Jung, Source Book of Jewish History, p. 139.

57. Roth, Personalities and Events, p. 274.

58. J. Maritain, Antisemitism, p. 27.

59. S. Friedlander, Pius XII and the Third Reich.

60. On the chilling dilemma of the Judenräte — News of the Yivo, Summer 1970.

61. P.E. Lapide in Jewish Heritage, Fall 1962, p. 30.

62. London Jewish Chronicle, June 21, 1963. Sister Marie Louise Gabriel reports (Jewish Affairs, Johannesburg, October 1962) that the Sisters take a leading part in collaboration with Jewish-Christian friendship groups in order to promote a better understanding of those of whom Cardinal Liénard in his Lenten Pastoral of 1960, "The Christian Conscience and the Jewish Problem," said: "They remain ever the Chosen People." It is obvious that there exists today a new climate in the Catholic Church. It is impossible to predict whether these sentiments will be translated into action and bear positive results, but it is evident beyond doubt that they are not prompted by conversionist motives, but by genuine sentiments of philo-Semitism.

63. Augustin Cardinal Bea, The Church and the Jewish People.

64. London Jewish Chronicle, November 18, 1966.

65. Ibid, October 23, 1970.

66. Zionist Record, Johannesburg. October 30, 1970.

67. Rabbinic studies were facilitated by a number of works which according to the scientific standards of the time represented a high standard of accuracy, such as the works of Buxtorf the elder, Buxtorf the younger, Sebastian Münster, Adrian Reland and others. Intensive Rabbinic studies were pursued in Germany, Switzerland, England, Holland and Sweden. G.A. Kohut in Israel Abrahams Memorial Volume 221 f. S.A. Hirsch, Early English Hebraists, Book of Essays, 3 f.

68. Opinion on Jewish writings submitted to Emperor Maxmilian I October 1510: "If the burning of Jewish literature were godly, laudable and beneficial to the Christian faith . . . whether to take, carry off and burn all the books of the Jews," is included in Augenspiegel (1511), a book that contains Reuchlin's entire controversy with the Dominicans. See Marcus, ib. pp. 159 ff; Hoexter-Jung, ib. p. 199.

69. J. Baron, Stars and Sand, p. 95.

70. Juedische Parabeln, Adrastea 7, 64.

71. Jewish artisan life in the time of Jesus, pp. 29 f, 51 f. Rohling's Talmudjude pp. 10 f. In his powerful defence of the Talmud against the misrepresentations of the notorious anti-Semite Rohling, Delitzsch writes that there are indeed among the Jews people who violate the laws of moral-

ity; but their actions are opposed to the ethical demands of the rabbis; the ethics of the Talmud is sufficiently pure and strong to condemn the deeds of evildoers who disgrace the Jewish community and human society.

72. Though Strack may not have been quite free from missionary motives, yet his services to Jewish studies were so remarkable that he deserves to be included among the genuine friends of the Jewish people and lovers of its literature. His defence of Judaism against the blood libel had remarkable effect in its days.

73. Henry Coudenhove-Kalergi, Anti-Semitism Throughout the Ages, pp. 219 ff.

74. The Jews, translation of F.W. Foerster's Die Juedische Frage by Brian Battershaw, p. 109 f.

75. J.H. Hertz, Sermons, Addresses and Studies, vol. 2, p. 98. D. Daiches, The King James Version of the English Bible, p. 163 f. F.F. Bruce, The English Bible, p. 106 f.

76. Graetz, History of the Jews, V 193 f, p. 312-314. J. Parkes, Judaism and Christianity, p. 147.

77. Introduction to Book of Offerings. See S. Rappaport, Jewish Horizons, p. 118 ff.

78. S. Rappaport, Jewish Horizons, p. 123 f. In his lighter moments Herford used to describe himself as a "Jewnitarian." For daring to break with a well-established theological tradition, Herford was attacked by Christians. His opponents condemned his rehabilitation of Phariseeism as a spiritual religion and saw in his enthusiastic appraisal of rabbinic teaching even an "excuse for the Crucifixion." See H.G. Wood, Peake's Commentary on the Bible, p. 666.

79. In the Manchester Guardian, Dr. E. Rosenthal wrote: "He has no peer in sympathetic understanding and scholarly presentation of Rabbinic Judaism," while Rabbi Dr. Altman declared, "No Christian of our time has made so deep an impression on his Jewish contemporaries as the late Dr. Herford did."

80. On G.F. Moore, S. Schulman in The Judeans, vol. IV.

81. World Jewry, September-October 1969. A History of the Jewish People, pp. 44 f. The "Foundations of Judaism and Christianity" constitutes a summary and culmination of Parkes's thought on Judaism and Christianity. It would be worthwhile to investigate what influence Parkes exercised on contemporary Christian thought. In possible contrast to the German friends and students of rabbinic literature, the English-American scholars of rabbinism appear to be free of missionary motives. The rabbinic studies of Rev. C.H. Box and Dr. W.O.E. Oesterly deserved special recognition.

82. Translated by S.H. Hooke, p. 258 f.

83. J. Bonsirven, Palestinian Judaism in the Time of Jesus Christ, p. 142.

84. On Pallière Marion Schwarze-Nordmann, Das Leben eines Noachiden.

85. Communion in the Messiah, p. 62 f.
86. Die Pharisäer, in Die Gemeinde, Vienna 29 May 1961. Prof. K. Schubert is the author of The Dead Sea Community, 1959, and Die Religion des nachbiblischen Judentums, 1955.

    In Summer 1978, Professor Schubert arranged a magnificent exhibition, "Judentum im Mittelalter" (Judaism in the Middle Ages), held in the Austrian Castle Halbturn.
87. London Jewish Chronicle, March 20, 1964. p. 9.
88. London Jewish Chronicle, October 14, 1966. p. 15.
89. F.C. Grant, Ancient Judaism and the New Testament, pp. 161 and 187 f.
90. London Jewish Chronicle, May 3, 1968, p. 22.
91. H.H. Rowley, Israel's Mission to the World, p. 125.
92. G.F. Moore, Judaism, vol., 1, p. 285.
93. Considerations on Representative Government. J. Baron, Stars and Sand, p. 131.
94. Faulhaber's collection of sermons preached in Munich in 1933, Judaism, Christianity, and Germany, translated by J.D. Smith, pp. 7 f, 16 f.
95. H.H. Rowley, ibid pp. 39 f.
96. J. Maritain, Anti-Semitism, p. 28.
97. Le Salut par les Juifs, Maritain, ibid. p. 28.
98. Thomas Newton, Dissertations on the Prophecies, vol. 1, p. 216 f. J. Baron, ibid, p. 71.
99. G.E. Lessing, Rettung des Hieronimus Cardanus, 1754.
100. Israel Zangwill, M. Hoexter — J. Jung, Source Book of Jewish History, p. 277; C. Roth, Personalities and Events in Jewish History, p. 69 f.
101. E.M. Arndt, Versuch in vergleichender Völkergeschichte, 1843, p. 19 ff.
102. A. Toynbee, A Study of History, vol. 12, pp. 479 f.
103. K.H. Cornill, The Prophets of Israel, pp. 178 f.
104. H.H. Rowley, Israel's Mission to the World, pp. 100 f.
105. R. Otto, The Idea of the Holy, p. 77.
106. H. Gunkel, What Remains of the Old Testament, pp. 52 f.
107. The Letters of Robert Louis Stevenson, vol. 2, p. 273 f.
108. On Herder, see J.L. Talmon, Herder and the German Mind, in The Unique and the Universal, p. 91 ff.
109. S. Rappaport, Jewish Affairs, Johannesburg, November 1959.
110. Fr. de Chateaubriand, Genius of Christianity, pt. 1, bk. 2, ch. 4.
111. J. Baron, Stars and Sand, p. 95 f.
112. Moses and his Laws, J. Baron, ib. p. 115 f.
113. J. Baron, ib. p. 137 f. J.H. Hertz, A Book of Jewish Thought, p. 143 f.
114. O. Rabinowicz, Winston Churchill on Jewish Problems, p. 27.
115. Hoexter-Jung, Source Book, p. 200 f.
116. L. Poliakov, The History of Anti-Semitism, p. 216 f. A reference to Luther as a righteous man of God (L. Haubner in The Christian Minister, Cape Town), September 1969, cannot be accepted in view of Luther's savage outbursts against the Jewish community. However, Luther's

greatness as one of the decisive personalities in the history of Western humanity must be measured by other standards as well.

117. H. Grotius, The Truth of the Christian Religion, pp. 208 f; On Grotius's sympathetic interest in Jews and Judaism, see I. Husik, "Law of Nature, Grotius, and the Bible," in Hebrew Union College Annual, vol. 2, pp. 381 ff.
118. G.E. Lessing, Nathan the Wise, IV, 7.
119. On Solovyev's religious attitude, E. Munzer, Solovyev Prophet of Russian-Western Unity. p. 2 f.
120. Ellen Key in Rahel Varhagen, p. 13. J. Baron, Stars and Sand, p. 67. Anti-Semites of the racialist variety maintain that Jesus was an Aryan. H.S. Chamberlain, notorious author of Die Grundlagen des neunzehnten Jahrhunderts, was convinced that Jesus did not belong to the same race as Abraham. He was sure that Jesus had fair hair and blue eyes, and the fact that He was the embodiment of all that is good was further proof that He could not have been Jewish. Chamberlain also laid great stress on the fact that Jesus was born in Galilee where a considerable section of the population was Greek. See J.L. Talmon, The Unique and the Universal, p. 152.
121. F.C. Grant, Ancient Judaism and the New Testament, p. 99.
122. Philip Friedman, Their Brothers' Keepers, p. 41.
123. E.A. Phillips, The Old Testament in the World Church, p. 35.
124. N. Soderblom, Christian Fellowship, p. 41.
125. N. Berdyaev, in Religions, Feb. 1939, pp. 13 ff.
126. A. van Selms in Jewish Affairs, Johannesburg, April 1965.
127. A.M. Ramsey, The Christian Minister, Capetown, October 1964.
128. T.G. Masaryk in C. Newman, Gentile and Jew, p. 68.
129. R. Bacon Opus Tertium. S.A. Hirsch, Book of Essays, p. 23.
130. L. Rosenthal in J.H. Hertz Jubilee Volume, pp. 351 f.
131. Jewish Heritage, Fall 1962, p. 40 f.
132. J. Abrahams, Jewish Life in the Middle Ages, p. 447.
133. J.E. Renan, Studies in Religious History, p. 168 ff.
     Renan's contributions to Jewish history and literature have a great value as pioneering works. Particularly notable are his editions of Adolf Neubauer's Les rabbins francais du commencement du quatorzieme siecle, and Les ecrivains juifs francais du xiveme siecle.
134. A. Bein in Between East and West (Memorial volume for Bela Horowitz), p. 170 f.
135. Graetz, History of the Jews, vol. 5, p. 27 f.
136. E. Wilson in Commentary, Oct. 1956. p. 329 f.
137. John Fiske, The Beginnings of New England, J. Baron, Stars and Sand, p. 457 f.
138. R.W. Emerson, Lectures and biographical sketches, p. 233 f.
139. H.J. Schoeps, Jewish Quarterly Review, Oct. 1956, p. 144.

140. W.E. Gladstone, Gleanings of the Past Years, vol. 7, p. 79 f. J. Baron, Stars and Sand, p. 133 f.
141. E. Wilson in Rogow, ed., The Jew in a Gentile World, p. 358 f.
142. W.B. Selbie in The Legacy of Israel, edited by E. Bevan and Ch. Singer, p. 407 f.
143. See Poliakov, The History of Anti-Semitism, p. 198 about the importance of the Reformation for the development of sympathy for the people of the law, especially through active contact of Christians with Jewish scholars.
144. James Truslow Adams, the American historian, stresses the alleged unfavourable effect which study of the Old Testament had on the Puritans. He states that they took special delight in the Old Testament. This did not, however, imply any love for the living Jew.
145. S. Schechter coined the unfortunate phrase of "higher anti-semitism," as being characteristic of every critical approach to the Hebrew Bible. See his Seminary Addresses, pp. 35 f.
146. N. Berdyaev, The Meaning of History, p. 86.
147. W.A. Irwin, The Old Testament, pp. 162 f.
148. B.W. Anderson, The Living World of the Old Testament, pp. 414.
149. Preface to Annals of the Roman People.
150. Richard Livingstone, The Future in Education, p. 77.
151. H. Butterfield, Christianity and History, pp. 68 f.
152. Joseph S. Bloch, Israel and the Nations, p. 219.
153. Rowley, Israel's Mission to the World, p. 113.
154. J.H. Hertz, A Book of Jewish Thoughts, p. 151.
    The optimistic view of human history has its roots in the Hebraic conception of the historical process as a progressive revelation of God's purpose; it was during the Enlightenment that it took on its modern garb, and in the nineteenth century it became the dominant mode of thought. It underlay the outlook of Tennyson, with his belief in the coming "Parliament of Man" and "Federation of the World." It underlies equally — though translated into other terms — the powerful Marxist interpretation of history, which also sees the history of mankind passing through well-defined phases, culminating in a classless society, so perfect that the ugly contrivance of the state will "wither away." Toynbee, A Study of History, vol. 12, p. 220.
155. Edwin R. Bevan in Singer, The Legacy of Israel, p. 38.
156. Wijnhoven, Jewish Heritage, Fall 1962, p. 40 f.
157. Baron ed., Stars and Sand, p. 26.
158. Dickens tried to make amends for the ill-feeling he engendered in creating Fagin, the criminal Jew in Oliver Twist, by portraying a sympathetic character, Ria, in Our Mutual Friend. E. Rosenberg, From Shylock to Svengali, p. 50.
159. David Hume, History of England, vol. 1. pp. 632 f.

251

160. J. Baron, Stars and Sand, pp. 216 f.
161. Jean Jacques Rousseau, Emile, translated by B. Foxley, pp. 267 f.
162. From the Declaration of Independence of the United States of America, 1776.
163. From the Virginia Act for Religious Freedom, 1786.
164. Act of Surinam, August 17, 1665. Raphael Mahler, ed., Emancipation: A Selection of Documents.
165. Austrian Edict of Toleration, 1782.
166. Hoexter-Jung, Source Book of Jewish History, p. 222.
167. Ibid, p. 235 f.
168. Hoexter-Jung, Ibid, p. 219 f.
    Parkes, Judaism and Christianity, p. 152.
    B. Dinur, Be-mifneh ha-dorot, pp. 275 f.
168a. Hoexter-Jung, Ibid, p. 168 f.
169. Rosenberg, From Shylock to Svengali, p. 331 f. Hoexter-Jung, Ibid, p. 204 f.
170. R. Mahler, ed. Emancipation, p. 28 f.
171. H. Alexander in National Jewish Monthly, April 1968.
172. Smuts' memorable address delivered in Johannesburg Town Hall on November 3rd 1919 is reprinted in Jewish Affairs, August 1970. E. Bernstein, the Legacy of General Smuts.
173. T.G. Masaryk and the Jews, ed. B.R. Epstein.
173a. Ch. Kegley and R.W. Bretall, The Theology of Paul Tillich, p. 15.
174. A.H. Friedlander, Reconstructionist, 12th November 1965. Wilson, Commentary, October 1956.
175. O. Rabinowicz, Winston Churchill on Jewish Problems, p. 25 f.
176. M.F. Modder, The Jew in the Literature of England, p. 260. On the subject of the contrasting representation of the Jew in English literature, Harold Fisch, The Dual Image. The dual image is based on the conflicting role which the Jew holds in the Christian conscience as the people who produced Christ and rejected him. The image of the Jew in literature is indeed a dual image: he excites horror, fear, hatred; but he also excites wonder, awe, and love. . . . The Jews were a deicide nation but they were also a nation which is redeemed, and on whose redemption the fate of mankind hangs. From this state of mind arises the two-fold image of the Jew in the Christian literature of the Middle Ages and beyond.
177. Matthew Arnold: Heinrich Heine.
178. Harry Jessey, The Glory of Jehuda and Israel. Magna Bibliotica Anglo-Judaica, ed. C. Roth, London 1937.
179. There is a large bibliography on George Eliot, her role in promoting Zionist thought and her celebrated Daniel Deronda. See the perceptive essay by Soi Liptzin in Jewish Book Annual 1951-1952, ". . . the wisdom and insight of the English novelist are apparent to Jews the world over

and tribute is being paid to this mid-Victorian seeress as a non-Jewish pioneer of Jewish rebirth."

180. Joseph II's prayer quoted in G.A. Kohut, ed. Nathan the Wise, p. 11. Raisin, Gentile Reactions to Jewish ideals, p. 619, unjustly attributed conversionist motives to Joseph II.

181. Herder was the first to undertake a comprehensive evaluation of Biblical literature from an aesthetic viewpoint. His main works in this field are Die älteste Urkunde des Menschengeschlechts, Solomons Lieder der Liebe, Vom Geist der ebräischen Poesie.

182. Quoted in Lady Magnus, Jewish Portraits, p. 146.

183. Letter to the "American Hebrew," August 17, 1932.

184. Reference to the famous saying by August Bebel, German Social Democratic Leader.

185. Thomas Mann, Seven Manifestos pp. 60, 70.

The Exchange of Letters between Thomas Mann and the University of Bonn which, at the beginning of the Nazi era, took away the honorary doctorate from its most distinguished son, has been reproduced in 1937 by the Friends of Europe (Publications No. 52). In his Foreword, J.B. Priestly writes: "Real patriotism brings us the duty — in Thomas Mann's fine phrase — of keeping pure the image of one's own people in the sight of humanity."

186. P. Berline, Jewish Social Studies, Oct. 1947, p. 271, p. 272 f.

187. Proclamation of Russian intellectuals, J. Baron, Stars and Sand, p. 234.

187a. Stefan Zweig, The Living Thoughts of Tolstoy, p. 12. H. Troyat, Tolstoy, p. 582.

188. Dubnow, History of the Jews of Russia and Poland, vol. 2, p. 387, vol. 3, p. 76.

Tolstoy's idealistic concepts led him to consider excessive materialism, the over-emphasis on technology and neglect of the great Christian truth, as the main reasons for Russia's defeat at the hands of the non-Christian Japanese. In his search for the guilty parties, he even began sliding imperceptibly towards anti-Semitism. "This debacle," he wrote on June 18, 1905, "is not only that of the Russian army, the Russian fleet and the Russian State, but of the pseudo-Christian civilisation as well . . . . The disintegration began long ago, with the struggle for money and success in so-called scientific and artistic pursuits, where the Jews got the edge on the Christians in every country and thereby earned the envy and hatred of all. Today the Japanese have done the same thing in the military field, proving conclusively, by brute force, that there is a goal which Christians must not pursue, for in seeking it they will always fail, vanquished by non-Christians." Troyat, ib. p. 588.

There is sometimes a thin line of division between pro-Jewish and anti-Jewish feelings, conditioned by changing situations and moods. Such has been and is until today the Jewish situation in the world.

Russian national pride wounded by the ignominious defeat in the Russo-Japanese war of 1905 looked for a scapegoat. Not even Tolstoy was quite above finding it in the Jews.

189. It may be asserted that Judaism rejects the doctrine of non-resistance to evil and all forms of pacifism. It demands action from its devotees, it teaches that there is evil in society and that it is man's duty to overcome it — if need be by force. Yet the idea underlying Jesus' teaching of "resist not evil" is paralleled in Jewish tradition, though it may not belong to its dominant trend. "Learn to receive suffering," the Rabbis teach, "and forgive those who insult you." "Belong ever to those who are persecuted," they exhort, "rather than those who persecute." Those who are insulted, but do not retaliate, who hear insults and do not reply, who love God and rejoice at sufferings, about them Scripture says: "Those that love Him are as the sun that goeth forth in its might."

190. L. Tolstoy, The Road to Live, authorised German translation — Fuer alle Tage, by E.K. Schmidt.

191. Simon Dubnow, Tolstoy and Judaism, vol. 25, 627 f.

192. The Meaning of History, p. 86 f, 91 f.

193. S. Zeitlin, Jewish Quarterly Review, July 1968, p. 76 f.

B. Malamud's The Fixer also creates in the reader the impression that the voice of humanity and reason was not heard in Russia.

194. On Mickiewicz and the Jewish Problem, A. Duker in M. Kridl, ed., Adam Mickiewicz (Symposium). English translation of Polish short stories on Jewish themes, J. Baron, Candles in the Night.

195. M. Debre, The Image of the Jew in French Literature from 1800 to 1908, p. 66, 68, 86.

196. Published on January 13, 1898 in Clemenceau's paper L'Aurore.

197. R. Kedward, The Dreyfus Affair, p. 71.

198. M. Bernard, Zola, p. 137 ff. Memorable is Clemenceau's editorial in L'Aurore of February 5th 1898: "We believe that we are still far removed from that time and that it is far easier to invent the steamboat, the telegraph and the Roentgen rays than to alter an iota of the atavism of our hearts. We have come to the point when the masses are roused by the cry of Long Live France! Long Live the Army! to plunder, arson and murder, and when the mere demand for justice exposes one to the charge of being a traitor or of being in the pay of the enemy. The latter is perhaps the less pardonable, for it has not even the excuse of mob frenzy and ignorance . . . . What does it matter to you whether Dreyfus is innocent or guilty? a general asked of Col. Piquart. You are not on Devil's Island. And in daily conversation we hear many people exclaim, apparently in order to acquit themselves of some doubt which may attach to them: 'Why should it concern us whether Dreyfus was judged aright or not! After all, he is only a Jew!' These words will remain in the memory of men, for they characterize an age."

199. Kedward, The Dreyfus Affair, pp. 75 f.
200. J. Maritain, Jewish Frontier, August 1944, p. 14 f.
201. Charles Peguy, Notre Jeunesse IV, p. 219. Gillet, Communion in the Messiah, p. 231.
202. C. Peguy, Man and Saints, M. Hindus in Contemporary Jewish Record, June 1945, p. 332.
203. E.M. Levy, The Jews and Ourselves. A "Quarterly on Judaism and Christianity in the World of Today," Summer 1965.
204. C.A. Lippman, Contemporary Jewish Record, February 1943, p. 91.
205. Paul Claudel, Symposium Les Juifs, Gillet, Communion in the Messiah, p. 233.
206. Jules Michelet, The Bible of Humanity, pp. 257 f.
206a. Curt Lang in AJR Information, March 1971, p. 6.
207. Jacques Duquesne in Wiener Library Bulletin, London, Spring 1967, p. 15. Ph. Friedman Their Brothers Keepers, p. 49 f.
208. Published in Paris in 1946; the latest English printing is The Schocken Books edition of 1967.
209. J.P. Sartre in New Outlook, Tel-Aviv, May 1967.
210. R. Minc in Jewish Heritage, Spring 1969, p. 58 f.
    Am Vasepher, Sept. 1966, p. 31 f.
211. Abraham Jonker, The Scapegoat of History.
212. The entire letter, a remarkable document, has been reprinted in Jewish Affairs, Johannesburg, September 1967, p. 51 f.
213. E. Tannenbaum, Jewish Affairs, May 1951, Jan Burger, Jewish Affairs, August 1960, vol. 15 p. 65 f.
    The unfortunate Nazi influence in the thinking of a section of Afrikanderdom after 1933 may be considered as a regrettable aberration. Its evaluation lies outside the scope of this study. On the subject of Jewish-Afrikaner relations, S. Rappaport, Early Jewish Africana in Bibliophilia Africana, III, 1978.
214. G. Saron and L. Hotz The Jews in South Africa, p. 212.
215. S.A. Jewish Times, 27th August 1953. On the historical interaction between Jews and Afrikaners, G. Saron in S.A. Jewish Times, 5th March 1971.
216. Aarne Sirala, Waterloo Lutheran University, Herzl Institute Bulletin, January 16th 1966.
217. L. Poliakov, The History of Anti-Semitism, p. 221.
218. Poliakov, ibid, p. 225.
219. F. Kobler, "Juden und Judentum in Deutschen Briefen aus drei Jahrhunderten," pp. 80 f.
220. Ibid, p. 98.
221. Goethe's "Conversations" (Gespräche) in answer to an effort to make the Jews an object of ridicule on the Weimar stage.
222. Kobler, Juden und Judentum, p. 144.

223. In a letter to Moses Mendelssohn dated Weimar, 10 October 1779, Herder asks Mendelssohn for a critical judgment on his works, calling Mendelssohn an honest (rechtschaffen) Israelite and stressing his reverence for Mendelssohn's knowledge of Hebrew and for the images of the prophets and teachers of Israel. This letter is a testimony for the tremendous encouragement which the champions of enlightenment and liberalism derived from the remarkable personality of Moses Mendelssohn. Kobler Juden und Judentum, p. 72.

224. Table Talk, August 14, 1833. Modder, The Jew in the Literature of England, p. 111, comments on the manner in which Coleridge mixed his original pro-Semitic judgments with conventional uncomplimentary views. On the one hand Coleridge notes the fact that the Jews were destined to remain a quiet light among the nations for the purpose of pointing out the doctrine of the unity of God, but he contradicts this sentiment by adding that the religion of the Jew is indeed a light; but it is the light of a glow-worm, which gives no heat, and illumines nothing but itself.

224a. Hertz, a Book of Jewish Thought, p. 170. Herbert Solow, Voltaire and Some Jews in Menorah Journal, April 1927. A Hertzberg, The French Enlightenment and the Jews overstates the case against Voltaire and the champions of enlightenment. — Saint Simon; J.L. Talmon, Israel Among the Nations, p. 14 fl.

225. E. Silberner in Jewish Social Studies, Oct. 1947, p. 339 f.

226. On socialist philo-Semitism and anti-Semitism, E. Silberner, Sozialisten zur Judenfrage (Berling 1962); Silberner, Historia Judaica, April 1948, on Proudhon's Judeo Phobia; also Historia Judaica, April 1949 on Karl Marx's anti-Semitism. Karl Marx, according to Silberner, is the founder of the anti-Semitic trend of modern Socialism.

226a. Human, all-too Human, J. Baron, Stårs and Sand, p. 170 f.

227. See Achad Ha-am, The Transvaluation of Values. Achad Ha-am gives Nietzsche's thought of the Superman a "Jewish quality." "Superman" represents "absolute ethics." See the perceptive essay by F. Lachover in *Bitchum umichutz lithchum* (Hebrew). Even if Nietzsche blames the Jews, he exalts them. He is astounded and amazed at their vital power, and even forgives them the creation of ethics which lead to decay. There is no connection between Nietzsche's belief in creative vitality reflecting the heroic quality of man and the monstrous disdain for all human virtues practised by the Nazis.

228. Beyond Good and Evil, article 250.

229. Ib. art. 52.

230. Genealogy of Morals III, art. 22.

231. Anti-Christ I, art. 24; Will to Power, art. 352; Ecce Homo. A. Stern, Contemporary Jewish Record, February 1945.

232. Talmon, The Unique and the Universal, p. 287.

233. J.L. Talmon, The Unique and the Universal, p. 117 f. A. Bäumler, one of the first Nazi theoreticians, proclaimed that "When we shout Heil Hitler . . . we are also hailing Friedrich Nietzche." Talmon, Ibid, p. 144.

234. Modder, The Jew in the Literature of England, pp. 133 f; Rosenberg, From Shylock to Svengali, pp. 61 ff; Fish, The Dual Image.

234a. Axel Springer, leading German publisher, interviewed in a BBC documentary, AJR Information, October 1971. Chancellor Helmut Schmidt's remarkable plea for honesty and tolerance, addressed to a gathering in the Cologne Synagogue to commemorate the 40th anniversary of the Kristalnacht, Jewish Affairs, Johannesburg, March 1979.

235. It is notable that the experience of American Jewry has been different from that of European Jewry. "If there has been occasional indulgence, by a minority, in vicious Jew-baiting and anti-Semitism, there have never been massacres of Jews, or pogroms, or inquisitions, or concentration camps. The influenza epidemic after World War I was not blamed on the Jews, and the South did not attribute its defeat in the Civil War to a Jewish conspiracy . . . Universities each year appear to make less use of 'quota' systems, and every year also sees an increase in the number of mixed fraternities and sororities on campuses." Rogow, The Jew in a Gentile World, p. 221.

236. Genuine and direct intimacy between Jew and Gentile is rare. Social emancipation was never and nowhere completely achieved. This was only partly due to Gentile exclusiveness; everywhere the Jews themselves wanted to preserve their social cohesion to avoid intermarriage, and maintain their religious and cultural character. There was an aversion to complete social amalgamation on both the Gentile and Jewish sides.

237. Tosefta Sanhedrin 13,2. The non-Hebraist may consult C.G. Montefiore — H. Loewe, A Rabbinic Anthology, p. 604.

238. "Bin kein Jud, bin kein Christ, bin ein wahrer Socialist" was a favourite motto of the Austrian Social Democrats before their elimination from political life in 1933.

239. The Society for Christian Jewish Co-operation in Düsseldorf under the leadership of Frau Elisabeth Cremers practiced active philo-Semitism during the Nazi era and is at present engaged in various activities in the field of promoting Gentile-Jewish friendship. The writer of these lines knows from personal contact that its work has been motivated by sentiments of Catholic charitable feelings towards the Jewish people.

240. Zionist Record, Johannesburg, March 16, 1979. An important source on human kindness and decency in Nazi Germany is: H.D. Leuner, "When Compassion Was a Crime" (Germany's Silent Heroes), with a foreword by the Honorable Terence Prittie.

241. See G. Hausner, The Indictment of Adolf Eichmann, in N. Glatzer, The Dynamics of Emancipation, p. 144 f.

242. See above p. 86.
243. Parkes, A History of the Jewish People, p. 222.
244. M. Zylberberg quoted by Joseph Leftwich in AJR Information, March 1959, p. 6. The story of how thousands of Poles defied Hitler in a doomed attempt to rescue the Jews of Poland has recently been told by K. Iranek-Osmecki, He Who Saves One Life, and by W. Bartoszewski — Z. Lewin in the volume "The Samaritans" — Heroes of the Holocaust. "The stake they set for my life was high . . . their own lives," says one of the survivors now resident in Israel, of her saviours.
245. Friedman, Their Brothers Keepers, p. 51.
246. Omer (Hebrew), 25 October 1968.
247. Marie Syrkin, Blessed is the Match, pp. 190 f. On Holland's assistance to its Jews during the Nazi era, see Lily Herzberg in Jewish Affairs, Johannesburg, December 1967. The author pays a striking tribute to the "great tolerance and humanism of the Dutch people" and the "ultimately unbreakable spirit of man." The article bears the title: "There is also pro-Semitism."
248. J.B. Agus, The Meaning of Jewish History, vol. 2, p. 445.
249. "Unbesungene Helden," AJR Information, January 1968.
250. Jerusalem Post, December 24, 1969.
250a. Federation Chronicle, Johannesburg, December 1965. H.J. Zimmels, "The Echo of the Nazi Holocaust in Rabbinic Literature," p. 339.
251. In a book published by the Danish Government, Denmark Besat og Befriet, Hartvig Frisch, the author devotes a chapter to Duckwitz in which he states that the rescue action to Sweden initiated by the then 39-year-old Duckwitz saved the lives of 6700 Jews, among them 1351 refugees from Germany, and 1376 half-Jews. The former Danish Prime Minister, Hans Hedtoft, asked a Jewish journalist, "Do you want to meet the German to whom Danish Jews owe their rescue?" It was Georg Ferdinand Duckwitz, A.J. Fischer in AJR Information, December 1969.
252. A complete factual story of the rescue of Danish Jewry is presented by Leni Yahil, "The Rescue of Danish Jewry — Test of a Democracy." An effort to record the Righteous among the Gentiles who helped rescue victims of Nazism is the book "The Legion of Noble Christians" by Gerald Green. The book tells of a mission sponsored by an American Jew and carried out by a Gentile to interview such rescuers. He wishes to search out, honour and perpetuate the deeds of noble Christians who through a variety of ways have aided Jews to elude death at the hand of the Nazis. While the tendency of the writer is praiseworthy, the subject is not treated with a view to provide documentary evidence, but a fictional reconstruction of possible motives and actions.